BLACK DIVA OF THE THIRTIES

BLACK DIVA

OF THE THIRTIES
THE LIFE OF RUBY ELZY

DAVID E. WEAVER

UNIVERSITY PRESS OF MISSISSIPPI   JACKSON

www.upress.state.ms.us

Excerpt on page 180 from *The Etude* (June 1993), "The Spirit of the Spirituals." © 1943 Theodore Presser Company. Used by permission.

Frontis: Ruby Elzy, 1937 (Photo by Woodards Studio, courtesy of the author's collection)

The University Press of Mississippi is a member of the Association of American University Presses.

12 11 10 09 08 07 06 05 04   4 3 2 1

∞

Library of Congress Cataloging-in-Publication Data

Weaver, David, 1952–
  Black diva of the thirties : the life of Ruby Elzy / David Weaver.
      p. cm.
  Includes bibliographical references and index.
  ISBN 1-57806-651-4 (cloth : alk. paper)
  1. Elzy, Ruby. 2. Sopranos (Singers)—United States—Biography.
I. Title.
  ML420.E555W4 2004
  782'.0092—dc22   2004001484

British Library Cataloging-in-Publication Data available

CONTENTS

Preface   vii

PROLOGUE: A Concert at the White House   3

Mississippi Jewel   9

Stumbling Upward   33

A Magnolia in Manhattan   57

The Birth of *Porgy and Bess*   80

"My Man's Gone Now"   99

Rising Star   114

"Serena Out West"   124

"Going Hollywood"   134

"Where Is Dis Road A-leadin' Me To?"   147

Porgy and Bess Triumphant   163

"I'm on My Way"   176

EPILOGUE: "Don't You Weep When I'm Gone"   188

Research and References   193

Acknowledgments   201

Index   204

PREFACE

The genesis of this book goes back to April 1998. I was working for WOSU, the public broadcasting stations of Ohio State University. At a luncheon for our new classical music station in Marion, Ohio, I was seated next to a charming woman named Madge Cooper Guthery. Despite her silver hair and sixty-plus-year career in broadcasting (in Marion she's renowned as "The First Lady of Radio"), Madge had considerably more vigor and vitality than people half her age at the luncheon. Talking together, Madge and I found we shared common interests not only in broadcasting, but in opera and theatre. I told her I had been studying voice since the age of eighteen, including a year spent at the University of Cincinnati, where one of my classmates was the noted black soprano, Kathleen Battle. It was then that Madge asked me a ten-word question that was to have a profound effect on my life:

"Have you ever heard of a singer named Ruby Elzy?"

"No, I haven't," I replied. "Who was she?" Madge told me that Elzy had been a classmate of hers, a 1930 graduate of Ohio State who had gone on to Juilliard. Elzy had won fame as the original Serena in George Gershwin's *Porgy and Bess*, but her promising career as an operatic soprano had been cut short when she died tragically at a young age. Exactly how she died Madge did not know. But she did recall that, "Everyone just loved Ruby. And she had one of the most beautiful voices I ever heard."

As it so happened, the 1937 Gershwin Hollywood Bowl Memorial Concert, in which Elzy had sung, had just been released for the first time on CD. Intrigued by what Madge had told me, I bought a copy. Listening to Elzy sing "My Man's Gone Now," the dramatic and difficult song that she had introduced in *Porgy and Bess*, I was stunned. Yes, her voice was indeed beautiful, vibrant and expressive, but there was something more. I had never heard a voice exactly like it. I was hooked.

Little did I know that Madge Guthery's question that spring day in Marion was going to set me off on one of the greatest adventures of my life. I eagerly began researching the life and career of Ruby Elzy, a task that would take more than five years to complete (and I really believe I am not through yet). Even though she was famous at the time of her death in 1943, the passage of time had relegated mention of her to mostly a line or two, a paragraph at most, in books about *Porgy and Bess* or the American musical theatre. Unlike her more well-known contemporaries Marian Anderson and Paul Robeson, Elzy had no permanent archive, where voluminous materials are centrally housed and extensively catalogued, as there are for Anderson and Robeson.

A major part of the problem was that what information there was about Elzy was widely scattered. It took a great deal of slow and painstaking effort, the help and guidance of many people across the country, and oftentimes just plain good luck over the course of five years to uncover what, in the end, was a wealth of material.

But I wanted more than just facts, names, dates, and places. I wanted to discover—and reveal—the personal side of Ruby Elzy. I wanted to show her not just as a gifted artist, but as a woman—a *black* woman—at a time in America when there were limited opportunities for both.

Fortunately, I was able to interview more than a dozen people who had known her personally—friends, family and neighbors from Mississippi, classmates from Rust College and Ohio State (including Madge), even fellow performers. Included in this latter group were the two remarkable women who played Gershwin's Bess between 1935 and 1943: Anne Brown, Elzy's friend and Juilliard classmate who created the role in 1935; and Etta Moten Barnett, who followed Brown as Bess in 1942. Their recollections of Ruby Elzy, Gershwin, and *Porgy and Bess* were indispensable.

My two biggest strokes of good luck came a few months apart. In the spring of 1999, I learned that Ruby Elzy's two sisters, Dr. Amanda Elzy and Wayne Elzy Bankhead, were living together in retirement in Columbus, Mississippi. That August, I visited them for the first time. Over the course of two days spent with them I recorded nearly four hours of conversations that shed tremendous light on Ruby, their parents, their experiences growing up as black children in Jim Crow Mississippi, and their own remarkable adult lives as educators. Their help, particularly in giving permission for me to obtain certain records that otherwise I could not have gained access to, was indispensable. Sadly, Wayne died in April of 2000 at the age of eighty-seven. I have continued to visit Amanda each year since.

A few months after returning from my first trip to Mississippi, I located the family of Dr. C. C. McCracken, the man who discovered Ruby Elzy at Rust College in 1927 and brought her to Ohio State. When I first made contact with them, all four of McCracken's children—Janet, Bill, Mary Ruth, and Ed—were living within a few miles of each other in the northwest Florida. Regrettably, Mary Ruth died before my first visit in July 2000. But I was fortunate to be able to meet and spend time with the other three siblings, who were an incredible source of help and information. Remembering their father and their close relationship with Ruby Elzy was a true labor of love, for as they all told me, "Ruby was a member of our family." Regrettably, both Bill and Janet have since passed on.

Their younger brother Ed is the last of Dr. McCracken's children remaining alive. The family historian, Ed has been an enthusiastic supporter and mentor of this project from the outset. His devoted wife Ruth has also been a great help, organizing materials and compiling for me a veritable treasury of Ruby Elzy resources. Among them are a collection of more than fifty letters (spanning a thirty-five-year period) between Dr. McCracken and Ruby, her mother, and others who were integral to Ruby's life and career. Ed and Ruth also provided me with photographs (many of them personally inscribed by Ruby) and copies of programs from nearly all of her major performances, including her Town Hall recital, White House concert, and the productions of *Porgy and Bess* and *John Henry*.

Most importantly, Ed and Ruth gave me a fifty-five-page manuscript—the beginnings of a biography that Dr. McCracken was writing in the early 1950s. Working closely with Ruby's mother Emma, Dr. McCracken had written a detailed account of Ruby's life from her birth in 1908 to her admission at Juilliard in 1930 that would have been impossible for me to otherwise obtain.

Heart disease forced Dr. McCracken to put the project aside incomplete in 1953. For more than four decades after his death in 1957, the manuscript and twenty pages of Dr. McCracken's research notes were stored in a number of boxes in Mary Ruth's garage. This material was uncovered for the first time in the spring of 2000. I am grateful to Ed and Ruth for generously giving me permission on behalf of the McCracken family to freely utilize this material in the writing of my own book.

In several instances I have reconstructed personal thoughts, conversations, and incidents in Ruby Elzy's life. In every case, these reconstructions are based on my interviews with her family and friends, from their correspondence, from Dr. McCracken's manuscript and notes, and from Ruby's own personal writings.

Hopefully, in the end I have achieved my goal to make this story more than a recitation of facts or a scholarly but distant treatment of its subject. I hope I have created for you, the reader, a candid and intimate portrayal of a beautiful and gifted individual who deserves to be rediscovered and remembered as one of the extraordinary women of her time—Ruby Elzy.

BLACK DIVA OF THE THIRTIES

PROLOGUE

A CONCERT AT THE WHITE HOUSE

Washington, D.C., was getting an early taste of winter that Wednesday afternoon. The skies were gray. The temperature, usually a mild fifty degrees at this time of year, struggled to get above freezing. Bureaucrats and secretaries, heading back from lunch to the government offices where they worked, pulled their coat collars up and walked a little faster.

It was December 15, 1937. America had entered the ninth year of the worst depression in its history. Yet here, ten days before Christmas, downtown Washington's fashionable department stores were crowded with shoppers. At Garfinkel's on the corner of 14th and F Streets, the display case in every bronze-framed window was decorated in red and green, silver and gold. Outside the revolving doors of the main lobby, Salvation Army bellringers competed with panhandlers for the pocket change of passers-by.

Traffic around the public buildings and monuments was heavy, as it always was. No one paid particular attention to a yellow taxi as it turned south off of Pennsylvania Avenue, pulling to a stop as it reached the east gate of the White House. This was the entrance where visitors on official business inside the mansion were checked in by the uniformed guards.

The driver turned to the attractive black woman seated in back. "Here you go," he said. Ruby Elzy looked at her watch. "My goodness," she said, "I'm twenty minutes early." She smiled at the driver. "Could we drive around the Mall once?" she asked. The driver nodded and eased the taxi back into the traffic.

If Ruby Elzy was unusually nervous and excited on this day, no one could blame her. Inside the White House, Eleanor Roosevelt, the wife of the President of the United States, was hosting her annual Christmas luncheon in honor of the wives of the justices of the United States Supreme Court. As was the tradition, a concert would follow in the East Room, presented by a leading singer or musician. Today that artist would be Ruby Elzy, invited to perform by the First Lady.

The event had attracted the attention of the press, and the *New York World Telegram* planned to run a story in its afternoon edition. It wasn't that the First Lady hosting a luncheon was newsworthy, nor even that an entertainer had been invited to perform in the White House—the Roosevelts had done that frequently. No, what made this concert a singular event was the artist herself.

It wasn't only that Ruby Elzy was black that had captured the attention of the press. It was that Ruby Elzy was black *and* one of the most acclaimed young singers of her time, a classically-trained soprano who sang Schubert and Verdi as well as she sang Negro spirituals, a performer as at home on the stages of New York City's Town Hall or the Hollywood Bowl as she was in the little church in Pontotoc, Mississippi, where she had first sung twenty-five years before.

The taxi passed by the Lincoln Memorial, with its imposing statue of the great Civil War president. Ruby's grandmother, Belle Kimp, had been born a slave in the first year of Lincoln's presidency. Today, Belle's granddaughter would be singing in the very house where Lincoln had signed the Emancipation Proclamation, freeing Belle and finally ending two hundred years of bondage for the black race.

Ruby had first visited Washington just after graduating from Ohio State University. Like any other tourist, Ruby had stood patiently in line, waiting her turn to see the Library of Congress and the U.S. Capitol.

Much had happened in the seven years since. From Ohio State Ruby went on to study at Juilliard. Less than a month after arriving in New York City, she landed her first job in a Broadway show. A few years later Ruby made her film debut in *The Emperor Jones*, co-starring opposite Paul Robeson. The screenplay was by DuBose Heyward; the writer from South Carolina took a liking to the singer from Mississippi, and during the film's production they became friends. When Heyward and George Gershwin began collaborating on an opera based on Heyward's novel *Porgy*, he urged Gershwin to audition Ruby. One hearing was all it took. Gershwin, impressed with Ruby's singing and acting ability, cast her in the important role of Serena. He wrote one of the score's greatest songs, "My Man's Gone Now," specifically for her. When the opera, now called *Porgy and Bess* premiered in 1935, Ruby Elzy was proclaimed a new star. It was a time in America when black classical artists were still a rare phenomenon. Only a handful had achieved any major success—singers Roland Hayes, Marian Anderson, and Paul Robeson, and composer William Grant Still. After *Porgy and Bess*, Ruby Elzy's name was now included in this select group of performers.

More recently, Ruby had won new acclaim for her performance at the Gershwin Memorial Concert at the Hollywood Bowl—broadcast worldwide by CBS—and for her solo recital debut in New York's Town Hall. In early December, Ruby had sung a private audition for Henry Jurge of Steinway and Sons. It was Jurge and Malvina Thompson Scheider, Mrs. Roosevelt's personal secretary, who were in charge of planning musical programs for the White House. When Jurge and Scheider recommended Ruby to the First Lady, she enthusiastically and immediately approved. Eleanor Roosevelt was one of the great champions of civil rights for blacks in the 1930s. Presenting an artist like Ruby Elzy symbolized Roosevelt's commitment to the cause.

By now the taxi had returned to the gate at Executive Avenue. Waiting to help Ruby as she got out of the cab was a tall man with eyeglasses and wavy hair. It was Arthur Kaplan, Ruby's principal accompanist since they had both been at Juilliard. Arthur Kaplan was white, making his musical association with Ruby unique for its time. Nearly all black singers performed with blacks at the piano, the notion being that few, if any, white accompanists would agree to be subservient to a black.

Ruby and Kaplan walked the stone path to the south entrance of the White House. The doorman was there to greet them. "Good afternoon, Miss Elzy. The First Lady is expecting you." Ruby beamed with pride. She and Kaplan were shown into the Gold Room, a private parlor for the First Lady's guests, which also housed the mansion's collection of gilded tableware, hence, its name.

Ruby looked herself over in a mirror. She had chosen her wardrobe carefully—black long-sleeved dress, black bolero jacket over a white blouse and black shoes. At first she thought to wear a hat, but remembered her mother's advice: "No fuss. Be simple and dignified." The hat went. Ruby did wear a special piece of jewelry—a mineral "tear of Christ" that had been a gift from her voice teacher, Lucia Dunham, on the night of her Town Hall debut. Ruby considered it her good luck charm.

She vocalized with a few scales. Singing early in the day was always difficult. She had risen early to warm up her voice and get rid of the huskiness. As she sang a little, the door opened and a young woman entered, an assistant to Malvina Scheider. "They're ready for you, Miss Elzy," she said. The woman escorted Ruby and Kaplan up the short flight of stairs to the East Room, where Eleanor Roosevelt was finishing her remarks.

"And now," said the First Lady, "it is my pleasure to introduce a young woman with a beautiful soprano voice—Miss Ruby Elzy."

Ruby smiled and bowed as she walked into the room and took her place in the curve of the piano. As Arthur Kaplan played the introduction to Ruby's first song, she looked out over her audience for the first time. Nearly fifty of Washington's most prominent, influential women were seated in front of her. At the front and center, of course, was Mrs. Roosevelt. Seated to her side was Mrs. Charles Evans Hughes, the wife of the current Chief Justice; to the other side of Mrs. Roosevelt sat her guest of honor, former First Lady Helen Herron Taft, the widow of the only man who had ever served as both President of the United States and Chief Justice of the Supreme Court. William Howard Taft had been elected President in 1908, the year Ruby was born.

Ruby began to sing. Her voice was a clear, vibrant soprano, and she had carefully chosen a program to show the range and artistry of that voice to the fullest. Her first song was "Nachtigal," a German *lied* by Brahms. Then came "Depuis le jour" from Charpentier's opera "Louise," a dramatic aria in French with a high B finish that had become one of Ruby's signature pieces. She followed it with an English art song "Blue Are Her Eyes" by Wintter-Watts, then Thrane's "Norwegian Echo Song," a song that had been one of her favorites since she was a student at Ohio State. Ruby closed with Lawrence Brown's arrangement of the spiritual, "You Hear the Lambs." When the last note died out, the audience broke out in sustained applause that continued well after Ruby had taken her bows and left the room.

Eleanor Roosevelt stepped forward and motioned for Ruby to come back. Taking her hand, the First Lady said, "Ruby, you have a beautiful voice. If you are able to do another, Mrs. Brandeis would like you to sing, 'Every Time I Feel the Spirit.' Would you?" Ruby smiled and said yes. She took center stage again, this time performing a capella:

Ev'ry time I feel de spirit, movin' in my heart,
I will pray.
Oh ev'ry time I feel de spirit,
Movin' in my heart,
I will pray.

Although she had been trained to sing art songs and operatic arias, no music suited Ruby Elzy's voice more perfectly, no music did she sing with greater feeling, than the spirituals of her people. For two minutes, under the spell of Ruby's performance, the East Room of the White House seemed transformed into an old-fashioned tent revival at a Southern Methodist camp meeting. When she had finished, Eleanor Roosevelt led her guests in a standing ovation for Ruby.

After the program, Ruby spent several minutes talking with the First Lady and her guests. Mrs. Taft and each of the wives of the Supreme Court Justices congratulated her. Alice Brandeis lingered to thank Ruby for the encore and to offer words of encouragement. Her husband,

Louis Brandeis, had been the first member of the Jewish faith to serve on the Supreme Court. His appointment by President Wilson in 1916 had set off a barrage of anti-Semitic hatred and protest. Mrs. Brandeis could appreciate the many obstacles Ruby had to surmount in order to become a singer.

"Ruby, you can be very proud," Mrs. Brandeis told her, "because you are achieving recognition not only for yourself, but for all the Negro people in America."

Mrs. Roosevelt asked, "Ruby, will you be staying long in Washington?"

Ruby replied, "I'd love to, but I'm afraid I can't. I'm singing tonight and have to catch the train back to New York City. In fact, I hope you won't mind if I use the telephone to call a taxi."

Mrs. Roosevelt said, "That won't be necessary, Ruby." She motioned to Malvina Scheider's assistant, standing nearby. The First Lady told her, "Have my car brought around for Miss Elzy."

The sleek black limousine arrived at the front entrance of the White House, and a uniformed chauffeur held the door as Ruby and Kaplan got into the back seat. As the car pulled from the winding driveway onto Pennsylvania Avenue, Ruby laughed and turned to her accompanist.

"Oh, Arthur," she said, "if only my friends back in Mississippi could see this little colored girl now."

MISSISSIPPI JEWEL

The voice of Ruby Elzy was heard in public for the first time on a spring day in 1912, at McDonald Methodist Church in the little town of Pontotoc, Mississippi. Her "debut" was a completely spontaneous performance that surprised the congregation and embarrassed her mother. Emma Elzy had a lovely soprano voice and sang in McDonald's choir, while her three small children sat in the front pew with Emma's mother, Belle Kimp. The choir had just finished the morning anthem, and was beginning to sing a hymn when suddenly a child's voice rose over all the others. It was little Ruby, singing her heart out from the front pew.

The worshippers laughed at first, but their amusement quickly turned to astonishment: this diminutive four-year-old had a voice that seemed well beyond her age. It had a clarity and power, a sweetness and beauty, that was thrilling. Emma blushed and cast a stern eye in Ruby's direction, but was helpless to do anything. The choir, led by its impromptu guest soloist, carried on. When the song reached its conclusion, the congregation erupted with applause and shouts of "Hallelujah!" Ruby Elzy had conquered her first audience. It wouldn't be the last.

Pontotoc, where the Elzys lived, was a small town of less than a thousand people in the northeastern part of Mississippi. Like all southern towns of that time, it was strictly segregated according to race. In Pontotoc, black families lived on either the northern or southern outskirts of the town. Belle Kimp's house was on the north side, on a grassy knoll called Church Hill for the three large churches that stood there. It was here on the raw Thursday morning of February 20,

1908, that Charlie and Emma Elzy welcomed their first child, a baby girl they named Ruby Pearl. Neighbors stopping by to see the newborn remarked that with her smiling face and sparkling eyes she was indeed a "Mississippi jewel."

About the Elzy side of the family not much is known. According to Ruby's sisters Amanda and Wayne, the Elzys were living in northwestern Mississippi, near the town of Holly Springs, when the Civil War ended in 1865. At some point over the next twenty years, they moved to Pontotoc, where Charlie was born on November 18, 1886. Charlie had at least two sisters, Amanda and Ada, and a brother, Ed, a talented athlete who grew up to play professional baseball in the Negro league.

About Emma Kimp and her family heritage much more is known, because Emma never tired of telling the story throughout her long and colorful life. Emma's great-grandfather arrived on a slave ship from Africa in the early 1800s and was sold straight off the docks in Norfolk, Virginia, to a Methodist minister named Stovall. When the reverend was called to pastor a church in Troy, Mississippi, he took his large family and all his slaves with him. Stovall's daughter later married a man named Kimp, and as a wedding present the reverend gave the couple several of his slaves, including Emma's great-grandfather. Kimp, like Stovall, was a devout Christian who did not believe blacks should be mistreated even though they were slaves. The blacks who served the Kimp household were given good food, clothing, shelter, and medical care. And even though it was against the law of the time, Kimp provided his slaves with a simple education, and taught them the Bible.

In 1835 Emma's grandmother Fannie was born. As was the tradition, Fannie took her master's last name as her own—Kimp. Later Fannie was married to another of Kimp's slaves, a man whose first name was Henderson. They began a family, which included their daughter Belle, born in 1862. When the Civil War ended, Fannie and Henderson decided to remain close to the Kimps in Troy. Belle grew up and married, and on May 23, 1886, she gave birth to her daughter Emma. Belle's marriage would not last, and soon she moved north—first to Algoma and eventually to Pontotoc, where Emma met Charlie Elzy, six months her junior.

It isn't known exactly when Charlie and Emma began to court, or for how long. They were married at McDonald Methodist Church on June 7, 1907. Ruby was born a little less than nine months later. More babies would soon follow: Amanda Belle in September 1909; Robert Isaac, Charlie and Emma's only son, in March 1911; and finally, Beatrice Wayne (always called Wayne) in November 1912.

The America in which Charlie and Emma were beginning their life together was undergoing an enormous transformation in the first decade of the twentieth century. The United States had become a world power only ten years before, with its victory in the Spanish-American War. The hero of that war, Theodore Roosevelt—the "Rough Rider"— was now President, and the whole country seemed to brim with same qualities as "TR" himself—bold, brash, energetic, and optimistic. In 1907, the year Charlie and Emma were married, a record 1,250,000 immigrants—mostly from Europe—arrived on Ellis Island in the New York harbor, all seeking a better life. America truly seemed to be a land of destiny, with its promise of freedom and opportunity.

But that promise was largely an empty one for the nine million blacks living in America—especially those in the Deep South. For them, life was difficult, and often dangerous. In the years immediately following the Civil War, blacks made significant political, economic, and social progress. Laws to guarantee their civil rights had been passed, and these laws were enforced by the Union troops stationed throughout the south. But Reconstruction ended in 1877, when President Rutherford B. Hayes pulled the last federal troops out. The white supremacists who had been kept in check now seized every opportunity to beat down those who once had been slaves. The hated "Jim Crow" laws were born in the Deep South states like Mississippi, eroding the gains that blacks had made and placing severe limitations on their rights. By 1900, conditions for blacks in Mississippi were almost worse than they had been before the Civil War.

It was the era of James K. Vardaman, a charismatic politician who was probably one of the most bigoted, racist men ever to hold public office in the United States. He was elected Governor in 1903, and under him life for blacks in Mississippi grew more intolerable—mob violence and lynchings dramatically increased during Vardaman's two terms as Governor. Such violence was not surprising, given Vardaman's remarks in 1907 that, "If it is necessary every Nigger in the state will be lynched, then it will be done to maintain white supremacy." It was pure venom, yet the majority of whites supported Vardaman. When he ran for the U.S. Senate in 1912, Vardaman won in a landslide, carrying seventy-four of Mississippi's seventy-nine counties.

But not all white Mississippians shared Vardaman's views, and there were many who had a patriarchal sympathy to the plight of blacks. Fortunately for the Elzys, Pontotoc was almost like an oasis in the desert. While the white population was clearly dominant, there was much less of the kind of hostility and violence that plagued other Mississippi towns, particularly those in the cotton-rich Delta. Whites in Pontotoc were much more tolerant and accepting of blacks as people at a time when that kind of attitude was clearly in the minority. It was even a source of pride in coming years. In the 1950s Dr. C. C. McCracken, the man who discovered Ruby Elzy and became her mentor, visited Pontotoc and talked to a number of residents who had known her. When he commented to one elderly white woman about the seemingly benign racial climate in the town, she pulled herself up grandly in her chair and said, "Yes, we were always very good to our Niggers in Pontotoc."

Charlie Elzy worked nine months of the year at the town's most prosperous business, the Pontotoc Cotton Seed Oil Pressing Company. The mill was owned by the Furrs, the county's most influential family. Although "king cotton" did not grow as abundantly in northeast Mississippi as it did in the Delta, it was still vitally important to the well-being of every family in Pontotoc. Charlie was a meal cook, and Emma recalled proudly that he was the highest paid worker on the line. The mill closed each summer for three months. During that time,

Charlie worked at whatever odd jobs he could find, such as delivering ice. But he was just as content to spend his time fishing and hunting with his buddies, or shooting dice at the local bars in the part of town appropriately called Rough Edge. Easygoing and likable, Charlie Elzy could always be counted on for a good time.

Although they tried to make their marriage work, in reality Charlie and Emma had little in common. Perhaps Emma Elzy would never find a man capable of matching her. She was a woman of great faith; the Methodist Church was the rock on which her life was built. She was also an optimist who always believed that a better life was ahead for herself and her children. Emma was unafraid of hard work, and hard work she did constantly. Each morning she taught five grades at the Pontotoc Colored School, which black children attended four months of the year. Once school let out at noon, Emma headed to the cotton fields, where she worked until sunset. At night, after supper was over and her husband and children were asleep, Emma worked again— laundering clothes for the Furrs and several other white families in town. It took until the early hours of the morning to get all the washing, drying, ironing, and folding done. After a few hours of sleep, Emma would be up again, delivering the finished laundry while on her way back to the little one-room school. In a way, Emma was the perfect model for the devout and hardworking Serena—the noble character that would one day be created by DuBose Heyward and George Gershwin, and played to great acclaim by her daughter.

Charlie, to his credit, more than pulled his load when there was work to be done. But he was not particularly ambitious. And when it came to religion or the responsibilities of parenting—well, that was "women's work," as Charlie saw it. So he left both up to Emma.

Ruby began helping her mother with the chores as soon as she was old enough. Side by side with Emma, Ruby worked in the garden, put her brother and sisters to bed, and helped with the laundry, neatly folding the still-warm clothes as soon as her mother finished ironing them. As Ruby got older, she took over the job of delivering the finished laundry. And whatever she did, wherever she went, she sang—neighbors could hear her coming all the way from Church Hill, laundry bag in tow, singing a spiritual, or perhaps a popular song of the day like "Down by the Riverside."

Despite the segregation in housing and in schools, the white and black children of Pontotoc often played together. Summers were spent chasing doodlebugs, fishing and swimming in the creek, and climbing trees. Ruby would remember these times fondly, and several of the friendships she made with her white playmates would last her entire life.

Growing older meant becoming more aware of the segregated society in which she lived. Yet Ruby seemed to be spared the kind of hatred and bigotry that plagued many blacks in the South. Her later success as a singer would be a source of pride for everyone in Pontotoc, whites as well as blacks. She in turn came to have respect and affection for the white people who had befriended her. Much of the credit for this must go to Emma Elzy: She instilled in each of her children that they should never feel animosity or resentment towards whites, and to pray for those who were intolerant.

The summer of 1913 arrived, and with it the three-month closing of the Pontotoc Cotton Seed Oil Company. Charlie took his last paycheck and went off for two days, drinking and gambling with his friends. When he came home, a frustrated Emma, unable to control herself any longer, took him to task as she never had before. Here they were, with little money to their names and a house full of young children, and he had wasted the last regular paycheck he would get for three months. Emma needed a responsible man upon whom she could depend, and she wanted their children to have a father they could be proud of. She pleaded with Charlie to think about what he was doing—if not for her sake, then for their children.

Exhausted after talking to him, Emma retreated to a corner of the room, in silent prayer. Charlie said little, if anything. Perhaps it pained him to hear what his wife was saying, for he knew it was true. To be and do what Emma wanted was not impossible. But it would mean a complete change of heart, mind, and attitude—changes that required a kind of discipline and effort that Charlie Elzy had never before shown in his life.

For the next few days, Charlie did stay close to the house, giving Emma more help. They spoke very little, and Emma thought it was best not to prod Charlie any further. She had said and done all she could; now she would leave it in God's hands.

More than sixty years later, in her late eighties, Emma vividly recalled the sweltering afternoon when Charlie came in the door after making a short trip into town. It was Friday, July 11, 1913. Charlie came in and said, "Emma, I haven't had any luck finding summer work here in Pontotoc. I think I'll try Tupelo or Corinth, maybe Memphis even. I need to go somewhere where I can get a job and make as much money as I can until the seed oil company starts up again."

Emma felt this was a good sign. Her husband at last was thinking sensibly, acting like a responsible man with a wife and a family. Charlie wanted to get on the road before dark. Emma fixed his supper, which they enjoyed together with their children. Then he packed a few belongings in a sack, and Emma wrapped up some extra food for him to take. Charlie Elzy said goodbye and stepped out into the waning daylight.

He never came back.

Emma later said Charlie must have decided that being a family man was just too much. For a while, she thought he would return, but he never did. Charlie wandered about the South, working at a number of jobs, never staying in one place for too long. He ultimately settled in St. Louis, where most of the Elzy family had already gone, including his sisters Amanda and Ada. He would remain there until he died.

When Charlie Elzy abandoned his family, Emma was twenty-seven years old. She was a poor black woman in the Deep South, with four children ranging in ages from five years to eight months. Her prospects looked worse than bleak.

But Emma Elzy was not a woman who could be worn down or put down. With an iron will, boundless faith and an almost superhuman capacity for hard work, she determined to pull through. Her husband was gone—so be it. She had no money—she would just have to work harder. She still had her children, and they needed her. For them, she needed to be strong and to carry on. And she did.

Ruby, the oldest child, saw what Emma endured to get them through the difficult times. The bond between the mother and her first daughter deepened. Throughout Ruby's career, in every story and every interview, she would always speak admiringly of her mother, and the sacrifices she made: "I don't need to do any guesswork when it comes to interpreting the emotions of my race. I know what sorrow means. When our little family was broken up, mother was left with four babies to bring up. I know what it means to work and pray and live rejoicing every day. Even then, mother was a 'glad' person. She dressed and fed the four of us before leaving for the battered old schoolhouse down the road where she taught all day and worked hard the rest. She was always sure the Lord would make things come out all right."

Fortunately, Emma did get help from her friends and neighbors in the church. Most importantly, she reached out to the two women in her life she knew she could depend on for anything—her mother Belle and her grandmother Fannie. They helped Emma with everything—caring for the babies, tending the garden, cooking and cleaning, even drilling Ruby on her ABCs.

It was great-grandmother Fannie Kimp, affectionately known as "Aunt Fannie," who became a guiding light for the oldest child. Awaking every morning at dawn, the old woman would open her front door and immediately burst into song, praising the Lord and thanking him for another day. Her high, clear soprano voice carried over a quarter mile. Ruby remembered that the neighbors, far from being annoyed, would laugh and say, "Everything must be all right over at the Kimp house—Aunt Fannie's singing!"

By now Ruby was her mother's main helper, carrying a burden almost as heavy as any of the adults. Her favorite time was at night. With her brother and two sisters fast asleep, Ruby helped Aunt Fannie with the great loads of laundry. As the white-haired woman worked, she told Ruby stories about what it was like being a slave on the great plantations. The child listened wide-eyed, learning of her heritage as an African. Aunt Fannie told Ruby she could be proud that she was 100 percent Negro—there was no white blood in any of their kin. They were as African now as the day they first arrived in America. Most of all, Ruby loved to have Aunt Fannie teach her the great Negro spirituals, and tell her the stories behind them.

Ruby loved the story of one spiritual in particular. Aunt Fannie told her that it was sung by the slaves as a secret signal. One slave would start the tune, and it would pass from slave to slave, one plantation to another, until all the slaves had been reached. It was a sign that a meeting would be held that night, by the moonlight. That old spiritual became one of Ruby Elzy's favorite songs. She did not know then, but singing it would one day change her life, and it would become a standard in nearly every concert she gave. It was called "Steal Away."

Steal away, steal away,
Steal away to Jesus.
Steal away, steal away
I ain't got long to stay here.
My Lord calls me by the thunder,
He calls me by the night.
The trumpet sounds within'a my soul
I ain't got long to stay here.

The young girl thrilled at these songs and stories, and memorized them all by heart. Aunt Fannie was happy, too, to see the spark in her great-granddaughter. Already Emma Elzy instinctively felt that her oldest child had been given a very special gift. And Emma knew if God *had* given her baby a voice, then He must also have planned for her to use it.

There was no money for music lessons, or for luxuries of any kind, in the Elzy household. With three adult women and four small children sharing the small house, taking care of the basic necessities was enough of a challenge. But this didn't stop music from being a vital part of the Elzys' lives, as Ruby would remember later: "In our home we had no instrument—not even a banjo. We were taught to love and appreciate the spiritual as a contribution of the Negro race which the race had evolved itself, and which still seems to me a higher achievement than the imitation of Western music."

McDonald Methodist Church provided a place where Ruby's love of singing could be given free rein. As she grew older, Ruby joined Emma in the choir, and when she was given the chance to sing solos—which was frequently—she never failed to thrill the congregation.

Years later Ruby said, "God gave me my voice. Whatever I've made of it is the Methodists' gift to the world!"

Like all the other black children in town, Ruby attended Pontotoc Colored School, the one-room school where Emma was the sole teacher. Mississippi law of the time made no provisions for the public education of black children beyond the fifth grade. While some larger cities had high schools for black children, Pontotoc was too small to have one.

In 1919 Ruby finished fifth grade. Bright, eager to learn, and mature for her age, she wanted very much to continue her education. Emma also wanted her to go on, but the question was how and where. As always, Emma prayed to God for guidance.

It was at this same time that Ruby first realized what she wanted to be. Jane Lathan, a white girl, was one of Ruby's best friends. Her mother was the town's most prominent musician and piano teacher. Ruby and June were always playing around the piano, or listening to Mrs. Lathan's phonograph, with its huge bell-shaped horn and the word "Victrola" richly carved on the side. From this machine came the sounds of beautiful voices, singing music like Ruby had never heard before. It mesmerized her, and she would ask Jane to play the same records over and over again. One day, Ruby and Jane were playing when they overheard Mrs. Lathan talking with some guests about a concert she'd seen in Memphis. The soloist was a famous soprano, singing a program of music just like Ruby had heard on the Victrola. Ruby listened spellbound as Mrs. Lathan described the beautiful woman in her elegant gown, the packed auditorium of people who rose to their feet applauding. The description created a vivid picture in Ruby's imagination, moving her in a way she had never experienced before. Excited, she ran all the way home.

Ruby breathlessly told Emma the whole story, in all its colorful detail. Then she said, "Mama, that's what I'm going to do someday. I'm going to sing in a big hall before a large group of people." Then, without pausing, Ruby lowered her head, almost as if an imaginary pin had burst her balloon. She said, "But I know that's too much for a little nigger girl to wish for." The look of disappointment in her daughter's face brought tears to Emma's eyes. She went quickly outside on the porch to compose herself and breathed a quick prayer that the Lord would help her find the right words to tell her child. After a moment, she went back inside to the kitchen, where Ruby sat weeping quietly at the table. Emma placed her hand under her daughter's chin, gently lifting it so they could look into each other's eyes.

"Ruby," Emma said, "if being a singer is what you really want, then just keep praying. And someday God will open the door for you to do it."

Ruby embraced her mother, grateful for her understanding and encouragement. But in truth, Emma Elzy *did* know that wanting to be a singer was a huge ambition—an almost impossible one for a young Negro girl in Mississippi. Blacks in the Deep South were destined, so it seemed, to a lifetime of menial servitude by the dominant white race that controlled everything. The tangible chains of slavery had been replaced by the invisible, yet equally heinous chains of discrimination.

Emma realized that if Ruby were to have even a remote chance of realizing her dream of becoming a singer, she would have to leave Pontotoc. She would need an education to prepare her. But where could she go? As Emma often did in her times of need, she turned to her church for help.

Sixty miles northwest of Pontotoc was the town of Holly Springs. Here in 1866 the Missionary Society of the Methodist Church founded

Rust College—one of the first colleges to be established for blacks in the South after the Civil War. Emma went to the Missionary Society and asked if they could find a place for Ruby at Rust. Rust was not only a college, but also had a high school. Maybe here Ruby could get the education she needed.

The news at first was not hopeful—students at Rust had to be at least fifteen years of age to enter the high school. The tuition, while modest by white college standards, was substantial for a single woman with four children. Undaunted, Emma met with school officials and pleaded her daughter's case.

"My daughter has a gift," Emma told school officials. "It needs to be nurtured and developed. She loves to sing more than anything else in the world. I've prayed to God that you can help my little girl."

The headmistresses in the E. L. Rust Industrial Home for Girls were two matronly, no-nonsense Methodist women named Rebecca Barbour and Ella Becker. As they saw it, there were three major obstacles to Ruby being able to attend Rust. First, of course, was the age issue—Ruby was four years younger than the minimum age of fifteen usually required of incoming students. Second, the Elzy family had almost no money to help support Ruby and all the expenses she would incur at Rust— tuition, books, supplies, room and board. If Ruby was to attend Rust, she would have to earn her keep. Finally, Barbour and Becker knew that in bringing Ruby to Holly Springs, Emma Elzy would be deprived not only of her eldest child but of her main helper in the home. It would mean a huge sacrifice for everyone involved.

Yet as Barbour and Becker listened to Emma's story, they couldn't help but be moved by her sincerity and faith, and her determination to see her daughter succeed. The two women decided to admit Ruby to the E. L. Rust Home for Girls. She would work to pay for her room and board. Ruby would take classes, for which Emma would pay tuition of ten dollars a month. When she reached age fifteen, Ruby could enter the high school at Rust. If she did well and continued to the end, she would graduate with a diploma. It was the opportunity Emma had prayed for. She and Ruby were both overjoyed.

In September of 1919, Ruby bade goodbye to her family and friends. For the first time in her life, she was off on her own, traveling to a new place, preparing for a new experience, a new adventure. It was a scenario that would be repeated many times in the coming years— Ruby would go from Pontotoc to Holly Springs, from Rust College to Ohio State University to Juilliard, from Broadway to Hollywood and eventually all across the United States. Only eleven years old, Ruby Elzy was already beginning a life that few people of her race and sex, in that period of American history, would experience.

Once at Rust, Ruby was put to work in the kitchen, cleaning the pails that were used to collect milk from the cows each morning. When she entered the high school in 1923, Ruby became one of the caretakers assisting Rebecca Barbour and Ella Becker. This was a special job, given only to those young women who were deemed by Barbour and Becker to be especially diligent and trustworthy. The caretakers helped look after the younger girls at the E. L. Rust Home.

One of Ruby's young charges was a bright girl from Corinth named Oneida Vanderford. The Vanderfords were one of the most prominent black families in Corinth; Oneida's father was an undertaker, a position of great importance in any black community. At first Oneida resented the idea of Ruby being her supervisor. "I didn't think I needed anybody to tell me to brush my teeth or go to bed," she recalled. But in time she became close to the older girl who was her caretaker, and Ruby in turn became fond of her young charge. What Oneida would remember most about Ruby was her smile and her singing, especially of spirituals.

Ruby often accompanied Oneida home for visits. "My Daddy missed me, being off at school so far away," Oneida said. "So every other week-end, I'd go back home to Corinth on a train called the 'dinky'—it was just an engine and three cars. Ruby would go with me, since I was so young. And sometimes she'd stay the weekend at our house." The Vanderford family became friends not only with Ruby but also with Emma Elzy. A few years later, soon after Ruby had gone north to study at Ohio State, Emma lost her teaching job in Pontotoc. Emma found a new job teaching near Corinth. The Vanderfords helped Emma get settled, and took her to Mount Moriah Methodist Church, where she became a member. Emma would remain in Corinth nearly all the rest of her life.

Like a number of other Negro schools and institutions located throughout the South, such as Booker T. Washington's famous Tuskegee Institute, Rust College was a vital force in the lives of black Mississippians. Here young blacks could get a high school diploma and then, if they wanted, a college degree. They could be trained in a profession such as teaching or law, or learn skills that would enable them to start a business. Most importantly, Rust College gave blacks the hope that they did not have to be shackled by the limitations placed on them by Jim Crow, doomed to spend their lives in the menial and meager jobs that white Mississippians expected them to take.

As a result, Rust College became a source of tremendous pride for blacks. And that pride was never greater than in 1924 when Dr. L. M. McCoy became the first Rust alumnus—and only the second black—to be appointed president. The Methodists who founded Rust in 1866 were white missionaries from the North. Ever since then, most of the faculty and administrators, like Rebecca Barbour and Ella Becker, had also been white. But the years following the end of World War I had signaled a change. More blacks assumed important teaching and administrative positions within the college, culminating in 1920 with the appointment of Professor Matthews S. Damage as Rust's first black president. Dr. McCoy followed Damage four years later.

Sixteen-year-old Ruby Elzy became one of Dr. McCoy's favorites almost from the minute he took office. He delighted in her enthusiasm, optimism, and vivacious humor, and when McCoy heard Ruby sing he was instantly captivated. It was not long before Ruby was being presented regularly at Rust functions, and McCoy beamed with pride at her every performance. Ruby told McCoy her dreams of a singing career. The president was sympathetic and encouraging—yet he also knew that such a career was far beyond what Rust could prepare her for.

During her years at Rust, Ruby Elzy blossomed from being a child to an adolescent to a woman. By the time she graduated from the high school with honors in 1926, she was a young beauty whose voice and personality were admired—especially by the boys. She was one of Rust's most popular students—and most sought-after girls.

Ruby remained at Rust to begin her freshman year of college in September 1926. The yearbook for 1926–1927 preserved in the school archives has the quaint features that all yearbooks seem to contain. Student nicknames, class predictions, and "best of" lists are all included. For Miss Ruby Elzy, the yearbook shows her nickname as "Rube." She is "most noted for" not her voice but "making eyes." Under "Hardest Job at Rust College" one of the tasks is "to convince Ruby Elzy that she can have but ONE Romeo." Finding dates for parties and dances was never a problem for Ruby; making the choice from among several young men was!

Ruby loved Rust College, and would remain close to Dr. McCoy until her death. The entire Elzy family—with the exception of Robert—would develop enduring ties to the school. Amanda followed Ruby to Holly Springs, graduating from the Rust high school in 1929, and five years later from the college. Baby sister Wayne, who graduated from Corinth High School, also got her bachelor's degree from Rust. Most importantly, Emma Elzy—deeply grateful for the opportunities Rust had given her children—became one of the college's most ardent volunteers and supporters, ultimately serving for many years on Rust's board of trustees. In 1988, three years after Emma's death, a new women's dormitory was opened on the Rust campus, near the place where the old E. L. Rust Home had once stood. The new facility was named the Emma Elzy Residence and Learning Center.

Ruby's freshman year at Rust included courses in English, Latin, math, history, and physical education. She also took what was called "Music–Voice" but in reality it was strictly a class in which students sang—there was no instruction in vocal technique, sight-reading, or other rudiments of music. It would be several years before Rust would develop a complete music curriculum. A dynamic woman named Natalie Doxey founded the Rust College A Cappella Choir, which under her direction became world renowned for its concerts and recordings with such noted artists as Leontyne Price. Unfortunately this all happened after Ruby had already left Rust; yet she and Doxey became good friends, and Ruby would return several times to perform at Rust as a guest artist.

Now nineteen, Ruby's desires to be a singer were stronger than ever. She performed often at Rust and represented the college at musical events throughout the state. Sometime in 1926, Ruby and a quartet from Rust sang a concert in Memphis, Tennessee. Ruby's solos drew enthusiastic applause, and afterward two white men came backstage, raving about her performance. They claimed to be from New York, and said they felt Ruby had great potential for a career on stage. They told her they would go back to New York, to make arrangements for her to come there and audition for several important producers and agents. When these arrangements were finalized, they would send her the money to come. Excited, Ruby went back home, telling Mama and everyone at Rust that her dream to be a singer was going to come true at last.

But time passed, and no word came from New York. Ruby never heard from the two men again. She was devastated—and more than that, embarrassed after telling everyone about her "big break." Her classmates at Rust couldn't resist teasing her, almost as if to say, "And did you really think that two smooth-talking white men were gonna waste their time and money bringing some little colored girl all the way to New York— just because they liked your singing? Girl, you really *are* a rube!"

Ruby's disappointment turned to anger when Miss Becker told her that dreaming of a singing career was foolish. For the first time, Ruby quarreled with Miss Becker, who was surprised at how upset Ruby became. Walking through the halls afterwards, Ruby, still shaking, bumped into Dr. McCoy. Sensing that something was wrong, the president invited her to his office.

"Ruby, I've never seen you look so unhappy. What's the matter?" McCoy asked.

"I am unhappy, Dr. McCoy." she replied. "I'm angry at Miss Becker because she was really mean to me today."

McCoy was surprised. "I thought you and Miss Becker were very good friends. What has she done?"

Ruby leaned forward. "Dr. McCoy, you know how much I want to be a great singer. But Miss Becker tells me my place is here in Mississippi, helping my own people, instead of chasing after this crazy dream to sing."

McCoy now understood the problem. Walking her to the door he said, "Ruby, you know I have many boys and girls here. I pray for them every night to do right and make good. Now I can't always pray for everyone by name, but I promise you that whenever I think of you, I'll pray for God to help to show you what to do with the voice He gave you. Will you pray, too?"

Leaving his office, Ruby looked back and said, "Yes, I will pray. And thank you, Dr. McCoy. I feel much better."

McCoy heaved a sigh as he watched Ruby go down the hall. He knew that Ruby *was* asking for the impossible. He also knew that part of the reason Miss Becker encouraged Ruby to stay in Mississippi was because she did not want to see Ruby hurt again, as she had been by the two New York men in Memphis.

No one knew it, but the answer to Ruby's and Dr. McCoy's prayers was already in the making. It would come in the form of yet another two white men from the North. They were not on a trip to find new musical talent, but instead were two educators on an assignment to help black schools throughout the South. One of these men would become Ruby Elzy's greatest friend, mentor, and champion.

Dr. Charles Chester McCracken—known as "C. C."—was a native of Bellefontaine, Ohio, born in 1882. A graduate of Monmouth College in Illinois, he had gone on to get his master's and doctoral degrees from Harvard. McCracken had moved successfully through a number of teaching and administrative positions at schools and colleges in Illinois and Ohio and since 1919 had served as professor of school administration at Ohio State University in Columbus. By 1927 he was a nationally recognized authority on the subject of educational organization and management. When the U.S. Office of Education appointed a commission to study Negro schools and colleges in the South, Dr. McCracken was a natural choice. He would join Dr. Walter C. John, an administrator from the Office of Education's headquarters in Washington, D.C., in visiting sixty schools over a two-month period, and in making their final report by June 30, 1927.

Rust College was one of the final stops on the itinerary. By the time McCracken and John arrived in Holly Springs in mid-May they had already been on the road for six weeks, and had visited more than fifty schools. It was a tedious and wearying routine of catching trains, tours of one campus after another, meetings with teachers and administrators, followed by nights sitting up in small hotel rooms to discuss and compare notes on what they had seen and heard during the day.

McCracken and John arrived at Rust College and were shown into the president's office. They pulled out the sixty-page questionnaire Dr. McCoy had sent to Washington, and carefully began to review it with him. The questionnaire was an integral part of their evaluation that, together with their site inspection, would help them to make recommendations to the educational commission on Rust's behalf.

Going over the long form took time, and as the morning wore on it became quite warm, typical for May in Mississippi. The windows in Dr. McCoy's office were open, and sounds from outside could be heard. One sound in particular became more and more distinctive, a sound that captured the attention of the three men. It was a beautiful soprano voice, singing "Steal Away to Jesus." Dr. McCracken later recalled that Dr. John grew increasingly agitated. He finally threw down his pencil and said, "Dr. McCoy, either we make their girl stop singing—or bring her in here to sing for us!"

McCoy laughed. "That's Ruby Elzy, one of our students. She's always singing. In fact, she's upstairs right now, practicing for a program. Would you like to hear her?" McCracken and John agreed at once, and official work was put aside to go to the auditorium above McCoy's office. Ruby was on stage with a violinist and a pianist and the Rust College Male Vocal Quartet. They were getting ready for a school program the coming weekend. McCoy said, "Ruby, these two gentlemen are visiting the campus and heard you from my office. They'd like to listen in on your rehearsal, if you don't mind." Ruby smiled, "Not at all, Dr. McCoy." Her smile and warmth struck an instant chord with McCracken. The three men took seats halfway back in the auditorium, and McCoy gave the signal for them to begin. McCracken and John, expecting to hear a Negro spiritual, were amazed when Ruby began to sing the "Inflammatus," a Latin liturgical piece that was vocally demanding. She sang it with ease, then several other classical songs before finally singing several spirituals. In all, she sang nine numbers.

Dr. McCracken later recalled that they moved to several different locations in the auditorium. Although Ruby's voice was not especially big, she had no trouble filling the large hall with her sound.

McCracken and John thanked Ruby and left the auditorium with McCoy. They could not believe they had heard such a voice in this small black college in the Deep South. McCoy invited them to lunch. The entire conversation was not at all about the survey, but about Ruby Elzy. McCoy shared the story of Ruby's background, of how well she had done at Rust in the eight years she had been there, about the mother determined to help her daughter get an education, and especially of Ruby's desire to become a singer.

"We don't have the kind of program at Rust to help Ruby realize her ambition," McCoy told them. "Perhaps you gentlemen could do something." But neither McCracken nor John had the connections, or the money, to help Ruby. They were educators, not agents or promoters.

The three men went back to Rust and finished work on the questionnaire by the early evening. That night at the hotel, McCracken and John once again talked about the young black girl with the phenomenal voice and the burning desire to sing. What a shame nothing could be done to help such a gifted talent. Ruby Elzy seemed destined to remain in Mississippi, her dream of a career as a singer unfulfilled, like the dreams of many young blacks in the South.

But Ruby now had an ally in C. C. McCracken. Not someone who would shrink away from challenges, McCracken was a man of high moral purpose and most of all a true educator who believed that everyone had potential and the God-given right to develop it. In his hotel room that night, McCracken found it difficult to sleep. Surely, he thought, God would not have given a person such a gift if He had not meant for her to use it. Dr. McCracken knew that Ruby Elzy deserved that opportunity, and that it was up to him to help her. Exactly how he would do that, he had not yet figured that out.

McCracken rose early and called Dr. McCoy to see if he could arrange another meeting with Ruby that morning. Dr. McCoy agreed, and when McCracken arrived in the president's office Ruby was waiting for him. They talked for a few minutes, and then McCracken asked her, "Ruby, can you sing a lullaby for me, or something from your childhood?"

Ruby replied, "Dr. McCracken, we didn't sing lullabies when I was little. But I would like to sing a song my grandmother, who was born a slave, taught me." She then proceeded to sing the old spiritual, "By and By, I'll Lay Down This Heavy Load."

Again her voice and expression moved McCracken, just as they done the day before. She sang several more songs for him and then he asked her to sit down.

McCracken said, "Ruby, if I could arrange it, would you be willing to come north to study and develop your voice? I don't have the money to pay for your training myself, but I might be able to interest others, if you're willing to work hard and make some sacrifices."

Ruby looked him squarely in the eyes. "Dr. McCracken, I don't even know if I *have* a good voice. But if I do, I would be willing to make any *discreet* sacrifice in order to improve it."

McCracken did not know then what Ruby meant; a few years later he learned about the two men from New York who had heard her in Memphis, and their failed promises that had caused her such hurt and embarrassment. She was not going to make the same mistake twice.

Yet Ruby sensed that this time things *were* different. She felt at ease with Dr. McCracken and confident that he was a man of his word. By the time they parted company it had been agreed: Ruby would talk to her mother and the officials at Rust, while Dr. McCracken would go back to Columbus and lay the initial groundwork needed to bring her to Ohio State University.

It was the beginning of a strong bond between this unlikely pair— the Harvard-educated professor and the poor but gifted black girl from rural Mississippi. In time, they would forge one of the most unique collaborations ever undertaken in the annals of the music world.

When Ruby shared the news with Dr. McCoy, he gave his immediate and wholehearted approval. Others at Rust were much more skeptical, especially Ella Becker. Dr. McCracken would recall that many questions were raised, mostly negative, some even insidious, about his motivations: Just who was this man to think he could help Ruby? What did he expect in return? Columbus was six hundred miles away. Ruby had no money for a train ticket, and even if she did, blacks in the South were prohibited from riding in the Pullman cars; how would Ruby get there? Ohio State was a large university—would it accept a Negro student from a small, non-accredited school down south? And even if it did accept her—how would Ruby's tuition and other expenses be paid? And finally, the most important, really the *only* important question: what would Emma Elzy say? Her consent would be needed for Ruby to go. Would Emma be willing to send her daughter far away, entrusting her care and education to a man—a white man at that—whom she had never even met?

Emma *was* upset when Ruby's letter arrived, talking about the professor from up north who had so generously offered to help her achieve her dream of becoming a singer. Ruby had written to tell her mother not to worry, that she would be all right. And if things did not work out as Dr. McCracken promised, she would come home at once.

Despite Ruby's reassurances, Emma hesitated to give her approval. In truth, Emma was agonizing over making a decision. It was the greatest dilemma she had ever faced, greater even than Charlie Elzy walking out. Emma had always told Ruby that if God wanted her to use her voice, He would help her find the way. Now a chance had presented itself, yet Emma was afraid to let Ruby take it. Sensing that her mother was about to say no, Ruby wrote again from Rust, this time in an almost desperate plea: "Mama, you said God would open the door for me. Now that He has, are you going to kick it shut—or will you let me go?"

Emma knew that Ruby was right. She had taught her children about faith and prayer, about trusting in God. Now it was as if she was being put to the test to see if that was what she truly believed. Emma knew there was only choice to make: she had to let Ruby go.

With Emma's approval, plans now had to be made for the trip north. The issue of travel was quickly settled: Ella Becker would soon be leaving for summer vacation in her hometown of Mansfield, Ohio. She would accompany Ruby to Columbus, letting Ruby travel as her maid—the only blacks who were allowed to ride in the Pullman cars. This would also give Miss Becker a chance to meet Dr. McCracken and make certain the proper arrangements had been made for Ruby's stay.

Dr. McCoy and the faculty took up a collection to pay for Ruby's train ticket and also a new outfit to wear for the trip. On the last day of school, Dr. McCoy and the faculty gathered in his office to present Ruby with her ticket and the new suit of clothes. Overcome, Ruby broke down, crying tears of both joy and sadness. She was excited for the opportunity that lie ahead, yet at the same time she was filled with regret at having to leave Rust College; it had been her home, and the faculty and students her extended family, for nearly half her life.

Although she had agreed to take Ruby to Columbus, Ella Becker still was not sold on the whole idea. She had not met Dr. McCracken during his visit to Rust and was not yet ready to completely trust him. In early June, shortly before she and Ruby were to leave, she wrote to Dr. McCracken:

> Dear Sir:
> I am writing you concerning Ruby Elzy, the girl you met at Rust College and in whom you so kindly became interested in the training and developing of her voice. . . . Ruby has always been a lovely girl—earnest and true. . . . Her mother is a widow with four children and a

mother to care for. . . . From the letter we gather that you will secure a scholarship which will take care of her musical training. . . . Something was said of you taking her in your home, that would be fine.

She is a pure, clean, happy-spirited girl. We took her to our best white physicians of our town. He gave her a thorough examination and he gave her a health certificate with no reservations.

Ruby cannot read music or play the piano. We are sorry for this for it surely will be a handicap. But may be it will be the voice which will count.

If her voice should fail in the test for Operatic singing, could she have the same opportunity of training for a voice teacher? I would prefer that she do teaching, but she prefers the other. . . .

Fortunately, McCracken had already written to Dr. McCoy about his initial arrangements for Ruby. McCoy shared this with Becker to reassure her that McCracken was sincere and that Ruby would be well cared for in Columbus. Now more at ease, Becker wrote again to McCracken:

President McCoy gave me your letter. This will be a wonderful opportunity that seldom comes to any person. I trust Miss Elzy proves worthy.

We leave Holly Springs Thursday 4 p.m., arrive in Cincinnati 9:45 a.m. Friday. Leave Cincinnati I think about 3 p.m., be in Columbus between 7 and 8 over the Baltimore & Ohio railroad. . . .

With the spring term at Rust ended, Ruby went home to Pontotoc for a short visit. It was a bittersweet reunion for Emma, but by now she had come to fully accept Ruby's leaving. Mississippi was too small, too confined to rein her daughter in. Ruby had been given a great talent, and it was her destiny to take that talent to the world.

The night before Ruby returned to Holly Springs, the Elzy house on Church Hill was filled with a constant stream of well-wishers—family, friends, and neighbors. It was a scene Ruby would never forget: "We sat on the floor, all of us. My grandmother asked me to sing 'Steal Away.' We sang our spirituals far into the night. All the community came to wish me goodbye when I left."

Ruby arrived back in Holly Springs early in the afternoon of Thursday, June 16, 1927. Ella Becker met her at the train station. Miss Becker said, "Now, Ruby, you give our luggage to the porter here."

"Yes, Miss Ella," Ruby replied, in her best impersonation of a maid. The conductor gave Ruby a careful look as she handed him her ticket. Once they took their seats in the Pullman car, Ruby and Miss Becker looked each other in the eye directly for the first time and broke out laughing.

The train pulled slowly out of the station, and soon the town of Holly Springs was out of sight. Ruby Elzy glanced out the window as the Mississippi countryside went rushing by. She was on her way north, to a new place, a new adventure. She did not know what to expect when she got to Columbus, but she was excited and unafraid. Whatever lay ahead, Ruby had faith that somehow, someway, she was on the path God meant her to take, just as Mama had promised.

The door had opened.

STUMBLING UPWARD

By the time C. C. McCracken returned to Columbus in early June, nearly a month had passed since the trip to Rust College. The tour of Negro colleges and schools with Dr. John had been completed and the report to the educational commission was ready to submit. As soon as he was back home, Dr. McCracken told his wife about Ruby Elzy, the young black woman gifted with a beautiful soprano voice whom he hoped to bring to study at Ohio State University. Since Ruby knew no one in Columbus, she would have to stay—at least initially—with the McCrackens. If everything worked out as planned and Ruby was admitted to Ohio State, Dr. McCracken would help her find a permanent home with a black family.

Cleo McCracken listened patiently to her husband. Many wives might have reacted in shock and dismay at the thought of a stranger being brought into their home, especially one who was black—after all, this was 1927. Yet Mrs. McCracken, whatever reservations or concerns she may have had, did not object. After fifteen years of marriage, no one knew C. C. McCracken better than his wife. She knew that he was serious and thoughtful—a man who always acted in accordance with his principles. Certainly he offered to help this young black girl because he felt she had talent worthy of development. Mrs. McCracken told her husband to go ahead with his plans and reassured him that Ruby would be more than welcome to stay with their family.

Dr. McCracken and Dr. McCoy had agreed that if Ruby failed to pass the preliminary tests, she would be sent home at once. But that posed a dilemma: there was no money for a return ticket. And there would be no one to accompany Ruby back to Mississippi—Ella Becker would be leaving Ruby in Columbus and going on to Mansfield to stay the entire summer. The first few days and weeks Ruby spent in Columbus were therefore critical. Her entire future would depend on how well she was able to handle the tests and trials given her. As the time for Ruby's arrival approached, the usually unflappable Dr. McCracken became apprehensive.

Yet there he was at Union Station when the train pulled in at 7:30 p.m. on Friday, June 17, 1927. Dr. McCracken would remember it vividly: "I stood at the top of the stairway in the main waiting room, my enthusiasm at a very low ebb. When Ruby appeared, she ran all the way up the stairs. She gave me a big smile and said, 'Dr. McCracken! My, but am I glad to see you!' Really, I was glad to see her too, and to finally meet Miss Becker in person. But I was still dreading the next few days."

Ella Becker said she wanted to hear Ruby sing once more before going on to her home in Mansfield. Dr. McCracken suspected that Becker's real desire was to see where Ruby would be living, and the people with whom she'd be living. Together the three made the short drive to the McCracken home at 172 East Lane Avenue, just north of Ohio State's sprawling campus. Ruby had brought along some music, and with Mrs. McCracken at the piano, she sang several numbers. Afterwards Ruby and Miss Becker went upstairs to see the room where Ruby would be staying.

Once they were alone, Dr. McCracken turned to his wife. Cleo McCracken was a conservatory-trained musician who, in addition to being a fine accompanist, had heard many of the great singers of the day in person.

"Well, what do you think?" McCracken asked her.

"I've never heard such a voice in my life," she said. Dr. McCracken smiled. Ruby had passed her first important test.

But all was not well when Ella Becker came back downstairs. She was not happy with Ruby's quarters—a room in the attic, only about twenty-five square feet. It had a bed, a chair, and some hooks on the wall for hanging clothes. McCracken explained that the room was only temporary—he was already working on finding Ruby rooms with a black family near campus. At this news, Ruby spoke up for the first time.

"Please, Dr. McCracken, can't I just stay here?" she asked. "Even though I'm a complete stranger in Columbus, I feel like I already know you. I told Miss Becker that room will be just fine."

McCracken said, "Ruby, Miss Becker is only thinking of your welfare. We know the room isn't much, and besides, it's almost summer, and that attic is going to get awfully warm."

Ruby smiled. "But remember, Dr. McCracken, I'm from Mississippi. That heat in the attic will make me feel right at home."

Everyone laughed, and McCracken said the incident revealed Ruby's sense of humor for the first time. It was a quality he found endearing and one that he would credit with helping her through many difficulties in the future. It was agreed that Ruby would stay, earning her room and board by helping Mrs. McCracken to take care of the house and the McCrackens' four children.

After Ella Becker left to catch her train to Mansfield, Ruby settled in for her first night in the small attic room. Although she was tired from the long train ride, there would be no sleeping late the next morning—Dr. McCracken had already set up her first important audition.

At 9:00 a.m. sharp, Dr. Royal D. Hughes arrived at the McCracken house. A huge, balding man with eyeglasses, Hughes was the director of Ohio State's Department of Music, which he had established only two years before. Like McCracken, Hughes held his doctoral degree from Harvard. It would be Dr. Hughes who would decide whether or not Ruby Elzy had the talent to enter his fledgling music program at Ohio State University.

Ruby entered the parlor, neatly dressed in the simple school uniform she'd worn at Rust College. Once again accompanied by Mrs. McCracken, Ruby began by singing several spirituals. Hughes closed his eyes as he listened to her. When Ruby finished her second song, Hughes smiled and nodded his approval to McCracken. But the smile left his face when Ruby announced her next selection—the "Shadow Song," an aria in French from the Meyerbeer opera *Dinorah*.

Hughes turned to Dr. McCracken and whispered, "Impossible. There's no way a girl who's had no vocal training, who can't even read music, can sing such a difficult piece."

Ruby began to sing. The aria *was* difficult. Ruby had learned it by listening over and over to a recording by one of her favorite singers, the great Metropolitan Opera soprano Amelita Galli-Curci. Yes, Ruby's performance did not have the famed diva's polish and finesse. The French diction was less than flawless. But the aria was suited perfectly to Ruby's clear and vibrant tone and to her instinctive ability to *act* with her voice.

Hughes could not believe his ears. He took over from Mrs. McCracken at the piano and accompanied Ruby through the remainder of her songs. She sang one hymn that required the voice to drop a full octave. When Ruby came to that point of the song, Hughes stopped playing until Ruby struck the low note. Her pitch was dead-on.

Afterwards, McCracken walked Hughes back to his house, a block away. Hughes told McCracken there were many obstacles that lay ahead. Ruby was only nineteen, too young for anyone to make predictions of future success. She lacked musicianship and could not read a note of music. But her voice had convinced Hughes. He told McCracken, "If she remains in Columbus, I'll teach her privately at no cost, even if we can't get her enrolled in the university."

The following night Ruby sang at the Hughes home. Thirty of Columbus's leading musicians showed up at Hughes's invitation to hear the young black soprano. These musicians were all extremely accomplished, and their assessment of her talents would be crucial. Dr. McCracken recognized one woman seated close to the front who was paying rapt attention to Ruby's performance. The woman was one of the principal violinists with the Columbus Symphony Orchestra, and was known to be very critical in her opinions of other musicians. She headed straight for Dr. McCracken when Ruby finished singing. McCracken braced himself in anticipation.

The woman shook his hand and said, "Whatever you do, don't let that girl go back to Mississippi. Her voice is magnificent, and she has the personality to sell herself to any audience." McCracken was relieved.

Since childhood Ruby had sung many times, before many audiences, mostly in her little church in Pontotoc and at Rust College. But in a true sense, the career of "Ruby Elzy, Soprano" began with that recital in the Hughes home on June 19, 1927. Sixteen years later, to the exact day, she would give her final public performance in *Porgy and Bess*.

Dr. McCracken marveled at how quickly Ruby adjusted to this new and different environment. She seemed very much at ease with people who were complete strangers. When Ruby sang, it was not only her voice that impressed; she had a poise and confidence that belied her nineteen years. That first weekend in Columbus, Ruby had won Dr. McCracken's admiration and respect. As far as he was concerned, the question of talent was settled. Now the task was to develop that talent to its fullest potential.

McCracken went to work preparing Ruby for admission to Ohio State. She needed a complete physical examination and, more importantly, an examination to test her IQ. There was the question of her work at Rust College and how it would be treated by Ohio State University (Rust was not yet an accredited school in 1927, one of the reasons for McCracken and John's visit). McCracken wanted Ohio State to accept Ruby's credits at Rust in full, allowing her to enter the University as a sophomore. But the greatest challenge would be finding the money to pay for Ruby's education.

All this was plenty to keep McCracken busy that summer of 1927, yet he took on still another task. Dr. McCracken knew that letting Ruby go had been very difficult for Emma Elzy. He knew how much Emma would miss her daughter and that she would be worrying about her. McCracken began writing to Emma, keeping her informed of everything. Two months after Ruby's arrival, he wrote to Emma about their steady progress:

> Ruby is very happy and has been during her stay in Columbus. We have not been able to give as pleasant a room as we wished that we

might up until last Saturday. She now has a very pleasant room on our second floor and she has made it very pretty and keeps it very nicely . . .

Upon her arrival in Columbus, I sent her to the University Hospital for a thorough physical and medical examination. The doctors reported that she is in the very best of physical condition. This I am sure will be satisfactory to you.

I had her given intelligence examinations by Doctor Maxfield of the University. He gave her the Binet Test and his written statement to me is that she shows an IQ 123, which is up to the average if not above average of our student body in the university. This means that she has mental capacity for doing regular university work.

President McCoy of Rust College sent me her credits. I have arranged for her entrance in Ohio State University and they will give her a full year's credit on her work in the Rust College which means that she will enter the Ohio State University on the first of October with the standing of sophomore.

The important consideration in her case was the matter of voice. I had her tested by Dr. Royal Hughes, head of the Department of Music, and other fine musicians in this city. They report to me that Ruby has a voice of very exceptional range and quality. We have not permitted her to sing in public. She has been singing to friends in our own home. Among those who heard her were the State Superintendent of Public Instruction, the dean of the college of education of the Ohio State University, the assistant superintendent of the Anti-Saloon League, and other men and women of similar standing.

My reason for having these people hear her sing is that I must arrange in some way to take care of her finances. With us she can make her board and room, but we are not able to pay her other bills. These persons who have heard her sing have been so delighted that they have given small amounts of money from time to time so that Ruby now has in the savings bank $35. I know where I can secure enough additional money to assure me that we can pay her tuition and buy her books for the first quarter of the college year. These bills will amount to approximately $100.00.

Emma deeply appreciated McCracken's thoughtfulness in corresponding. Although the two had never met, they were now partners working toward a single goal—to help Ruby to fulfill her dream to sing. Emma wrote to McCracken:

> Of course Ruby has written me all the time how happy she is and how so very nice you all are to her. . . . Dr. McCracken, I do appreciate all that's being done for my child. I wish I had words at my command to express how much I do appreciate your kindness and how thankful I am to you all and my heavenly Father. I get awfully blue to see her some time especially when the rest of my little family and I assemble in the home for our night's rest. The only consolation I have is I prayed to the Lord to help me to make such a man and women out of them as He would be pleased with.
>
> I am so thankful because all the wonderful things that are being done for Ruby is an answer to my prayer. Oh, how can I realize such great things being done for my precious little daughter? You are wonderful people with big, big hearts to do so much for a poor little black girl. I am indeed proud to know she is in the best of health and so proud she has a mental capacity to do regular university work and so thankful she can enter the university. Thank you for the great things you all are doing for my precious little girl.

The correspondence begun that summer sparked a friendship between Emma Elzy and the McCrackens that would continue for more than thirty years—long after Ruby's death.

Dr. McCracken's efforts to have Ruby sing for important people began to pay off. In September 1927 McCracken was engaged to give the keynote address before the Ohio Teachers Institute in Bellefontaine, Ohio. He arranged for Ruby to give two short concerts, which were announced in the *Bellefontaine Daily Examiner:* "A unique feature of the Institute will be the appearance Monday, September 5, of Miss Ruby Elzy, a lyric soprano of unusual personality and talent.

Her presence is made possible through Professor Charles McCracken, of Columbus, who will appear on the program Monday evening."

Ruby's performance was a great success, and the following day the *Daily Examiner* gave her a headlined story:

Miss Ruby Elzy Delights Large Audience of Educators

> Miss Ruby Elzy . . . sang a group of spirituals which showed the great beauty of her voice. The possessor of a voice said to be equal, if not superior, in its upper range to that of any known soprano, Miss Elzy is quite unspoiled and natural before her audience. In the afternoon she sang a group of classical numbers . . . (and) in response to the enthusiastic desire of her listeners, she encored with another group of spirituals.

In the coming years, Ruby would be acclaimed by the nation's most renowned critics in America's greatest newspapers. But the review from that small town Ohio newspaper in 1927 would remain one of her most cherished.

McCracken saw the Bellefontaine program as an important step for Ruby, as he wrote to Emma Elzy: "While they [the Teacher's Institute] will not pay her a great deal, they will give her some compensation for her appearance. I am doing this in order that Ruby may see that it will pay her to go on with the development of her voice. Some day, she will be drawing very considerable sums for her appearance if nothing happens to her voice."

That summer, Ruby gave several church concerts at which collections were taken up after she sang; one congregation's free-will offering amounted to more than fifty dollars, a huge sum in 1927. Dr. McCracken wrote to several civic organizations, such as the Columbus Rotary Club, telling Ruby's story and asking their help in supporting her education. From these letters came a number of gifts, ranging from twenty-five cents to twenty-five dollars. Everything was put into a special account for Ruby that Dr. McCracken set up. He taught Ruby how to keep the books—another way in which she was learning to become self-sufficient. By September, Ruby had enough money in the account to cover the tuition and all her living expenses for the fall quarter. In September 1927 Ruby Elzy entered the sophomore class at Ohio State University.

By this time, Ruby had become a full member of the McCracken family. Earlier in the summer, just after Ruby's arrival, Cleo McCracken had been stricken with a life-threatening illness. A physician was called in late at night, and he decided that emergency surgery was needed at once. Cleo McCracken lay on the sofa, her husband and family anxiously waiting for the ambulance to arrive that would take her to the hospital. As the attendants lifted Mrs. McCracken onto the stretcher, Ruby, standing in the doorway, began to sing:

His eye is on the sparrow,
And I know he watches me.

In every crisis of her life, or of those whom she loved, Ruby Elzy turned to song—especially a spiritual—to express her feelings in ways that spoken words alone could not express.

Cleo McCracken's surgery was a success, but it would be several weeks before she would be allowed to return home. Once she did, she would still need at least a month of convalescence. With help from Mrs. McCracken's parents (who lived next door), Ruby took charge of the house. Her experience as Ella Becker's assistant in the E. L. Rust Home for Girls came in handy, as Ruby now became caretaker for the McCrackens' four energetic children—Janet, age thirteen; William, ten; Mary Ruth, eight; and the baby, Edward, who was only five.

The two boys were especially rambunctious, and Ruby had her hands full with them. As William "Bill" McCracken remembered, "My favorite time with Ruby was Saturday night, when we took our baths. Ed and I would run upstairs and hide under our parents' bed. Ruby would stand at the staircase and holler in this stern voice, 'William! Edward! Don't you make me come up there and get you! You get down here *right now* and get into this bathtub!' She pretended to be mad, but she ended up laughing almost as much as Ed and me were."

Ruby was a natural at taking care of children, just as she had proven with her own siblings and at Rust College. She developed a deep and lasting bond with each of the McCracken children. The youngest—Ruby always called him "my Edward"—became her favorite. The McCracken children returned her love and devotion completely.

Shortly after Mrs. McCracken came back home, Dr. McCracken took their eldest daughter Janet to a recital. It would be very late when they got back home. Ruby put the younger children to bed, and helped Mrs. McCracken into her bed as well. When he and Janet arrived home, Dr. McCracken went up to his bedroom and was surprised to see Ruby sleeping on the rug next to Mrs. McCracken's bed.

Dr. McCracken woke Ruby up and asked, "Ruby, why didn't you go to bed upstairs in your room, instead of laying down on this hard floor?"

She answered, "Dr. McCracken, if I'd gone upstairs, I would've slept so soundly Mrs. McCracken couldn't have awakened me with a clap of thunder. So I just curled up on the rug. That way, if she needed me, I'd be right here. I wasn't about to leave until you came back home." Dr. McCracken later wrote, "Ruby then went on to bed, satisfied that she had done her duty. But she had left us with a feeling that we had found a real and true friend."

In October 1927, Mary Ruth McCracken had her ninth birthday. Mrs. McCracken was still weak from her recent illness, so Ruby and Janet took charge in preparing an elaborate meal, followed by cake and ice cream with all the trimmings. When they had finished, Dr. McCracken announced a special treat: he was taking everyone downtown to catch the stage show and a movie at the Keith-Orpheum's Palace Theatre.

Mrs. McCracken remained at home resting, while everyone else piled into the family car for the short ride downtown. When they arrived at the theatre, Ruby stayed with the children while Dr. McCracken bought the tickets.

They went up to the ticket taker, who let Dr. McCracken and the children in. But when Ruby presented her ticket, he refused. "No coloreds allowed," the man told her. Dr. McCracken immediately protested, then tried the tactic that had worked when Ella Becker brought Ruby on the train. "She's our children's maid," Dr. McCracken said; "she should be allowed in with our family." It was no use—the man said it was the theatre's policy to exclude blacks for evening performances. Ruby could not even sit in the upper balcony, the section of the theatre where blacks were usually relegated.

The McCracken children were now joining in a loud protest against the ticket taker. They had become fiercely protective of Ruby, and if she could not go in, they would not either. The box office manager ended up refunding Dr. McCracken's money, and the family headed back to the car. The doctor and his children were all upset; Ruby had not yet said anything.

Things seemed even worse when the car would not start. Dr. McCracken tried several times with no luck, and it looked as if they all might have to catch the streetcar home. Then Ruby spoke for the first time.

"Maybe this car objects to having a nigger in it," she said with a big smile. Her remark broke the tension, and everyone burst out laughing. It even seemed to help the car—when Dr. McCracken tried the starter again, the engine turned over and they went home.

Dr. McCracken later recalled, "We all felt so sorry for Ruby—I had never dreamed that she would be refused admission, even when she was with our family. After we got home, we decided to put on a show of our own. Ruby was not barred from this one—in fact she was the star. Several years later, she would be singing to audiences in Columbus, the size of which would make any theatre manager turn green with envy."

Dr. McCracken knew that racism and bigotry were not confined to the South; there was plenty of it in the North as well. But not until he began to help Ruby Elzy did C. C. McCracken come to fully appreciate the ugliness and injustice that blacks in America were forced to endure as a part of daily life.

Yet, as sorry as Dr. McCracken felt for Ruby, he also knew that prejudice was something she would have to deal with throughout her life, an obstacle she would have to find the strength to deal with on her own terms. And deal with them she did, in ways that McCracken came to admire: "No one sensed more keenly than Ruby how important it was that she be able to deal with those who objected to her because of her race. To me, she possessed three qualities which helped to do that. First, she had a marvelous sense of humor, coupled with an engaging personality that made her instantly likable. Second, she had a brilliant mind and an ability to analyze people and situations quickly and accurately. Third, and most important, she possessed the unique gift that was hers alone and which enabled her to break down almost any barrier—her voice."

Ruby would face prejudice not only in the outside world, but even at Ohio State. In her first quarter, Ruby was put into the new University Chorus, directed by Royal Hughes. On the second day of school, two students from Texas approached Hughes after class.

"We don't have to sit next to colored people where we come from," they told Hughes, "and we don't intend to sit next to one here." The students wanted Hughes to move Ruby. Embarrassed, Hughes asked Ruby if she'd mind sitting in the back. She graciously agreed.

A month later the same two students came again to see the director. "Dr. Hughes, we'd like to ask if you would apologize to Ruby for us. We've come to really admire her, and would consider it an honor to sit next to someone with such a wonderful voice." Ruby had triumphed once again over those who would mistreat her.

When Ruby began attending Ohio State in 1927, there were three hundred students in the Department of Music, which was part of the College of Education. Although Ruby was planning for a career as a singer, her degree from the university would qualify her to teach public school—something that Miss Ella Becker back at Rust very much wanted her to do.

The first year at Ohio State was difficult for Ruby, and even more so for Dr. Hughes. It seemed that singing was all Ruby wanted to do, but Hughes wanted her to develop into a complete, well-rounded musician. It was a slow process, but Ruby eventually learned how to read music. She also learned how to play the piano, at least enough to accompany herself as she practiced singing.

In addition to music, Ruby took courses required as part of the College of Education's curriculum. She took Spanish and also French, learning how to speak and sing it correctly—no more imitating Galli-Curci records! At Ohio State, Ruby was given the opportunity to have the kind of education Emma Elzy had fervently prayed for her daughter to receive. Ruby worked hard, not wanting to disappoint her mother or Dr. McCracken, who by now had become not just Ruby's adviser and mentor but almost her surrogate father. Throughout the remainder of her life, there would be no two people Ruby relied upon or trusted more than Emma Elzy and C. C. McCracken.

Ruby lived with the McCrackens until December 1927. Dr. McCracken suffered respiratory problems that worsened in cold weather, so the family spent each winter in Florida. Ruby at first moved in with a family that was white, but they treated her as little more than a servant. When Dr. McCracken returned and found out, he removed Ruby from the home at once and severed all further relations with that family. He then found Ruby a home near campus with a black family, the Taylors. Mr. Taylor worked as a laboratory assistant at the university.

Ruby's third move in less than a year alarmed Emma, who wrote a heartfelt letter to Cleo McCracken in March, 1928:

> My Dear Mrs. McCracken,
>
> If for any reason you should think I shouldn't write this letter, please forgive me for I don't mean anything that would make any one feel bad. But Mrs. McCracken I am so worried tonight. I am compelled to write. My reason for writing is this. I received a very sweet letter from Ruby today that she had moved her boarding place. Again, she told me how

very happy she was and how so very sweet you were seeing that she had a nice comfortable place, but I am worried. I would like to know of you why my child has to change homes so much.

Please don't think hard of me for asking, I guess I wouldn't be so crazy about my four children if they had a father to care for them, but since they don't I will admit that I really act silly about them sometimes, but they are my heart. I don't want her thrust out in the world amid temptations of a wicked world unprotected. I had rather go to my grave than to fail to raise pure worthy Christian leaders for my race. I have never been to any of the great Northern cities, don't know anything about them, but I do know Mrs. McCracken, the exodus of the last few years of my race from the South carried all kind, both good and bad to Northern cities and so many of them have taken up with the evil side of life.

Please don't place her with any people you don't know. I am writing her advising her about the evils of life. Yet, I know she needs protection. Please let me know about her. Anything should come up in her life that's not agreeable let me know at once for I wouldn't let her stay in Columbus one day if I knew she wasn't or didn't have the care of a Christian home.

Fortunately, the Taylors did keep a good Christian home. They were Baptists, however, not Methodists as were the Elzys. Dr. McCracken recalled Ruby coming over to see him, soon after she moved in with the Taylors. He could see Ruby was clearly distressed about something. It turned out that the Taylors had invited Ruby to a prayer meeting at their church.

"Dr. McCracken," Ruby said, "if I wrote home to Mama that I'm mixing in with the Baptists she'll think I'm on my way to Hell in a hurry." McCracken couldn't keep from laughing. He encouraged her to go along, reassuring that nothing bad would happen. Ruby did, and when she came back the next week told him, "Dr. McCracken, I never would've guessed those people were Baptists, they were so nice and pleasant to me." She smiled at McCracken and said, "I guess they're not going to Hell after all." McCracken smiled and nodded. Ruby was having her attitudes challenged; her view of the world was growing and maturing. In years ahead, Ruby would sing in churches of all denominations, not bound by whether or not they happened to be of the same faith as hers. Her voice had come from God, and was meant to share with all God's peoples, regardless of where they happened to go to church.

Ruby celebrated her twenty-first birthday in February 1929, a month that would mark several important milestones. On February 4, Ruby was one of seventeen sopranos chosen to sing in the first Columbus performance of Ernest Bloch's tone poem *America* with the renowned Cleveland Orchestra. More than three thousand people heard the concert in Memorial Hall. Even though she was not a soloist, the experience of performing with the great orchestra to the huge audience was thrilling for Ruby.

Even more thrilling was the opportunity three days later to meet tenor Roland Hayes, by far the most celebrated black singer of that time. Dr. McCracken had met Hayes in Chicago a few months before. Knowing that Hayes was soon to appear in Columbus, McCracken asked him if he could take time to meet and hear Ruby. The generous Hayes, always eager to help young black artists, agreed.

Ruby sang for Hayes, accompanied by Dr. Hughes. When she finished Mozart's "The Violet," Hayes leaned forward in his chair. "Delicious," he said, "simply delicious." Ruby was genuinely humbled at his words of praise. McCracken had hoped that meeting the great tenor would inspire Ruby, and it did. Hayes became one of Ruby's most ardent supporters, writing to McCracken:

> I wish to express my appreciation of Miss Ruby Elzy, whom you introduced to me in Columbus. . . . Miss Elzy has a very unusual coloratura soprano voice which is worthy of development. I would even consider that she possesses a voice like which there are very few on the concert stage at the present time. Aside from the wonderful voice,

which Miss Elzy possesses, she has a natural artistry and the personality that make her especially attractive to the listeners. I consider that you are rendering to the Negro race and to society at large, a very real service in the part that you are taking in assisting Miss Elzy in her musical training. If I can at any time (help) you in advising as to the best methods to be followed in future training or as to any other phases of Miss Elzy's work, I shall be glad to be at your service for I believe that she has a real future.

A few hours after her private audition for Hayes, Ruby sang three solos with the University Chorus in a special program that was broadcast live on WEAO (today WOSU). It was the first time Ruby sang on radio, a medium that in the coming years would carry her voice into millions of homes across the United States.

Except for a few short visits home to see her mother, who was now living and teaching in Corinth, Mississippi, Ruby spent her summers in Columbus, taking classes and continuing her voice lessons with Dr. Hughes. The first school year had been the most tenuous, due to the constant worry over finances, but Ruby had made it through. She made money by performing occasionally, but Dr. McCracken and Dr. Hughes strictly controlled her appearances, thwarting anyone whom they felt was trying to exploit Ruby. By now they operated like a well-oiled machine: Dr. McCracken managed Ruby's finances and provided overall guidance to her career; Dr. Hughes supervised her musical and vocal training; and Cleo McCracken advised Ruby on personal matters, such as grooming and wardrobe. Ruby placed her complete confidence in their advice and judgment, and always acted accordingly. As Dr. McCracken recalled, "We played the game together—real teamwork."

During the 1928–1929 school year Ruby received her first scholarship, a $250 grant from the Presser Foundation, which had been established by Theodore Presser, music publisher and founder of *Etude* magazine. The foundation awarded scholarships to deserving music students at schools throughout the United States. One Ohio State student received the award each year, selected by the University's Board of Trustees. When Ruby received the first of her two Presser awards (she was chosen again in 1929–1930), the chairman of Ohio State's board was a man named Julius F. Stone.

Stone was an industrialist and one of the wealthiest men in Columbus. He had quietly followed Ruby's progress during her first year and was well aware of Dr. McCracken's efforts on her behalf. After the board voted to give Ruby the Presser Foundation scholarship, Stone decided to get personally involved. He contacted McCracken and told him that whatever additional funds were needed for Ruby's tuition and expenses, he would provide. There was one caveat: Ruby was not to be told who was helping her. McCracken agreed, and in December 1928 the first of Stone's checks in the amount of $250 arrived to support Ruby's tuition for the winter quarter. By the time she graduated in June 1930, Stone had anonymously given Ruby a total of $1,000. McCracken kept his promise—to the day she died, Ruby never knew the name of her benefactor. Thanks to Stone's generosity, Ruby's finances at Ohio State were never again a worry.

By now, Ruby was becoming well known. In April 1929, she was featured in a cover story in the *Columbus Dispatch*: "Cotton Patch Singer, 'Find' of Professor, Groomed at University for Concert Career." The article, written by Anne Schatenstein, ran two pages and included Ruby's picture. The reporter spent an afternoon at the McCracken home, interviewing both Dr. McCracken and Dr. Hughes. Ruby talked for several hours and even sang for Schatenstein. The reporter noted: "Her attachment and pride in her race is very keen. When Miss Elzy sang the spirituals of her people, she seemed imbued with regal supplication to her Deity for her race. Her dignity, poise, and self-possession is a thing of beauty when she sings."

Dr. McCracken would later say that, from the time the article appeared in the *Dispatch*, the people of Columbus, Ohio, would claim her as their own. Madge Cooper, a student who was in the University

Girls Glee Club with Ruby, said, "Everybody adored Ruby. It didn't matter that she was black." Incidents such as what had happened with the two Texans in Ruby's first year had ceased, at least on campus. McCracken wrote, "The entire city, as well as the University, fell in love with her." The story attracted national publicity for Ruby, and McCracken and Hughes were besieged with offers for her to appear.

One intriguing call came from a Miss Henrietta Davis, a teacher who was in charge of the school music program in Upper Arlington, a suburb of Columbus near the university campus. Davis read the *Dispatch* article and thought Ruby's story would make a unique play with music. Davis wanted it to be presented in her school, using students from the fifth and sixth grades.

The idea immediately appealed to Ruby, who chose to write about the night she left Pontotoc to begin the trip to Columbus. That incident had been one of the most moving parts in the *Dispatch* story. Ruby went to work on the play, which she decided to call *Stumbling Upward*. There were characters named Sarah, Susan, Jim, Dr. Smith, Dr. Williams—all of them representing real people in her life. Mama, Grandma Belle, Aunt Fannie, brother Robert, sisters Amanda and Wayne, Dr. McCoy and Dr. McCracken—they were all in there with Ruby, who named her own character "Ann."

Ruby sat on the parlor floor in the McCracken house every night for several weeks, writing dialogue and then reading to the family for their reactions. She would then show her work to Henrietta Davis, who would offer comments and suggestions. Ruby included nine spirituals in the play and taught them to Davis's students. She also helped Davis cast the leads and coached them on Negro dialect. Ruby loved working with the children—all of whom were white—and felt immensely proud that she was helping them to learn about and appreciate her race. *Stumbling Upward* was presented at Upper Arlington High School on May 9, 1930. For her efforts, Ruby was paid an honorarium of ten dollars.

Dr. McCracken always advised his students to copyright their works, to protect their creative rights. He told Ruby she should copyright her play, and as always, she followed his advice. On May 22, 1930, the Copyright Office of the United States recorded filing number D–5744 for *Stumbling Upward*—"A play in two acts by Ruby Pearl Elzy." Ruby's original application, showing she had paid the requisite fee of one dollar, is still on file in the Copyright Office in Washington, D.C. Ruby Elzy was now an author as well as an accomplished singer; but within a year, *Stumbling Upward* would become a quagmire not only for Ruby but also for her mentor, Dr. McCracken.

In September 1929, Ruby entered her senior year at Ohio State. After living for two years with the Taylors in their small house, Ruby needed more space. Dr. McCracken arranged for her to move in with the Greene Harris family. Mr. Harris, the postmaster at Ohio State, was the kind of upstanding, church-going gentleman Dr. McCracken knew would meet with Emma Elzy's approval. The Harris house at 2839 Indianola Avenue was large and comfortable. Ruby enjoyed staying with the Harrises and their four children. The youngest, Norman, was only seven when Ruby came to stay with them. Norman Harris still lives in the house and remembers when Ruby Elzy was a boarder there.

"She had a friend who'd come over, and they would take me down to High Street and buy me ice cream," Harris said. He recalls hearing Ruby practice in the living room. "Although I was too young to know much about music, I knew she had a beautiful voice," he said.

Mr. Harris's job meant that he got up before dawn, so the whole family would retire early. One night, Ruby sang a program across town, wearing for the first time a beautiful dress that Cleo McCracken had made for her. When Ruby got home, she found that she had forgotten her key; the Harrises had already gone to bed and Ruby did not want to disturb them. She quickly decided there was another way to get in. Ruby's room was at the front of the house, just above the large brick covered porch. By climbing from the brick railing, she could shinny up the drain spout onto the porch roof and get into her room through the open window.

Ruby began to climb. When she reached the porch roof, she lunged from the spout to the window. As she did, Ruby heard a huge rip. Her new dress was split in back from the waist to the ankles, ruining it completely.

The next day an embarrassed Ruby went over to see Dr. and Mrs. McCracken, certain they would be angry that she had been so careless. But when she told them the story of what had happened, instead they burst out laughing. Ruby's hilarious description of herself, dangling in mid-air between drain spout and window with the rear end of her dress ripped out, was too much. Cleo McCracken reassured her, "Don't worry about the dress, Ruby. We'll just make you a new one." Ruby was both relieved and grateful. Soon, Mrs. McCracken made a beautiful pink gown, one that would get a great deal of use in Ruby's final months at Ohio State.

Under Dr. Hughes's tutelage, Ruby's voice matured into a full coloratura soprano, with a range from a low B to a D above high C. Her repertoire expanded considerably, and she could sing in four languages—English, French, Italian, and German. During her last year at Ohio State, Ruby began performing more frequently. She gave concerts at the Western College for Women in Oxford, Ohio, and also at Knoxville College in Tennessee. Dr. McCracken and Dr. Hughes decided that Ruby would be given a singular honor before graduating—she would be the first student at Ohio State University to give a recital open to the public.

The question now facing Ruby was—what would she do after graduation? She would have a degree in education, and Ella Becker was already hoping Ruby would come back to Mississippi to teach. But Hughes and McCracken both felt Ruby should go on with her studies, to continue her preparation for a career on stage. But where she should go to study and how to pay for it were major concerns.

Dr. Hughes wrote to the renowned Curtis Institute of Music in Philadelphia. Curtis wrote back promptly that they were not interested, even to hear Ruby audition. It looked as if Ruby would have to teach, at least for a while. She was offered the position of supervisor of music in the Negro schools in Birmingham, Alabama. But McCracken advised her instead to take a position teaching music at her old school, Rust College. Dr. McCoy knew that Ruby hoped to go on with her singing career. If she would get the opportunity to go on with her studies abroad or at a major conservatory, McCoy would be willing to release her from her contract, which Birmingham or another place probably would not do. Ruby agreed to go back to Rust.

Ruby's graduating recital took place in University Chapel on May 27, 1930. The auditorium was filled to capacity; Madge Cooper said, "There wasn't a single seat unoccupied, and the people who didn't have seats were standing shoulder to shoulder." Ruby was dressed in the new pink gown made for her by Cleo McCracken. She would be accompanied by her good friend Olive Jones, who was white.

Ruby had saved all the money from her singing engagements to bring her mother up from Mississippi. Emma Elzy sat in the front row, seated next to Dr. George Rightmire, the President of Ohio State University, and his wife.

Olive Jones began the introduction to Ruby's first song, a French aria by Meyerbeer. As Ruby sang, she noticed her mother lower her head and clasp her hands, as if in prayer. When Ruby finished, the audience erupted in applause, which seemed to catch Emma off guard. Ruby sang in French, Italian, and German, and closed with a set of spirituals.

It was hot in the packed hall, and at one point Ruby smiled to the audience and fanned herself with a program, as if to say, "I'm hot, too." Her gesture brought laughter to everyone but Dr. Hughes, upset that Ruby had not maintained what he considered the proper concert decorum. Yet Ruby's small act had shown one of the qualities that endeared her to audiences—the ability to empathize with them.

When her program was finished, the applause was deafening, and Ruby was called back for many bows. She held up her hands and announced that she would do an encore, another spiritual that she would sing unaccompanied. It was the number McCracken had first heard her sing that spring morning three years earlier—"Steal Away."

Before she began, Ruby said, "There is someone here tonight who can sing this better than I." She motioned to Emma in the front row. "My mother can beat me all to pieces." The audience applauded Emma, who had tears streaking down her face.

After the concert, Mama joined Ruby for a huge party given at the McCracken house on Lane Avenue. Emma was dazed at the number of people who wanted to shake her hand, to tell her how much they admired her daughter. A reporter from Ohio State's newspaper, *The Lantern*, interviewed Emma, who said, "It is so wonderful. We are poor people and I could never have given Ruby the training she has had. It is to people like Dr. C. C. McCracken and Dr. Royal D. Hughes, her teacher, that she owes her success."

Later that night, after they left the McCrackens', Ruby did have one question for Emma: "Mama, why did you have your head down when I was singing my French aria?" Emma blushed and admitted, "Honey, I didn't *know* you could even sing in French! Mama thought you'd forgotten your words and was praying to God to help her baby to remember!" The two women laughed all the way back to the Harris house, where Mama was staying with Ruby.

On June 10, 1930, with Mama looking on, Ruby graduated from Ohio State with her Bachelor of Science in Education degree. She ranked first in her class of students from the Department of Music.

In a few days, Ruby left Columbus to begin a month of performances that Dr. McCracken had arranged for her throughout the East and Midwest at Methodist Church summer conferences. When the tour was completed, she would go on to Rust to begin teaching.

Saying farewell to Dr. McCracken was difficult for Ruby, much more difficult than the farewells at Rust College three years before.

A month after Ruby bid them goodbye, she poured her heart in a letter to the McCrackens:

> You can never know how hard it was to leave you, to feel that I wouldn't be there any more for any length of time, to feel that now I am through at Columbus. I've learned to love every one of you very much. I shall always love you. The 3 years I've spent in your circle have all been beautiful. If I hadn't known the love, friendship and harmony of a home, I would have certainly learned from your circle—such beautiful love and harmony between every member.
>
> Your children have made me love children, made me try to judge all children by yours and try to bring them up to your standard. I hope you will always have that love and respect for your home and each other that you have. The result will be that you'll always be happy. I hope you love Ruby half as much as she loves you. Even after you are grown men and women, I'll still love you as my Janet, Mary Ruth, William, and Edward. Please remember that you have helped me form ideals as much as "Mother and Daddy" have. You can each in your own way do much for our Father's world.
>
> Dr. McCracken, I'll never feel wholly that you aren't the "boss." It's an opportunity that comes once in a lifetime to have a boss like you. Ask Mrs. McCracken if that isn't true (smile). I shall always weigh your advice more carefully than ordinary advice because I've found that it has never been wrong.
>
> If all mothers were like you, Mrs. McCracken, there would be no pain. There'd been no disobedient children. You have done so much for me. You've been so considerate of everything. We all know that you are the power behind the throne. I love you very much and have so much faith in your decisions. It has been more than a privilege to know you.

Ruby's performances that summer at Methodist camps and conferences in Wisconsin and New York were immensely successful. When she returned south, Ruby gave six concerts in her native Mississippi;

then it was on to Holly Springs. Ruby arrived at Rust College in early August to begin teaching music, much to the delight of Miss Ella Becker.

But Mother Elzy was right—Mississippi was too small for Ruby. Emma's daughter had a great talent and had shown she deserved the right to share that talent with the world. Ruby's life was moving forward like a train in motion, picking up steam as it went.

The next stop would be New York City.

A MAGNOLIA IN MANHATTAN

In mid-June 1930, less than a week after he watched his protégé graduate from Ohio State, Dr. McCracken went to Chicago for an educational conference. Also attending was Edwin Embree, president of the Julius Rosenwald Fund. Rosenwald was a Jewish merchant and philanthropist who had risen from being a clerk to chairman of Sears, Roebuck & Company. Rosenwald supported many causes, but the one he was devoted to above all others was the Negro. In 1917 he had created the Rosenwald Fund to support projects in health, education, and the arts, all to benefit black Americans. Rosenwald Fellowships were awarded for talented black writers, artists and musicians, and Dr. McCracken felt Ruby was an ideal candidate to receive one.

By chance, McCracken and Embree were seated together at a conference luncheon. McCracken knew this was his chance, and introduced himself to Embree.

He said, "Mr. Embree, I'd like to make an appointment with you while I'm in town, to discuss a young Negro soprano whom I think deserves the Rosenwald Fund's consideration."

Embree politely declined. "I'm sorry, but I'm just getting ready to go out of town," he said, and started to walk away. But when he saw the look of disappointment in McCracken's face, Embree paused and said, "All right, Dr. McCracken. I'll give you five minutes right here and now to tell me about this girl."

McCracken took a deep breath. He proceeded to tell Embree the highlights of Ruby's background, finishing with two minutes to spare.

Embree was impressed. He told McCracken the Rosenwald Fund would be willing to help Ruby study abroad. They had recently awarded a fellowship to a young contralto from Philadelphia, sponsoring her for a year of study in Germany. Her name was Marian Anderson.

McCracken said, "Frankly, I don't think Miss Elzy is ready just yet for Europe. But I think she would really benefit from attending a good school right here in the states."

Without hesitation Embree said, "Send her to Juilliard. You go ahead and make the arrangements. I can promise her a $1,200 fellowship from the Rosenwald Fund."

When Ruby heard the news, she was ecstatic. Dr. McCracken had come through again for her. But there was one drawback: it was already June, past Juilliard's admission deadline for the new school year beginning in October.

By August 1930, Ruby had finished her summer performances at Methodist camp meetings and conferences and had joined the faculty at Rust College. A month later came word from Juilliard: Ruby would be granted a special audition on Monday, October 6. If accepted, she would begin class that same week.

Dr. McCoy kept his promise and released Ruby from her teaching contract at Rust. Before she left Mississippi, he advanced a full month's salary to help cover the cost of her trip to New York. There would be no Ella Becker to accompany her this time, no McCracken family to stay with. Ruby made the trip to New York alone and took a room at the YWCA.

The Juilliard School (or the Institute of Musical Art, as it was called then) was located on Claremont Avenue, within sight of Grant's Tomb. Ruby arrived early on the appointed Monday, more nervous than usual; so much was riding on this one audition. Chairing the audition panel was the dean of the school, Dr. Frank Damrosch. He was a brilliant musician and educator, and the younger brother of one of America's greatest conductors, Walter Damrosch.

Ruby was called in to sing promptly at 12:30. She offered a short but diverse program that showcased her voice and technique at their best. Once she had finished, Ruby was asked to wait in the lobby. Within ten minutes, the auditioning committee had reached their decision.

Dr. Damrosch came out where Ruby was seated. "Miss Elzy," he said, "welcome to Juilliard."

As excited as Ruby was, there was little time for celebration. The fall term was to begin the following day. She had to register for classes and get her books and other materials. But by late that afternoon, everything was ready, and Ruby boarded the subway back to the Y, located in Harlem on West 137th Street, just a block from Lenox Avenue.

It was an exciting time to be in Harlem—the vibrant, pulsating center of black life in New York. The "New Negro Movement"—known today as the Harlem Renaissance—was ten years old when Ruby came to New York in 1930. The movement covered roughly the two decades between the world wars. It was a dazzling period when the most brilliant and creative minds in black America came together in Harlem to forge what would be the greatest flowering of black literature, theatre, and music in history.

At the heart of the movement were people such as poets James Weldon Johnson and Langston Hughes, fiction writer Zora Neale Hurston, and painter Jacob Lawrence. These gifted artists lived and worked in Harlem, presided over and encouraged by the grande dame of black society, Miss A'Lelia Walker, daughter of Madame C. J. Walker. Into this unique world now stepped the young soprano from the Magnolia State. Within a few years Ruby would become a friend and colleague to many of those in—and herself a respected member of—the "New Negro Movement."

Settling in New York, Ruby was happy to find that she would once again be close to the McCrackens. Saying goodbye to them had been the most difficult part of leaving Columbus. Rust College was more than six hundred miles away from Ohio State, and Ruby knew it would be a long time before she would see her mentor and his family again.

In August 1930 Dr. McCracken went to New England, sent on yet another federally sponsored survey, this time of Eastern land-grant colleges. Among the schools he visited was the Connecticut State Agricultural College (today the University of Connecticut), whose governing board was looking for a new president. When the college trustees met C. C. McCracken, they knew they had found their man. Their offer came as a complete surprise to Dr. McCracken, who had never aspired to be a college president. But the opportunity was too good to pass up. In September, just as Ruby was leaving Mississippi for New York, Dr. McCracken moved his family to the quaint town of Storrs, where the college was located. It was only a two-hour commute by train from New York. Ruby and her "beloved McCrackens" would be able to see each other often.

Ruby had been in New York barely a week, but she already had a home (even if it was only a room at the Y), her classes at Juilliard, and the Rosenwald Fellowship to pay her tuition. All she needed now was a job—preferably singing—to help cover her living expenses.

From another black singer staying at the Y, Ruby learned that a Negro chorus was auditioning for new members. Its director was a man who would, over time, become a friend and mentor almost as close to her as C. C. McCracken.

His name was John Rosamond Johnson.

Rosamond Johnson—as he was best known—was the younger brother of James Weldon Johnson, one America's greatest black poets and a leading figure in the Harlem Renaissance. The brothers had started their careers together with a friend named Bob Cole. The trio became immensely popular in vaudeville and on Broadway for their songs and sketches. In 1900, James wrote a poem that he hoped would inspire the Negro people, instilling in them a pride that would help them rise above the prejudices of Jim Crow. Rosamond set the poem to music, and "Lift Every Voice and Sing" was born. Within a decade, the song was known to every black child in America, and was called "The Negro National Anthem."

In 1928 Rosamond and James collaborated on one of the most popular collections of the "New Negro Movement": *The Book of American Negro Spirituals*. Ruby had gotten a copy of the book while she was a student at Ohio State and had sung many of Rosamond Johnson's arrangements.

Ruby contacted Johnson and asked if she could audition for him. One song was all it took for Johnson to offer her a place in his chorus at a salary of twenty-five dollars per week—a sizable sum at the time. And Ruby would need to start right away—the Rosamond Johnson Choir was set to open in a new show on Broadway in a few days.

That a young singer could arrive in New York and within a week make her debut on Broadway is a scenario so unlikely that it almost seems like a contrived story—yet that is exactly how it happened. On Tuesday, October 7, 1930, Ruby Elzy stepped on to a New York stage for the first time in a show called *Brown Buddies*. The star was the greatest and most popular black song and dance man in the world—Bill "Bojangles" Robinson.

Billed as "a Negro musical comedy in two acts," *Brown Buddies* was a loosely plotted show about a company of black soldiers leaving St. Louis and going off to fight in what then was called "The Great War." With the incandescent Robinson in the lead, *Brown Buddies* was a two-hour romp with all the stereotypical characterizations of blacks that had become commonplace in American entertainment. Ruby's main contribution was in several spirituals Johnson had arranged. Three high C's were called for, and none of the other sopranos in the choir had them. With Ruby's fluid voice, high notes were no problem.

Brown Buddies proved to be a hit, making things hectic for Ruby during her first three months in New York. She would attend classes at Juilliard all day, then grab a quick dinner before catching the subway to the Liberty Theatre, where *Brown Buddies* was presented eight times a week. Ruby's part in it was small, but no matter—she was on Broadway. Thanks to the twenty-five dollars a week she was earning, she was even able to move out of the YWCA into her own apartment.

Nonetheless, Ruby was relieved when *Brown Buddies* closed in January 1931, after 111 performances. Juilliard was a difficult and demanding school with high standards. Students were treated as the professional musicians they were all aspiring to become. In her first year Ruby studied piano, sight-singing, music theory, English diction, and Italian. Most importantly, she was studying voice with Lucia Dunham.

Dunham's career at Juilliard would encompass more than four decades. She was an accomplished singer herself who had performed on the operatic stage and in concerts with both the San Francisco and New York Symphony Orchestras. Yet her true gift was teaching. Dunham's greatest strength as a teacher was her belief that singers must also be actors. Her philosophy appealed at once to Ruby, with her own innate dramatic sense. It would be Lucia Dunham, building on the foundation laid by Royal Hughes at Ohio State, who would transform Ruby Elzy into an accomplished artist, and more importantly, into a singing actress.

Ruby enjoyed being in a place where everyone and everything revolved around music. She made friends easily among her fellow students. It was at Juilliard that Ruby met Arthur Kaplan, the young pianist who would later accompany her many times, including the concert at the White House.

There were a number of black students at Juilliard. One girl in particular, also a soprano, would become a friend to Ruby.

Anne Wiggins Brown was four years younger than Ruby when she came to Juilliard, right after graduating from high school in her native Baltimore, Maryland. Anne's background could not have been more different than Ruby's. Her father, Dr. Harry Brown, was a prominent physician and one of the leading black citizens in Baltimore. Dr. Brown was able to provide his wife and three daughters with money and material things Ruby could only dream of. The Browns were a proud family and extremely sensitive to any racial prejudice. Yet interestingly, there was considerable white blood (as well as Native American) in the Brown line. Anne herself was fair enough to often be mistaken for white. Ruby would tease her friend at times by calling her "Yaller"—the term blacks used for Negroes who were light-skinned. Anne's temperament was very different from Ruby's. Ruby tried to understand those who were prejudiced against her and to persuade them to change by her own actions and attitudes. Rarely did she strike out in anger. Anne Brown was the opposite; as a child, she got into a fight with anyone who taunted her.

With a quick temper and an iron will, Anne was always ready to battle those whom she felt had slighted her because of her race.

Like Ruby, Anne Brown studied voice with Lucia Dunham, who called the two black sopranos "my prize pupils." Within a few short years, Dunham's prize pupils would collaborate to make theatre and musical history.

Dr. McCracken, now installed as President of Connecticut State Agricultural College, began engaging Ruby frequently as a guest soloist for events on campus. Ruby often spent holidays with the family in the president's residence in Storrs. She still relied on Dr. McCracken's advice, and he continued to take time working on her behalf, especially with the Rosenwald Fund.

Dr. McCracken had kept Edwin Embree apprised of Ruby's progress under Lucia Dunham and asked the Rosenwald Fund to consider supporting Ruby for another year. In the spring of 1931, Embree notified Ruby that the Rosenwald Fund would grant her a second $1,200 fellowship—a rare privilege, as the fund usually would only provide support for one year.

Ruby could not help but be pleased. She was performing regularly with the Rosamond Johnson Choir, and Johnson was now planning a series of concerts in which he and Ruby would appear together as a team. Her voice was getting better every day under Lucia Dunham's tutelage. And now her finances for the 1931–1932 school year at Juilliard were assured, thanks to the Rosenwald Fund.

Everything was going well—until April 1931. Back in Columbus, Ohio, Henrietta Davis wanted to again produce *Stumbling Upward*—and to have it published as her own work. When she found out Ruby had copyrighted it, Davis was furious. She hired a lawyer, a Mr. H. W. Arent, who wrote to Ruby:

> April 2, 1931
> Dear Miss Elzy,
> I have recently been consulted by Mrs. Henrietta K. Davis and
> retained by her to take proper proceedings to set aside the copyright of

"Stumbling Upward," which was copyrighted in your name under the date of May 22, 1930. Mrs. Davis was quite surprised when she was officially informed that this copyright of something that she had written had been effected in your name. She is of the opinion that you did not do that, but that it must have been done for you by Dr. C. C. McCracken, who was then a member of the Education faculty in this University. I cannot believe that either you or Dr. McCracken appreciated the possible consequences of what has been done here. The story copyrighted, to which Mrs. Davis also wrote the music for a two-act operetta, was written by her. To have the story copyrighted as it has been in your name, asserting as the application does that you are the author of it, it is not only dishonest but makes those responsible for it liable to proceedings which it would be most unfortunate to have to go through. Before the institution of such proceedings, I am writing to inquire whether you are willing to make such proceedings unnecessary by an assignment of the copyright to Mrs. Davis. I shall be greatly obliged if you will advise me as to your attitude at your earliest convenience in order that proceedings may not be unduly delayed.

The letter caused Ruby great anguish. That Henrietta Davis would claim *she* had written Ruby's life story—and that Ruby had stolen it— was absurd. Davis hoped her lawyer's threat of legal action would intimidate Ruby, and at first it did. But then Arent made the mistake of going after C. C. McCracken:

April 2, 1931
Dear Sir,
The composition of Mrs. Davis was copyrighted in the name of Ruby Pearl Elsey on May 22, 1930 after it had been performed May 9, 1930. It is assumed here that you had this copyright made for Miss Elsey, who was reputed to be your ward. In view of the undoubted facts, this action on your part is most astonishing from several points of view. Aside from the manifest unfairness to Mrs. Davis of such

procedure, I cannot believe that you comprehended the possible consequences of what you have done, if you are responsible for the copyright
of this composition.

I have written Miss Elsey a letter of which I hand you herewith a
copy. If you are still interested in Miss Elsey, you may feel called upon as
her friend to advise her with reference to this situation. As you see, I am
giving her a chance to undo this wrong by assigning the copyright to
Mrs. Davis. If she expresses a willingness to take this step I will prepare
an assignment and send it to her for execution. If not, I shall have to
institute the proceedings suggested above. I will appreciate a reply at
your convenience.

If Arent thought McCracken would persuade Ruby to assign the
copyright for *Stumbling Upward* to Davis, he could not have been
more wrong. Furious, McCracken wrote back:

April 6, 1931

Dear Mr. Arent,

Your letter was evidently written without a full knowledge of facts
involved. May I suggest the following:

First, Ruby Elzy is not and never has been my ward.

Second, Mrs. Davis came to me—as the advisor of Miss Elzy—and
requested that Miss Elzy write the story of her life to be presented as a
play in Upper Arlington. Mrs. Davis offered to divide the proceeds with
Miss Elzy in order, as she said, to assist Miss Elzy financially in getting
her education. After the play was over, Mrs. Davis did not offer to
divide the proceeds. Finally, as a friend of Miss Elzy, I notified Mrs.
Davis that if Miss Elzy did not receive some return, I would call the
matter to the attention of the Board of Education of Upper Arlington
and ask them to see that Miss Elzy received satisfactory compensation.
Mrs. Davis at once sent her a small amount of money, which was not in
keeping with the amount of work Miss Elzy had done, and the matter
was dropped.

Third, the most that Mrs. Davis could claim in any case would be joint authorship. If you have read the play you cannot help being aware of the fact that the story of it was supplied by Miss Elzy.

Fourth, before Miss Elzy made application for the copyright, Mrs. Davis was informed that such procedure was contemplated. She raised no objection whatever. Fifth, the play in itself has no real value and the copyrighting of it was more for the novelty of securing a copyright than because of any value which the composition possessed.

I expect to be in New York within the next ten days or two weeks and would like to have action in this matter delayed until I have the opportunity to talk with Miss Elzy. If Mrs. Davis is willing to agree to a joint copyright, I presume that there would be no question.

Incidentally, I might say that Miss Elzy could produce plenty of witnesses in Columbus to show that she wrote this play as the story of her life. I shall write you further as soon as I can see Miss Elzy.

Several more heated letters were exchanged over the next few weeks. Much to Ruby's relief, Dr. McCracken acted on her behalf; she could never have afforded a lawyer. Davis persisted, through her attorney. McCracken was leaning toward advising Ruby to assign the copyright to Davis just to settle the matter.

At about the same time, the board of trustees of the Connecticut State Agricultural College held their spring meeting. Afterwards, Dr. McCracken took aside one of his trustees, who was a United States District Attorney. McCracken laid out the facts of Ruby's case and showed the attorney the correspondence from Arent.

The attorney read the letters and told McCracken, "There's no reason at all why Miss Elzy should assign the copyright. It's clearly her story."

McCracken then asked the attorney what he should do about Arent and Davis and their threats of lawsuits.

"Tell them to go to hell," the attorney said.

Whether or not McCracken followed that advice exactly, the letters from Columbus soon ceased. *Stumbling Upward* remained on the official copyright register of the United States as "a play in two acts by Ruby Pearl Elzy." The copyright passed to Emma Elzy after Ruby's death in 1943.

Soon after the Arent-Davis situation was resolved, Ruby finished her first year at Juilliard. She planned to spend the summer in Ocean Grove, New Jersey, where she had been engaged to direct a choir. Lucia Dunham, pleased with Ruby's progress during the year, asked Ruby to keep in touch with her. Dunham would be vacationing during the summer in California. Ruby promised to write her teacher.

Two months went by, however, and Dunham heard nothing from Ruby. Concerned, she decided to write to Dr. McCracken:

> August 16, 1931
>
> My Dear Dr. McCracken,
>
> Have you any news of Ruby Elzy? I am troubled at hearing nothing from her since June first when I requested her to write me, before July 15th about herself and her summer activities. . . .
>
> I cannot think it is mere carelessness on her part. She made very solid progress, both technically and artistically and I trust nothing has occurred to retard it now. . . .
>
> Sincerely, Lucia Dunham

The McCrackens, too, had not heard from Ruby. Dr. McCracken wrote to Ruby, and shared with Dunham what he found out:

> August 25, 1931
>
> Dear Mrs. Dunham,
>
> Like you, I became worried because I had heard nothing from Miss Elzy. She expected to be at Ocean Grove, New Jersey. I wrote her last week asking what had become of her, and I received an immediate reply in which she stated that she did not go to Ocean Grove for the summer,

since they would give her only her board and room. She felt that it was not right for her to leave her roommate in New York with the full charge for room during the summer. Consequently, she remained in New York getting what work she could.

Evidently, she has not been able to get any regular work, but has managed to live through the summer. She stated that she has been singing quite a bit this summer, and that her voice seems to be in unusually good condition. I take it therefore that she is getting enough to eat, and is taking reasonably good care of herself. I do not understand why she has not written you, but I shall forward her a letter at once, asking that she let you know as to her whereabouts.

McCracken then did write again to Ruby, reminding her that her career depended on more than just her voice:

August 25, 1931

Dear Ruby,

I am enclosing a copy of a letter from Mrs. Dunham. I feel that this should have your immediate attention. You will recall that I suggested to you that attention to your correspondence, particularly of such nature as with Mrs. Dunham, is exceedingly important in light of future developments.

For Ruby to have been out of touch for two months with people she cared about was completely out of character. And while the job situation certainly had an impact on her that summer, there was more to it than that. Something unexpected had happened, something she was not yet ready to share with others, not even with her mother or with Dr. McCracken.

Ruby Elzy had fallen in love.

His name was Gardner Jones, Jr., and he was by accounts of those who knew him an impressive man—handsome, tall, and slender. He had graduated from college with a degree in journalism and worked for the *Afro-American Journal*. The *Journal*, published in Baltimore, was one of the leading Negro publications in America, and Jones was the editor of their Brooklyn office. In that capacity he met many of New York's most prominent blacks, those who were already established as well as those who were on their way up, like Ruby Elzy.

Few details of Ruby's relationship with Jones are known, but clearly it had become very serious by the summer of 1931. When the choir job in Ocean Grove did not pan out as expected, Ruby was probably as relieved as she was disappointed. Yes, she would have no steady job or income for the summer—but at least she could stay in New York, close to Gardner.

As Dr. McCracken wrote to Lucia Dunham, Ruby had told him her voice that summer was in "unusually good condition." Perhaps it was because of her newfound romance. Whatever the case, she would soon have the chance to use her voice again, in her second Broadway show. For Ruby, it would be a production that was memorable in several ways.

Fast and Furious began rehearsals in early August 1931. Billed as "A Colored Revue in 32 Scenes," the show was typical of the genre: comedy routines, sketches, dances, solo songs, and big choruses, usually singing spirituals. It was cut from the same mold as *Shuffle Along*, the 1921 hit by Eubie Blake and Noble Sissle that had marked the first major Broadway hit by a team of black collaborators. Ten years later, the novelty of the all-black revue was finally running out of steam. *Fast and Furious* would be one of the last shows of its kind.

But the company that producer Forbes Randolph put together for *Fast and Furious* was one of the most dazzling arrays of black talent ever assembled. Rosamond Johnson composed and arranged special music for the show. Zora Neale Hurston—one of the greatest writers of the Harlem Renaissance—contributed several original sketches, as did Jackie Mabley (long before she adapted the moniker "Moms"). The cast included not only Johnson, Hurston, and Mabley, but also Tim Moore (later famous as "Kingfish" in the 1950s TV version of *Amos and Andy*), Juano Hernandez, and Etta Moten.

And then of course, there was Ruby. She appeared in several sketches and choral scenes, but her big moment came in the second act. Standing alone in front of the curtain, Ruby sang Mack Gordon and Harry Revel's song "Where's My Happy Ending?" It was her first Broadway solo.

Fast and Furious played two weeks of tryouts in Brooklyn before it opened on Broadway at the New Yorker Theatre on September 15, 1931. Despite the heavyweight talents involved in the show, critics panned it almost unanimously. The watermelon-patch jokes and "here come de judge" skits were no longer funny. The songs were largely forgettable (Ruby's solo number was not mentioned in any of the reviews). The "colored revue" was passé. Serious musicals like Kern and Hammerstein's *Showboat* were what drew audiences now. *Fast and Furious* closed after seven performances.

During the show's run in September 1931, Ruby and Gardner Jones, Jr., got married. The newlyweds moved to a large apartment on West 115th Street in a more upscale part of Harlem. Ruby was now a soloist at Mount Calvary Methodist Church; every Sunday after the last service, she and her husband enjoyed going for a walk or a picnic in Central Park, five blocks from their home.

Gardner came to every performance of *Fast and Furious*, just to hear his bride sing "Where's My Happy Ending?" In time, the title of the song would prove unfortunately prophetic, as far as Ruby's marriage was concerned. But for now, she truly *was* happy.

Ruby's second year at Juilliard began a few weeks after her wedding. She was now taking the advanced level of the previous year's courses. She also began studying German, a requisite for any singer planning a career on the concert stage.

Rosamond Johnson was becoming a more and more important part of Ruby's musical life. On February 5, 1932, they gave their first joint recital together in Harrisburg, Pennsylvania. Several weeks later, on February 29, Ruby joined Johnson at the WEAF studios in New York City for a program called *Parade of the States*, a weekly series billed as "a musical tour of the United States" and broadcast over

NBC. Ruby sang two songs in a tribute to her native Mississippi. The program would mark her debut on national network radio.

Ruby was now wondering what she should do after her graduation in June 1932. Should she study in Europe or continue at Juilliard? If she did go to Europe, either Gardner would have to give up his job or Ruby would have to go without him. As much as she felt a year of study in Europe would benefit her, Ruby could not bear the thought of making her husband give up his career—or worse, of her spending a year alone overseas.

She decided to remain at Juilliard, and once again asked Dr. McCracken to help her with the Julius Rosenwald Fund. But this time, McCracken hesitated:

> March 30, 1932
>
> Dear Ruby,
>
> Last fall at about the time of your visit to Storrs, I wrote a letter to Mr. Embree of the Rosenwald Foundation recommending that they grant you a scholarship for next year. I notice that the date on the letter is November 28th. But I did not mail it.
>
> My reason for not mailing this was that you stated to me that you did not intend to inform the Rosenwald Foundation nor Mrs. Dunham that you were married. I believe that you are quite familiar with my thinking in this regard. While you may very properly appear on stage as Ruby Elzy, I am convinced that in any matters of an official nature or that involve money you should be known by your married name. You have written me that you did not inform Mrs. Dunham that you are married and that you did not intend to do so. For this reason I never mailed the letter to Mr. Embree. It is still lying in my desk unsigned.
>
> I think that a request might very properly be made of the Rosenwald Fund for a continuance of the scholarship and I should be glad to write Mr. Embree if you are willing that I tell him that you are married and give him your correct name. In this case I think it would be far better for you to notify him of your marriage before I write him.

It was true—Ruby had not told her teacher or anyone at Juilliard about her marriage, concerned that it would jeopardize not only her fellowship but her ability even to continue in school. Many educational institutions at that time did not allow married students. Yet when McCracken's letter came, Ruby realized that she had been wrong to conceal the truth. She also hated the thought that she had let Dr. McCracken down.

Ruby told Dunham and Juilliard about her marriage and also wrote to Embree at the Rosenwald Fund. Dr. McCracken then did as he promised, asking Embree to support Ruby for a third year. But by now, the effects of the Great Depression, which had begun with the stock market crash of October 1929, were beginning to have a severe impact on the national economy. Rosenwald was being inundated with requests by talented black artists who had nowhere else to turn for funding. Most fellowships were awarded for a single year, and Rosenwald had already given Ruby two years of support. Embree told McCracken and Ruby it was time for Rosenwald to help other deserving artists.

Ruby then applied for the Katherine McGill Scholarship, the most competitive and prestigious prize awarded at Juilliard. More than twenty students auditioned. The field was gradually narrowed down by the judges until only two candidates remained: Anne Brown and Ruby Elzy. As the final step of the competition, Ruby and Anne each had to present a short recital. When the results were announced, the judges had awarded the Katherine McGill Scholarship to Anne Brown.

It was a discouraging blow for Ruby. Without the scholarship or another source of support, continuing her education would be extremely difficult.

On May 31, 1932, Ruby graduated from Juilliard, receiving her diploma in voice. All the music departments were represented in a special program. The voice department was represented each year by the winner of the Katherine McGill Scholarship. Anne Brown sang Berlioz's "La Captive" as Ruby looked on.

With graduation behind her, Ruby took a job in Bayhead, New Jersey, as a teacher and music director at a Methodist Church summer camp. Gardner went along, too, taking time off from his work for the *Afro-American Journal*.

While they were in Bayhead, good news came from Juilliard: Ruby had been awarded the Faculty Scholarship, a special grant for post-graduate study. The recipient was chosen by the dean, with the faculty's approval. Dr. Damrosch had chosen Ruby. The coming year at Juilliard was now assured.

Besides winning the scholarship the high point of Ruby's summer came when she and Rosamond Johnson performed together in Westport, Connecticut. With her usual humor and flair, Ruby wrote about the concert—and her life on the Jersey shore—to the McCrackens:

July 29, 1932

My Dearest Friends:

It has been a long time since I've heard from you. I wrote you of my graduation, but you must have been in the midst of your very busiest season, commencement. So I am not surprised that I haven't heard from you. I do hope everybody is well.

Gardner and I are both so fat and working very hard here for the summer. Work for him got rather dull for the summer. Salaries were all cut so we decided if I was to have money for next year, we'd better spend July and August in the country and go back to New York for winter. At that time I wasn't sure that I'd be granted a scholarship from the institute, but just the other day I received a letter saying that I'd been granted one, so that worry is over. So we'll be about $300.00 ahead when we get back to the city. . . .

We are having a fine time here. We live only 3 blocks from the Atlantic Ocean and can swim in the afternoon. I am just about 3 shades dark. You'd probably have to have a searchlight to see me in the daytime (smile).

I went to Westport Connecticut Sunday July 24th to sing at the summer home of Miss Lillian D. Walk, who is at the head of the Henry

Street Settlement House at New York. Mr. J. Rosamond Johnson and I gave the recital, a program of which is enclosed. There were about 300 guests present, among whom were Jane Addams of the Hull House, Mr. Nikolai Sokoloff, director of the Cleveland Symphony, Miss Hughes, the manager of the orchestra, Fannie Hurst, the writer, and many others whose names you would know.

Mr. Sokoloff seemed very interested. We only sang spirituals, as you see. He wanted me to sing something else, but I hadn't any other music with me. So he asked me then, to send him a complete list of my present repertoire and if he could find use for the songs, he would certainly do so, which seemed to me encouraging. Many, many people spoke of how the program was enjoyed. Mr. Johnson and I may do some further concert work this winter.

I sang for Harry Burleigh for the 1st time on June 30. He was quite effusive in his praise of my work. My voice is fine this summer I am getting so much rest. And so much exercise too because my work gives me a lot of exercise, besides the dips I take in the afternoon.

I hope you are all having a wonderful summer. I will be very happy to have a letter from the family when you can find the time to write. All my love to all of you.

Ruby returned to New York in September to begin her third year at Juilliard. She was also performing frequently, and on February 8, 1933, gave her first major solo recital in New York City at the Union Baptist Church. She recruited a large number of notable patrons for the concert, including Nikolai Sokoloff, conductor of the Cleveland Orchestra, who had become an admirer after hearing her recital with Johnson the previous July in Connecticut.

In June 1933, Paramount Pictures offered Rosamond Johnson a contract to arrange and conduct his choir in the musical sequences for a film they were about to begin shooting on Long Island. Johnson signed the contract, and hired Ruby to join the picture as his assistant music director. The film was to have a lasting impact on Ruby Elzy's life and career. It was *The Emperor Jones*.

The star was Paul Robeson, without a doubt the most famous black man in America at the time. Handsome, athletically built, and charismatic, he also possessed a rich, resonant bass-baritone that was one of the truly great voices of the twentieth century. Robeson had created the role of Joe in the London production of *Showboat*, where his singing of "Ol' Man River" tore the house apart at every performance. Robeson had starred in Eugene O'Neill's *The Emperor Jones* on Broadway in the mid-1920s. Now he would be making his screen debut, recreating the role that had first won him great acclaim (actually, in 1925 Robeson had made one silent picture for pioneer black filmmaker Oscar Micheaux).

O'Neill's play is about a Negro porter named Brutus Jones who commits murder then flees to a tropical island. There he becomes a tyrant ruling over the natives as the "Emperor" Jones until he himself is killed. The play as done on stage is quite brief. The film producers decided a prologue was needed, showing the events leading up to Jones's escape to the island, which is the starting point of the play.

To write the prologue and screenplay, producers hired DuBose Heyward. Heyward was a poet and author best known for his 1925 novel *Porgy* about the Gullah blacks of Heyward's native Charleston, South Carolina. Two years later, the book had been adapted into a hit Broadway play by Heyward and his wife Dorothy, who also was a writer. Rumors had been circulating since then that a number of composers, including Jerome Kern and George Gershwin, were anxious to turn *Porgy* into a musical, perhaps even an opera, but so far nothing had come of that.

Heyward's opening scene in *The Emperor Jones* was in a church where Brutus Jones's friends are holding a service to bid him farewell. The Rosamond Johnson Choir would be playing the congregation and would be singing several spirituals. Since Johnson himself was then appearing in a Broadway play, Ruby took over directing the rehearsal of the musical numbers. Most of the chorus members were from the North, so Ruby coached them in how a Southern revival meeting was conducted.

Ruby put the choir through their motions in rehearsal, as Heyward and director Dudley Murphy observed from the sidelines. There was a small speaking role that was yet to be cast, the role of Brutus Jones's girlfriend Dolly. As Heyward and Murphy watched Ruby at work, they realized she had the exact combination of sweetness and strength they were looking for in Dolly. One afternoon, Ruby went from being Rosamond Johnson's assistant to Paul Robeson's co-star.

The film marked the beginning of another important relationship that would impact tremendously on Ruby's life and career. DuBose Heyward took an instant liking to Ruby, and soon the genteel writer from Charleston and the black soprano from Pontotoc were friends. They talked frequently during breaks in the filming. Heyward was fascinated by Ruby's background—it had the same kind of drama and poignancy he loved to write in his own novels.

The Emperor Jones was shot at Paramount's Astoria Studios on Long Island in July 1933. In addition to Robeson and Ruby, the cast included Dudley Digges, Frank Wilson, Jackie Mabley, and Fredi Washington, whose light skin caused a panic among studio bigwigs. When the first rushes were shown, Washington looked so fair that it appeared as if Brutus Jones was kissing a white woman—an absolute taboo under the strict Hollywood production code of the 1930s. All of Washington's scenes as Undine had to be reshot with the actress wearing make-up to darken her skin and to look, as one studio boss put it, "more Negro."

When the film opened in New York in September 1933, it drew favorable reviews, mostly on the strength of Robeson's towering performance. Unfortunately, *The Emperor Jones* did poorly at the box office. Black patrons in the North embraced the film, but white audiences stayed away. And the film was not shown at all in the South.

Over time, however, *The Emperor Jones* came to be regarded as a classic. In 1999 it was named by the Library of Congress to the National Film Registry, a distinction given only to those motion pictures deemed to be "culturally, historically, or esthetically significant."

Ruby was proud of her performance as Dolly. Though it was a small role, she played it convincingly, as Heyward and Murphy felt she would. And her musical contributions, in tandem with her mentor, Rosamond Johnson, were a memorable part of the film. Ruby had entered yet another new field and had proven herself a worthy talent. She hoped to make more movies in the future, a desire that would ultimately be fulfilled.

In April 1934, Ruby sang a complete recital before Dr. Damrosch and the entire faculty and student body of Juilliard. It was the final part of her examination in order to receive the Certificate of Maturity, a special diploma conferred only to those Juilliard students deemed ready to embark on a professional career. Following Ruby's performance, Damrosch and the faculty unanimously voted to award her the certificate.

A few days later, on May 10, Ruby sang in what was probably the most unusual and memorable program during her Juilliard career. It was called "The Negro in Music." The presiding host was Harry T. Burleigh, regarded as the dean of Negro spiritual composers and arrangers. Burleigh had been an enthusiastic supporter of Ruby's since July 1932. In addition to Ruby, six other black Juilliard students sang in the concert, including Anne Brown. Ruby sang "Cabin Boy" and "City Called Heaven," the latter song given an ovation so tumultuous that Ruby was called back for an encore. The finale was Ruby, Anne Brown, and a mezzo named Carmen Shepperd in a trio singing Harry Burleigh's arrangements of "Were You There?" and "Sinner, Doan Let This Harvest Pass."

On June 2, 1934, with Mama and Gardner in the audience, Ruby graduated from Juilliard, receiving both her graduate diploma in voice and the coveted Certificate of Maturity. Although Ruby would keep learning and developing her talent, her formal education was now ended. It was time to begin her career.

Ruby went back to Mississippi, where she gave homecoming concerts in Pontotoc, Corinth, and Holly Springs. The audiences were huge and, remarkably for the south, included whites as well as blacks. It was thrilling for Ruby. In her own way, she felt she was helping bring people of different races together. It was a worthy use of the talent God had given her.

Returning to New York, Ruby joined an ambitious venture called the Aeolian Opera Company. What made the troupe unique was that it was comprised of all black singers. It was the idea of Peter Creatore, an Italian whose immigrant father Giuseppe was second only to John Philip Sousa as America's greatest bandleader. Creatore, an admirer of black talent, felt the exclusion of Negroes from the Metropolitan Opera and other major American companies was a disgrace. He hoped to prove to white audiences and critics that blacks had the voices to sing the great works of opera. Creatore assembled a company of the finest black singers in the East. Both Ruby and Anne Brown were recruited, as were two other singers with whom they would be sharing a stage in the near future—Todd Duncan and Abbie Mitchell.

Creatore announced an ambitious summer season that would include *I Pagliacci, Rigoletto, Lakme,* and *Carmen.* For Ruby, it would be a dream realized—to follow in the footsteps of Amelita Galli-Curci and the other great sopranos whose voices she had heard so long ago on Mrs. Lathan's Victrola.

The new company made its debut at the Mecca Temple in Manhattan on July 10 with a double bill of *The Emperor Jones* (an operatic version of the play, with music by Louis Gruenberg) and *Cavalleria Rusticana.* Ruby, who was slated to make her debut in one of the later productions, watched from the house. Jules Bledsoe was nearly as great a Brutus Jones as had been Paul Robeson, while in *Cavalleria* the standouts were Todd Duncan as Alfio and Abbie Mitchell as Santuzza.

Reviews the following day were positive. But before the next production could be mounted, the company folded. Creatore had bankrolled the company in hopes that he could find other backers. None came forward, and Creatore was unable to go it alone. The Aeolian Opera Company came to a sudden and sad end.

For Ruby it was just one more disappointment; she had had them before and knew she would have them again. All she could do was keep singing and praying, remembering Mama's credo that "the good Lord will make it all turn out right in the end." Ruby was never one to dispute Mama. And sure enough, things would soon turn out right.

DuBose Heyward had embarked on a new project, an operatic version of his most popular novel. He would be collaborating with America's most renowned composer, George Gershwin. Heyward felt the work was ideally suited to the singing and acting talents of his friend Ruby Elzy.

The opera would be called *Porgy and Bess*.

THE BIRTH OF PORGY AND BESS

On November 3, 1933, soon after the release of *The Emperor Jones*, and as Ruby was in her final year at Juilliard, a two-paragraph story ran in the theatre section of the *New York Times* under the following banner:

To Present 'Porgy' as a Musical Show
Guild to Sponsor New Version—
Gershwin Brothers and Heyward to Collaborate

In the seven decades since that brief announcement appeared, millions of words have been written and spoken about the work that became known as *Porgy and Bess*. Probably no other creation for the American stage has been more discussed, analyzed, and dissected, nor caused more controversy and contention. It has been the subject of symposia, books, articles, and several documentary films. *Porgy and Bess* stirs passionate arguments between those who hail it as a work of genius and those who condemn it as an outdated, negative portrayal of black culture. Yet regardless of where one's sympathies may lie in this ongoing debate, one fact remains indisputable: *Porgy and Bess* is the most popular opera America has ever produced, beloved not only in the United States but by audiences around the world. With its powerful combination of song, dance, and drama, *Porgy and Bess* is a timeless classic.

And it made Ruby Elzy a star.

The opera had its genesis in the early 1920s, around the same time that a young Ruby Elzy was at Rust College. DuBose Heyward was a successful insurance salesman in his native Charleston, South Carolina; but his true love was writing. He had already won some attention for his poetry and now was giving thought to writing a novel. The Heywards were one of Charleston's oldest aristocratic families—one of their ancestors, Thomas Heyward, Sr., had been a signer of the Declaration of Independence. The family fortune had long vanished by the time DuBose was born in 1885. Heyward's mother was a noted authority on Charleston's blacks, the Gullahs (the name was said to be derived from Angola, the region in Africa from where they originally came). Mrs. Heyward had written a book about the Gullahs and had passed on her interest and appreciation in their unique culture to DuBose.

Heyward walked every day from home to his insurance office past a crumbling neighborhood known as Cabbage Row. Once an elegant section of Charleston where aristocrats lived in stately homes, it was now a poor ghetto of Gullah families. The men labored on the waterfront as fishermen and stevedores. Heyward had spent one summer of his youth working beside them as a cotton checker. The women of Cabbage Row cared for their children, cooked, and cleaned; a few were servants for wealthy white families. Each morning the cries of vendors, hawking their strawberries, crabs, and honey, filled the air. The sights, sounds, and smells of Cabbage Row lingered with Heyward as he spent the day engaged in the insurance work he found dull.

In 1924, a newspaper story caught Heyward's eye. It was about a crippled Negro beggar named Sammy Smalls, who had been arrested for assault. The people of Cabbage Row called him "Goat Cart Sammy," because he made his way around town in a cheap, wooden wagon, pulled by a goat notorious for its foul odor. Intrigued, Heyward clipped the story out of the newspaper.

Before long, Heyward was at work on his novel, drawing on all his observations and experiences. The setting of his story was a rundown Charleston neighborhood he called Catfish Row. It had a huge and colorful retinue of people. There was Maria, a boisterous shopkeeper; the hard-working fisherman Jake and his wife Clara; a slippery dope peddler named Sportin' Life; the sultry yet tragic Bess; and Serena, the devout woman whose husband Robbins is killed in a fight over a crap game by Bess's boyfriend, the hulking stevedore named Crown. At the center of it all was a crippled beggar riding in a goat-pulled cart. Heyward titled the book after his hero, whom he named Porgy.

When it was published in October 1925, Heyward's novel was an immediate success with both critics and readers. Two years later, Heyward and his wife, Dorothy—herself a brilliant dramatist—adapted the book for the Broadway stage. Produced by the prestigious Theatre Guild, *Porgy* was again a sensation, giving nearly four hundred performances.

From the beginning, *Porgy* seemed like a natural for the musical stage. One composer in particular who thought so was George Gershwin.

Gershwin was interested in serious as well as popular music, having produced his unforgettable *Rhapsody in Blue* when he was only twenty-five years old. Yet the musical idiom that intrigued him most was opera. He had already made one attempt at it, a one-act piece in 1922 called *Blue Monday* (billed as "an opera a la Afro-American") about a murder in Harlem. Cast with white singers performing in blackface, the opera was panned by critics and pulled after only one performance. Gershwin himself acknowledged its shortcomings, yet he was anxious to try opera again. All he needed was the right material. From the moment he first read *Porgy* in a single, all-night sitting, Gershwin knew this was exactly the story he had been looking for.

Heyward was elated when Gershwin wrote him proposing they collaborate. Heyward was anxious to proceed, but quickly came to realize that the restless Gershwin was a man in perpetual motion. It would be nearly eight years between the time Gershwin first contacted Heyward and the actual start of their collaboration.

Two incidents finally prompted Gershwin to act. First, in 1930 he was engaged to compose an opera for the Metropolitan Opera. Gershwin immediately thought of *Porgy* but withdrew the idea when he realized the Met would not cast black singers, something he insisted on.

At about the same time, Jerome Kern and Oscar Hammerstein II, who had adapted Edna Ferber's novel *Showboat* into a colossal hit, approached Heyward. They proposed turning *Porgy* into a musical comedy starring Al Jolson, who had built his career singing "mammy" songs in blackface. Jolson had read *Porgy* and realized it would be the role of a lifetime.

Heyward hesitated. He wanted the musical of *Porgy* to be authentic, performed by black actors, not Al Jolson in burnt cork. The Theatre Guild's 1927 play was cast with brilliant black actors; couldn't a musical be done that way, too?

Heyward and Gershwin were of like mind: *Porgy*, a story about black life in Charleston, needed to be played by black actors. Gershwin, realizing that if he did not act soon Heyward would find another collaborator, told the author he was at last ready to begin work. The proposed production with Kern, Hammerstein, and Jolson was abandoned. The Theatre Guild stepped forward and said it was willing to produce *Porgy* with a black cast. Heyward and Gershwin signed a contract with the Guild in October 1933, a few weeks before the announcement in the *New York Times*.

The collaborators set to work. Gershwin lived in New York, where he was under contract to CBS for a weekly radio series that would last through June. Heyward did not like New York at all, so he worked on the libretto from his home in Charleston. As soon as Heyward finished a section he would send it off to New York, where Gershwin set it to music. The lyrics for the opera were a joint effort between Heyward and Gershwin's gifted brother, Ira. It was a unique arrangement that worked remarkably well.

Once the radio series ended for the summer, Gershwin went to South Carolina for a two-month working vacation. He rented a rustic cabin on Folly Island. With Heyward at his side, Gershwin immersed himself in the culture of Charleston and the Gullahs. Heyward was amazed at Gershwin's ability to take the complicated, strange rhythms of the native music he heard and immediately absorb it into his own composition. The music of the Gullahs—especially in their religious ceremonies—would influence Gershwin's score for *Porgy and Bess*, making it much more authentic and true to the people it portrayed.

From the beginning, it was clear that one of the most monumental tasks of the production would be casting. The performers needed to be singers as well as actors. And Gershwin wanted trained voices that could handle the demands of the score he was creating. They began to search conservatories and colleges across America for new talent. Ultimately, more than a thousand black artists would be auditioned.

It was DuBose Heyward who first brought Ruby Elzy to George Gershwin's attention. In a letter dated March 2, 1934, Heyward wrote to Gershwin: "I'm going to ask Rosamond Johnson to get in touch with you and ask for an appointment to bring a girl to sing for you. I think she has the exactly quality for Clara. Also I want you to talk to Rosamond about working for you. I think he's first class."

Gershwin did meet Johnson by the end of March. Soon afterward, based on Heyward's and Johnson's enthusiastic recommendations, Gershwin invited Ruby to sing for him.

It was a late spring day in 1934 when Ruby made the trip by subway to Gershwin's lavish penthouse on Riverside Drive. He greeted Ruby and her accompanist, and showed them in to the huge living room, its walls adorned with the exquisite art Gershwin loved to collect. Gershwin seated himself in a plush chair as Ruby took her place in the nook of the magnificent grand piano. She had chosen "City Called Heaven" to sing, the same spiritual she had performed to a standing ovation at Juilliard just a few weeks before. The song called on every bit of dramatic power and vocal skill a singer could muster.

Ruby had done many auditions before, but never had one been more important. Her natural talents, honed by seven years of study and training, came together to create this three-minute drama of a sinner's repentance and salvation. Gershwin sat transfixed. Ruby had come prepared with other songs, but Gershwin had heard all he needed to hear. Rising from his chair, he came over to the piano and extended his hand to Ruby. "Miss Elzy," he said, "I would love for you to be in my opera."

Now came a crucial question: which role in the opera was right for Ruby? Originally, Heyward had thought Ruby would be perfect as Clara, the wife of the fisherman Jake. It was a small part, yet important.

But there was another role, one that required more range and depth, not only in its singing but especially in its acting demands. Next to Bess, this was the largest and most important female role in the opera. It was Serena, who is widowed when her husband Robbins is killed by Crown. In Heyward's story, Serena is one of the most respected leaders in Catfish Row, a devout woman of such faith that her prayers can help to heal the sick.

Ideally, the actress playing Serena should be middle-aged. In the Theatre Guild's 1927 production, the role had been created by Rose McClendon, renowned as the "Sepia Barrymore." She was the greatest black actress of the Harlem Renaissance. McClendon was forty-three years old when she played Serena.

Ruby was only twenty-six when she auditioned for George Gershwin. Yet from the moment he heard her, he felt that she had the voice and demeanor he wanted in his Serena. She was young, it was true—but with the right costuming and make-up, she could be made to look older. What was important was that she could *act* the role convincingly. Gershwin consulted with Heyward, and the two men agreed: Ruby Elzy would play Serena.

It was a great opportunity for Ruby and also a tremendous responsibility. Yet she approached the role with confidence. In large part she owed this confidence to Lucia Dunham, saying, "She not only taught me singing but acting, too, for it is her theory that a singer *must* be an actor. When I came to the role of Serena, I was prepared for it."

Anne Brown, Ruby's classmate at Juilliard, had written to Gershwin asking for an audition. Gershwin cast her as Bess. Lucia Dunham must have been immensely proud that her "two prize pupils" were about to star in the most talked-about production of the season.

Gershwin's Porgy would be Todd Duncan, who had been with Ruby and Brown in the short-lived Aeolian Opera Company. A professor of voice at Howard University in Washington, D.C., Duncan was tall and handsome with a rich, resonant voice—Gershwin called him "a black Lawrence Tibbett" (Tibbett was then the reigning baritone at the Metropolitan Opera).

The plum role of Sportin' Life went to John W. Bubbles, of the renowned vaudeville team Buck and Bubbles. Though not a trained musician like the others, Bubbles was a brilliant dancer with an infectious personality. He, Duncan, Brown, and Ruby were the only four principals personally chosen by George Gershwin.

The cast was filled out by Warren Coleman, a rugged and handsome bass-baritone, as Crown; the veteran soprano Abbie Mitchell as Clara (the role Heyward originally intended for Ruby); baritone Edward Matthews as Jake; and Georgette Harvey as Maria, a role she'd also played in 1927. She was the only member of the stage play to also appear in the opera. Both Matthews and Harvey would become close friends of Ruby's.

Gershwin spent nine months composing his opera, often calling his singers in as he worked on a particular scene or musical number. In a sense, his work was tailored to the voices he had chosen. He would write some of his greatest music for Serena, and Ruby would later recall, "I was with Gershwin when 'My Man's Gone Now' was born."

There are many unforgettable moments in *Porgy and Bess*, and Serena's aria, coming in the "saucer burial" scene, surely ranks among them. Serena's husband Robbins, murdered by Crown, has been laid out in the parlor of his home. A saucer is placed on his chest, where neighbors can put in money to help pay for his funeral. If enough money is not collected, Robbins' body will have to be given over to the medical school. It is an emotionally charged scene, as Serena sings, "My man's gone now, . . ." This powerful aria challenges the vocal and dramatic talents of the greatest sopranos. As sung by Ruby Elzy, "My Man's Gone Now" would become one of the masterpieces of American musical theatre.

Dr. Charles Chester (C. C.) McCracken, who discovered Ruby Elzy at Rust College and became her lifelong friend, counselor, and mentor. (Courtesy of the C. C. McCracken family)

Four generations of Kimp Elzy women, circa 1914. Emma Elzy holds her youngest daughter, Beatrice Wayne. Seated below, left to right, are Emma's mother, Belle Kimp, and Belle's mother, Fannie. (Courtesy of Dr. Amanda Elzy)

One of the earliest photos of Ruby Elzy, taken around 1928. She is seated in the McCracken children's wagon in front of their home in Columbus, Ohio. (Courtesy of the C. C. McCracken family)

The C.C. McCracken family in the parlor of their home in Columbus. Clockwise from left to right: Mary Ruth, Janet May, Charles William and Mrs. Frances (Cleo) McCracken. The youngest, James Edward (Elzy's favorite), sits on his father's lap. Elzy lived with the McCrackens and cared for the children when she first came to Ohio State and remained close to the family until she died. (Courtesy of the C. C. McCracken family)

Ruby Elzy in 1930, the year she graduated from Ohio State. (Photo from "Makio," 1930 yearbook, courtesy The Ohio State University Archives)

Ruby Elzy with Paul Robeson in her screen debut, the 1933 United Artists film version of Eugene O'Neill's *The Emperor Jones*, starring Robeson in the title role. Elzy became friends with author DuBose Heyward, who wrote the screenplay. It was Heyward who later recommended Elzy to George Gershwin for *Porgy and Bess*. (Photo from the Billy Rose Theatre Collection, The New York Public Library for the Performing Arts, Astor, Lenox, and Tilden Foundations)

From 1935, the brilliant trio that created *Porgy and Bess*: George Gershwin, DuBose Heyward, and Ira Gershwin. (Photo from the Robert A. Wachsman Collection, courtesy of the Jerome Lawrence and Robert E. Lee Theatre Research Institute, The Ohio State University Libraries)

Elzy on radio, a medium that brought her voice to millions of listeners across America. She made her radio debut in 1929. During her career, she appeared on all the major networks, performing with such personalities as comedian Fred Allen and singer Bing Crosby. In 1935–36, she played a recurring role on the NBC series, *The Melody Master*. (Courtesy of the C. C. McCracken family)

Elzy as Serena (Photo by George Gershwin, courtesy of the Theatre Collection, Museum of the City of New York; gift of Mr. and Mrs. Ira Gershwin)

Curtain calls in Boston for the world premiere of *Porgy and Bess* on September 30, 1935. From left to right: Georgette Harvey, Elzy, Todd Duncan, Anne Brown, Rouben Mamoulian, George Gershwin, DuBose Heyward (partially obscured by Gershwin's left shoulder), Warren Coleman, Abbie Mitchell and Edward Matthews. (Photo by Richard Tucker, from the Robert A. Wachsman Collection, courtesy of the Jerome Lawrence & Robert E. Lee Theatre Research Institute, The Ohio State University Libraries)

This beautiful portrait was used frequently by Elzy in her publicity and concert programs. It was taken in 1937, a significant year during which she starred at the Apollo Theatre, sang in the Gershwin memorial concerts in New York and at the Hollywood Bowl, made her recital debut at Town Hall, and entertained Eleanor Roosevelt at the White House. (Photo by Woodards Studio, courtesy of the C. C. McCracken family)

Elzy as Ella Jones with Jess Lee Brooks as the Reverend Jones in Hall Johnson's musical play *Run Little Chillun*. The show opened in 1938 and ran for nearly a year in Los Angeles. It was a major success of the Federal Theatre Project, one of the most innovative yet controversial programs of FDR's New Deal. (Photo from the Federal Theatre Project Collection, National Archives and Records Administration)

One of several photographs of Elzy as Serena, taken on December 30, 1935, by noted author and photographer Carl Van Vechten. (Photo from the Library of Congress, Prints & Photographs Division, the Carl Van Vechten Collection)

Paul Robeson and Elzy teamed again in 1939 for Jacques Wolfe's musical version of Roark Bradford's novel *John Henry*. Despite acclaim for the two stars, a weak script and the producer's financial troubles caused the show to close after only a week on Broadway. (Photo from Photographs and Prints Division, Schomberg Center for Research in Black Culture, The New York Public Library, Astor, Lenox, and Tilden Foundations, courtesy of the Museum of the City of New York)

Elzy in Hollywood. After the short run of *John Henry*, Elzy returned to the west coast and married actor/singer Jack Carr. In 1940 she made her first and only commercial recording for Decca, singing Harold Arlen's "Where Is Dis Road A'leadin' Me To?" from his *Reverend Johnson's Dream*. From that period is this photo, inscribed to Arthur Kaplan, Elzy's long-time accompanist. (Courtesy of Michael Kaplan)

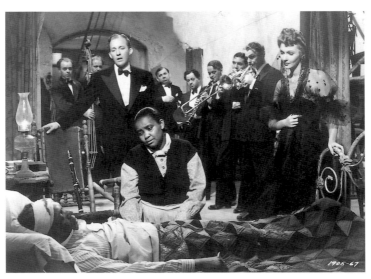

The high point of Elzy's film career came in Paramount's 1941 hit, *Birth of the Blues*, in which she sang W. C. Handy's classic "St. Louis Blues." Elzy is surrounded by Eddie "Rochester" Anderson (lying on bed), Bing Crosby, and Mary Martin. Crosby called Elzy a "truly great artist," and signed her to the talent agency managed by his brother Everett. (Courtesy of the Billy Rose Theatre Collection, The New York Public Library for the Performing Arts, Astor, Lenox, and Tilden Foundations)

Elzy and three of her co-stars from Cheryl Crawford's revival of *Porgy and Bess*: Harriet Jackson, J. Rosamond Johnson, and Edward Matthews, boarding a train for Washington, D.C., and a veterans benefit performance in April 1942. In addition to performing, Johnson was a noted composer, arranger, and choral conductor. A musical mentor to Elzy, Johnson gave her her first job on Broadway. (Photo from the J. Rosamond Johnson Collection, courtesy of Photographs and Prints Division, Schomberg Center for Research in Black Culture, The New York Public Library, Astor, Lenox, and Tilden Foundations)

Elzy as Aida, the Ethopian princess immortalized in Verdi's masterpiece. Her manager, Mark Byron, had this shot taken of Elzy in costume to promote her debut in the role. Tragically, her dream to sing on the grand opera stage would never be realized. (Photo by J. Abresch, courtesy of the C. C. McCracken family)

Ruby Elzy's last formal portrait, taken in the summer of 1942, less than a year before her death at age 35. (Photo by J. Abresch, courtesy of Dr. Amanda Elzy)

Gershwin finished composing in January 1935 and then began the momentous work of orchestration. Later that summer, anxious to put some of his completed score to the test, Gershwin asked CBS boss William Paley to lend him a transcription studio and the forty-three-piece CBS orchestra, and Paley agreed. On July 19, 1935, Ruby, Abbie Mitchell, Eddie Matthews, Todd Duncan, and Anne Brown joined Gershwin at the CBS studios in Manhattan. Sound engineer Jean V. Grombach was in the control room.

The music captured by Grombach on record that afternoon would become a historic treasure. With Gershwin himself announcing the numbers, playing the piano solos and conducting the orchestra, the principals of what was still then being called *Porgy* sang what would become some of the most beloved music ever written for the American stage: Mitchell singing "Summertime," Matthews doing his "A Woman Is a Sometime Thing," Duncan and Brown on their duet "Bess You Is My Woman Now," and Ruby Elzy singing "My Man's Gone Now." It was the first time Ruby or any of her fellow singers had put their voices on record, and it would provide a permanent legacy of their remarkable talents.

A month after the session at CBS, rehearsals were at last ready to begin. Rouben Mamoulian, who had staged the 1927 play and was now one of Hollywood's leading film directors, was put in charge of the production. Alexander Smallens was engaged to be the show's musical director. He was assisted by Alexander Steinert, who coached Ruby and the other principals in their individual roles.

Rehearsing any piece for the theatre is difficult, and *Porgy* was no exception. It would be a month of hard work and long days and nights as the cast went endlessly through their paces, but there were few complaints. Steinert would recall with admiration, "There was a great bond which united all those connected with the opera—a kind of fraternity which seemed to exist between the members of the company, the authors, the stage directors, and the producers."

Todd Duncan remembered one particularly exhausting day when Gershwin was present as they rehearsed "Oh, Doctor Jesus," the scene in which Porgy, fearful that the woman he loves is going to die from a fever, implores Serena to pray for Bess:

> We singers were very tired, tired enough fortunately to set up the exact atmosphere required for the prayer. It must've been our tenth consecutive trial. . . . Miss Elzy went down on her knees as if her own mother had been ill for weeks; she felt the need for prayer. Two seconds of silence intervened that seemed like hours, and presently there rose the most glorious tones and wails with accompanying amens and hallelujahs for our sick Bess that I ever hope to experience. This particular scene should have normally moved into the scene of the Street Cries, but it did not. It stopped there. The piano accompaniment ceased, every actor—and there were 65 of them—had come out of his rest position. . . . Rouben Mamoulian was standing before us quietly . . . his face (lighted to) sheer delight . . . and then George Gershwin, like a ghost from the dark rows of the Guild Theatre, appeared before the footlights. He simply could not stand it. He knew then, that he had put down on paper accurately and truthfully something from the depth of soul of a South Carolina Negro woman who feels the need of help and carries her troubles to her God.

If Duncan's words were a tribute to Mamoulian's direction and Gershwin's composition, they were also affirmation of the talents of Ruby Elzy, actress and singer, playing her role to dramatic and musical perfection.

A few days before the premiere, the opera, now officially called *Porgy and Bess* (Heyward had suggested the new title after the Guild expressed concerns that audiences would confuse it with the earlier play version), was performed in concert before an invited-only audience at Carnegie Hall. It marked the first and only time Ruby Elzy sang on that world-renowned stage. With the entire cast of soloists and chorus, accompanied by a symphony orchestra, Gershwin's opera was performed in its entirety. It would be more than four decades before the full version was heard again.

The world premiere of *Porgy and Bess* took place at the Colonial Theatre in Boston on September 30, 1935. The bravos that opening night were deafening; curtain calls lasted nearly half an hour. Several pictures exist of the company taking their bows; in these the close relationship between Ruby, Todd Duncan, and Anne Brown is very evident—Ruby stands behind the kneeling Duncan, her right hand on his shoulder. To their left stands Brown, holding Ruby's hand. Standing center stage, resplendent in white tie and tails, is a beaming George Gershwin.

The week-long run in Boston was sold out, but with New York looming ahead revisions were being made. *Porgy and Bess* might indeed be an opera, but it would still be playing in a Broadway house. At more than three hours it was far too long for audiences used to Gershwin's musical comedies. The composer obliged Rouben Mamoulian's request for additional cuts before the New York opening. Conductor Alexander Steinert marveled at how calmly Gershwin watched as his labor of love was reduced by almost a fourth.

Ruby's music was not exempted from the cuts. A duet Gershwin had written for Serena and Bess to sing for Clara's orphaned son called "Lonely Boy" was deleted. In its place was inserted a reprise of "Summertime," sung only by Bess. After the Boston opening, the dramatic trio "Where's My Bess?" with Porgy, Serena, and Maria was truncated and made into a short solo for Porgy. Ruby was undoubtedly disappointed with these changes. But at least she still had "My Man's Gone Now" and "Oh, Doctor Jesus."

The official Broadway premiere came at the Alvin Theatre on October 10, 1935, exactly eight years after the premiere of the play. Celebrities packed the house: writers Edna Ferber and Fannie Hurst were there; from opera and classical music came Lily Pons, Kirsten Flagstad, Jascha Heifetz, and Fritz Kreisler; Gershwin's friends and colleagues Richard Rodgers and Irving Berlin were also on hand to cheer his latest creation. Every major newspaper and magazine sent both their theatre and music critics to cover the premiere, unprecedented for any previous work. Ruby had her own "claque" rooting for her: Gardner, Mama, Lucia Dunham, and her "beloved McCrackens," too.

If Boston had given *Porgy and Bess* a warm welcome, then New York's reception was tumultuous. The applause and bravos went on and on; people seemed reluctant to leave the theatre. From the opening lovely strains of "Summertime" to the rousing finale of "I'm on My Way," the performance was brilliant.

Afterwards, Ruby joined Gardner, Mama, and the McCrackens for a celebration at their apartment. Then it was on to another party. Millionaire publisher Condé Nast was hosting the official post-premiere gala at his Madison Avenue penthouse. There were three orchestras playing, and once Gershwin arrived, he took his usual place at the piano. Despite having just performed, Ruby and all her fellow cast members joined Gershwin and sang through the entire score again, just for the guests at the party. It was after six the next morning when Ruby got home.

Audiences in two cities had loved *Porgy and Bess*, but now would come the reaction of the one group in whose hands the fate of the show rested: the critics.

It became almost a myth in later years that *Porgy and Bess* was a failure at first because of the overwhelmingly negative reviews it received from major critics. True, there were some stinging barbs thrown at Gershwin's creation, such as Virgil Thomson, who called it "crooked folklore and half-way opera," but most critics applauded *Porgy and Bess* as something unique and original. That, in fact, was part of its problem: many reviewers had trouble defining just exactly what the show was—whether or not it was a genuine opera or simply a musical on a grander scale than normal. Brooks Atkinson of the *New York Times,* who gave it a favorable review, later joked that "the drama critics praised the music and the music critics praised the libretto."

But while critics were mixed in their reactions to the work itself, they lauded the talented cast, and Ruby received some of the best reviews in the production. Olin Downes of the *New York Times* said, "Miss Elzy's Serena was equally in key with her part, and distinguished by truly pathetic expression," adding "The prayer of Serena for Bess is eloquent, original and the most poetical passage of the whole work."

A. Walter Kramer in *Musical America* wrote, "For sheer intensity of expression, the arioso 'My Man's Gone Now,' sung by Ruby Elzy, the Serena of the opera, in the 'saucer burial' scene of Act I, is one of the score's highest achievements. Miss Elzy's delivery of this music is a masterpiece of its kind."

Ruby's most memorable notices came from *Stage* magazine. Music critic Marcia Davenport wrote that the saucer burial was "a scene to glorify any opera . . . [it] mounts vitally and tensely . . . to the point where Serena begins to sing 'My Man's Gone Now.' And this is the point where this opera can stand comparison with anything written in many, many years. Forbiddingly difficult, Miss Ruby Elzy sings this dirge in a high, piercing soprano voice that embodies every shade of difference between the black throat and white. The burden is a wail, a minor arpeggio for which the composer's direction is glissando—something that demands a violin rather than a voice. The singer has it. She distills heartbreak from this extraordinary piece of music. . . . Miss Elzy is a notable artist."

Drama critic Ruth Woodbury Sedgwick praised Todd Duncan for creating "a new Porgy with sensitivity and sustained power," but was less enthusiastic about his co-star: "Anne Wiggins Brown, who is Bess . . . stands only on the threshold of her part." Then Sedgwick turned to the opera's second female lead:

"Before Ruby Elzy, however, a young graduate of Juilliard and another amateur player, one pauses with awe. This girl plays Serena, the gentle woman of God immortalized once by Rose McClendon. Always exactly right, at times her acting takes on real stature. At Robbins' wake, as she crouches before his bier, the shadows across her tired face, her hands stretched out to Maria on one side and Clara on the other, her angelic voice lifted, she becomes for a stabbing moment a symbol of all the patient sorrow in the world. As she sings 'Oh, Doctor Jesus,' while Bess is lying ill, she almost makes visible her rapt vision."

Ruby Elzy, only twenty-seven years old and in her first major role, was being hailed as a new star.

Playing Serena would prove a challenge for Ruby, whose life and career now revolved around her busy schedule at the Alvin Theatre. Things had yet to settle down when Gardner wrote to the McCrackens a few days after the opening:

October 13, 1935. Sunday Afternoon.

My dear Dr. McCracken,

I wanted to write you and send you the clippings since Friday, but such a busy weekend has made it impossible until now. As you will note, the papers were very kind. It seems that the show will have at least one season run on Broadway and another on the road.

Ruby is feeling fine. She is resting plenty and eats quite heartily. The matinee performances are quite tiresome for her and we find that she is not able to get much rest on Sundays, since many friends drop in then. We are planning to come down next weekend. We'll write you again if this is certain.

Dr. John and Dr. and Mrs. Belknap had dinner with us today. They came to the show last night which was quite a surprise to us. We had expected them next weekend and did not know they were in the theatre until they came to Ruby's dressing room after the night performance. They left for Washington on the four o'clock train.

We certainly enjoyed your being with us Thursday. We hope when you come again, you'll be able to spend a few days. It would be very nice and we would also have an opportunity to take you to many places of interest in the Community.

We are going to an affair tonight that's being given for Mr. Mamoulian. So I suppose I'll have to start preparing. We'll write you again during the week and keep you posted of all the happenings as

well as further clippings. Love to Mrs. McCracken and the children. Tell
Janet don't fail to write us when she is coming to New York.

Sincerely yours, Gardner and Ruby.

P.S. Ask Edward if he'd like to spend Thanksgiving with us?

Eight performances a week as Serena was demanding both physically and vocally. As Gardner noted, there seemed to be an endless
stream of people visiting, and Ruby was gracious to them all. When a
group of students from Delta Omicron, the music faculty at Ohio State
University, came to see *Porgy and Bess*, Ruby not only arranged tickets
but hosted them for dinner in her home. After she left for the theatre,
Gardner escorted the students on to the show. A few weeks after the
opening, George Rightmire, the president of Ohio State, came with his
wife to see the opera. Again, Ruby entertained them over dinner, and
Mrs. Rightmire invited Ruby to be their guest at the president's house
on her next visit to Columbus. Barely five years ago, Ruby had been a
humble student at Ohio State. Now she was friends with the university's first family. It was a heady experience for the little black girl from
a small Mississippi town.

Porgy and Bess was making Ruby and her fellow cast members,
especially Todd Duncan and Anne Brown, well known. A story
with her photograph ran in black newspapers throughout the United
States. But the attention came not only from the Negro press: she was
also the subject of a full-length article in the *New York Herald-Tribune*
titled "One Benefactor After Another Paved the Road for Ruby Elzy." It
covered her background in Mississippi, her discovery by Dr. McCracken,
her education at Ohio State and Juilliard, and her selection by
Gershwin to play Serena.

The opera was also opening up new opportunities for Ruby and her
fellow stars. On Sunday, December 1, 1935, the same day the story about
Ruby ran in the *Herald-Tribune*, Ruby joined Duncan, Brown, Abbie
Mitchell, and the Eva Jessye Choir to perform excerpts from *Porgy and
Bess* with conductor Frank Black and the NBC Symphony Orchestra on

The Magic Key of RCA, a popular weekly program of classical music. A few days later, NBC's Publicity Department sent out a news release:

Ruby Elzy, Negro Soprano
Joins "Melody Master" Cast

Ruby Elzy, hit of the Negro operetta "Porgy and Bess," which the Theatre Guild is presenting on Broadway, has been engaged to sing and play a new role in "The Melody Master" series beginning Sunday, December 8, at 11:00 p.m., E.S.T., over an NBC-WEAF network.

As "Ruby," the new maid at the home of the genial Clem Clemens, the Melody Master, the young Negro soprano will participate in the weekly songfest from the mythical town of Willow Heights.

The program's title role was played by Jack Norworth. A veteran song and dance man, Norworth was also a songwriter who had composed, among other hits, "Take Me Out to the Ball Game." Ironically, it was Norworth who in 1927 was headlining at Columbus's Palace Theatre on the night Ruby, accompanying the McCrackens, had been refused admission to see the show on account of her race. Now she was co-starring with Norworth on network radio.

Ruby enjoyed being part of *The Melody Master*, which featured important guest stars each week in addition to the regular cast. In Ruby's second week on the show the guest was Carrie Jacobs Bond, one of America's greatest women songwriters. Ruby sang Bonds's "A Little Bit o' Honey," and led the company in "A Perfect Day" with Bonds at the piano. *The Melody Master* was making the lovely voice and warm personality of Ruby Elzy familiar in homes across the United States.

One of Ruby's ardent new fans was the celebrated writer Carl Van Vechten. Considered one of the important "Negrophiles" of the Harlem Renaissance, Van Vechten was an influential devotee of black talent and culture. In addition to being a prodigious writer, he was also a fine amateur photographer. Most of his subjects were the black figures he admired, such as James Weldon Johnson, Paul Robeson, Rose McClendon, and Zora Neale Hurston. When Van Vechten saw Ruby in *Porgy and Bess*, he was immediately captivated by her performance. On December 30, 1935, Ruby went to Van Vechten's Manhattan studio, where he shot a series of photographs of her as Serena. Today the originals of those photos are part of the Van Vechten Collection in the Library of Congress.

Ruby was now working seven days a week. From Monday through Saturday (including matinees Wednesday and Saturday) she was on stage in *Porgy and Bess*. Sunday was her one day off from the opera; yet instead of resting, she would go to the WEAF studios for the dress rehearsal and live broadcast of *The Melody Master*. It was a demanding workload that would tax anyone.

It finally caught up with Ruby a few days after her session with Van Vechten. Winters up north were always hard on Ruby, and she came down with a high fever and bronchitis. Too ill to get out of bed, Ruby missed an entire week of performances in *Porgy and Bess*. Helen Dowdy, who played the smaller roles of the Strawberry Woman and Lily, filled in as Serena. Ruby returned to the cast on January 10 for the final two weeks of the show.

By then it was apparent that *Porgy and Bess* could not continue much longer. The entire production was an enormous financial burden for the Theatre Guild. The huge cast and orchestra were costly—even sellout houses for every performance were not enough to cover the weekly payroll. Plus, the Depression was still going on. *Porgy and Bess* had opened in September with a top ticket of $4.40, a sizable price for 1935. The Guild lowered that to $3.30 in December, hoping it would help attract audiences through the slower winter months, but to no avail.

On January 20, 1936, *Porgy and Bess* closed after 124 performances. It was a long run for an opera, though not for a production on Broadway. The Theatre Guild's only hope to recoup its initial investment of seventy thousand dollars was to send the show on the road. The *Porgy and Bess* tour would open in Philadelphia on January 27 and travel from there to Pittsburgh, Chicago, and Detroit, winding up in Washington, D.C.

The Philadelphia leg of the tour was difficult for Ruby, who was still not fully recovered from her illness. Dr. McCracken had resigned from his college presidency in Connecticut the previous August to become director of higher education for the Presbyterian Church of America. The McCrackens now lived in the suburbs of Philadelphia, and hosted a party for the *Porgy and Bess* cast in their home. Ruby was anxious to see her old friends again.

What should have been a joyful reunion turned out to be anything but. Weak after the performance, Ruby asked if she could lie down, and the McCrackens led her upstairs to the guest bedroom. John W. Bubbles did not believe she was sick. Ed McCracken, then thirteen years old, said, "Bubbles had had too much to drink, and he was getting pretty mean. He insisted that Ruby come down and join the party. My Dad told him Ruby was too ill. Bubbles said if Ruby wouldn't come down, then he was going upstairs to see her. My Dad stood in front of the staircase and said, 'No you're not.'"

Bubbles was a man who got violent when he'd had too much to drink. He pulled out a knife and said, "I'm going up to see Ruby *right now*," and lunged at Dr. McCracken. "Everyone let out a gasp, and I was really scared," Ed McCracken recalled. "Fortunately, Todd Duncan and several others jumped Bubbles and got the knife away from him before he could hurt Dad." The incident frightened everyone, and the party soon broke up.

As the tour proceeded, it was clear that box-office receipts would not be enough to save *Porgy and Bess*, nor to justify continuing the tour beyond the dates already committed. The week-long run in Washington, D.C., marked the final performances of *Porgy and Bess*. The opera ended as it had begun—in controversy.

Trouble was brewing even before the company arrived in Washington. The National Theatre, where the opera was to be presented, was strictly segregated. Todd Duncan was a Washingtonian,

Anne Brown was from nearby Baltimore. Even though they were the stars of *Porgy and Bess*, under the theatre's policies none of their family members or friends would be allowed in to see them perform. In many ways it was a precursor to the celebrated incident three years later when Marian Anderson was refused permission to sing at the D.A.R.'s Constitution Hall, which led to her famous Lincoln Memorial concert.

Brown and Duncan immediately protested not only to the management of the National Theatre and the Theatre Guild, but personally to Gershwin. Their efforts caused such a commotion that both were threatened with being fired from the show and fined by the actor's union; but neither budged.

Like Duncan and Brown, Ruby had faced discrimination throughout her life and career. Yet she never felt confrontation was a solution. At the same time, she was also loyal to her friends and colleagues, whom she felt were being unjustly pressured. After all, the National Theatre was wrong, not Duncan or Brown. Ruby joined the others in the cast in signing a petition in support of Brown and Duncan. It gave the National Theatre an ultimatum: if it did not amend its policy of segregation, the company of *Porgy and Bess* would refuse to perform.

Boxed into a corner, the harried impresario in charge of the theatre offered a number of halfhearted compromises: blacks could sit in the balcony for all performances; there would be special performances for black audiences only; blacks could sit in designated sections on the main floor for matinees, and so on. The cast held firm: blacks would be allowed to see any performance of *Porgy and Bess* with no seating restrictions whatever.

Finally, the National Theatre management gave in. *Porgy and Bess* opened on March 16, 1936; blacks were present at all eight performances, seated in every section of the hall. There were no repercussions and no incidents, as the manager had feared there would be. He remarked later that what he found most surprising was that "not even one white person asked for a refund."

Unfortunately, despite the success of *Porgy and Bess* in playing to an integrated audience, the National Theatre was unwilling to change its standing policies. After *Porgy and Bess* the theatre went back to being a segregated house. It would not become fully integrated until 1955. But Anne Brown and Todd Duncan, joined and supported by Ruby Elzy and the others in the company, had made theatre history that winter in Washington, and had advanced the cause of civil rights for blacks one step further.

With the tour ended, Ruby went back to New York City. After nearly a year of steady work, she now found herself without a job. Not only was *Porgy and Bess* finished; her illness and the Guild tour had forced her to drop out of the cast of *The Melody Master* in January 1936. The series came to an end a few months later after only a single season on the air.

But what to do next in her career was no longer Ruby's first priority. The ill health and fatigue of the past few months were merely symptomatic of a deeper problem that was eroding her once boundless energy and indomitable spirit.

The relationship between Ruby and Gardner had been strained for some time. Throughout the final months of *Porgy and Bess*, Ruby put on a brave front to her friends and colleagues. Now, as she returned to New York, Ruby's marriage was on the verge of collapse. It was too difficult to think of work when her heart was breaking.

The darkest period of Ruby's life had begun.

"MY MAN'S GONE NOW"

When Dr. McCracken and his family saw Ruby off at the train station following the Philadelphia run of *Porgy and Bess* (and the upsetting incident with John W. Bubbles in their home), they knew something was wrong. The state of Ruby's physical and mental well-being genuinely concerned them as they bade her goodbye. It would be nearly nine months before they heard from Ruby again:

> December 11, 1936
>
> My Dearest Dr. and Mrs. McCracken,
>
> Please don't show this letter to the children. Just tell them the good things in it.
>
> This time I know it will be harder than ever for you to forgive me. . . .
> I have what seem to me very good excuses for everything except not writing and telling you my conditions. Let me please tell you and then judge me, because I love you so much it would mean a great loss to me, more than you even realize to lose your friendship.

So began the longest letter she would ever write to the McCrackens, recounting in detail what probably was the most difficult year of Ruby's life. The sweet taste of success she had enjoyed in the fall of 1935 with her acclaimed performance in *Porgy and Bess* and her role on radio's *The Melody Master* had turned bitter all too soon. By the spring of 1936 Ruby was back in New York City, the tour ended, her stamina weak, her promising career stalled, her finances in ruin. But the most tragic and traumatic setback of all—and certainly a major cause for her other difficulties—was the failure of her marriage.

The McCrackens had seen signs of it the year before. Since she had married, Ruby had always visited the McCrackens with Gardner at her side. But Ed McCracken remembers a time when Ruby came alone by train. She was visibly upset, yet she found it difficult to explain what exactly was wrong. Finally she said, "Dr. McCracken, would you mind if I sing?"

Ed McCracken said, "Ruby sat at the piano and accompanied herself as she sang 'Nobody Knows the Trouble I've Seen.' I'd never heard her sing it more beautifully or with more feeling. Tears were streaming down her face, and by the time she finished, every one of us were in tears, too."

As always, Ruby could open up her heart through song more than she could with words alone. Once she did, she was finally able to tell Dr. McCracken her troubles. For some time Ruby and Gardner had been quarreling over money. The arguments had become more frequent and more strident. Ruby had begun to fear that it might put an end to her marriage.

It was not that they were not making money. Through some political connections Gardner had made from his work for the *Afro-American Journal*, he had taken a job in government. He earned a good salary and Ruby, between her stage and radio work, was making almost a hundred dollars a week—a sizable sum for the mid-1930s. They enjoyed a comfortable lifestyle unusual for a young black couple during the Depression, moving into a larger apartment on Seventh Avenue that Ruby furnished beautifully. She loved to entertain in her home, whether her guests were the young Delta Omicron students from Ohio State or its president, Dr. Rightmire, and his wife.

Ruby had always entrusted Gardner with their finances, but he proved to be no better than his wife at managing money. The troubles increased when Gardner had to pay political bosses a kickback in order to keep his job. It seemed now that no matter how much money came in, it was going out even faster.

Ruby had heard rumors that Gardner was gambling, and she grew suspicious that that was where all their money was going. It was one thing she could not tolerate; Ruby knew the anguish her own father's gambling had caused her mother, and how it had contributed to their breakup. When Ruby questioned Gardner about it, he exploded. From that point on, hardly a day went by without an argument. The stress of this, combined with Ruby's heavy workload, led to her illness in December 1935.

But Ruby still loved Gardner and determined to do all she could to salvage what had been for so long a happy marriage. As the *Porgy and Bess* tour moved on to Chicago, Ruby asked Gardner to join her. She hoped that, with time away from New York and the pressures of his job, she and Gardner could rekindle the deep feelings they still had for each other. Unfortunately, it had the opposite effect: by the time they returned home in late March they were barely speaking.

Although Ruby blamed their finances for her marital woes, there is another possible cause, too. When they married in September 1931, Gardner Jones was an up-and-coming figure in the black community as Brooklyn editor for the *Afro-American Journal*, an important newspaper. Ruby was a student at Juilliard, a talented but still unknown singer. During the first few years of their marriage, they lived on Gardner's salary, while Ruby's schooling was supported by her scholarships.

Now, four years later, it was Ruby who was garnering all the attention and acclaim. She was a rising star on Broadway and radio and for the first time was probably making as much, if not more, money than her husband. Perhaps this sudden reversal in their roles was difficult for Gardner Jones to accept.

Back in New York, Ruby and Gardner returned to the apartment on Seventh Avenue but communicated very little with each other. Gardner went back to work. Ruby attempted to resume singing, but her heart was not in it. Still hoping her marriage could somehow be saved, and badly in need of emotional support, Ruby asked her mother to come to New York. Emma Elzy had grown close to her son-in-law, and he in turn was very fond of her. Perhaps Mama could help heal the rift. Emma, teaching in Corinth, promised Ruby she would come as soon as the school year finished.

Ruby's spirits were momentarily lifted when she got a call from George Gershwin. He was planning his annual summer all-Gershwin concert with the New York Philharmonic-Symphony at the mammoth Lewisohn Stadium. This year, in addition to works such as *An American in Paris* and *Rhapsody in Blue*, Gershwin wanted to include an entire segment of *Porgy and Bess*. Was Ruby available to appear as a guest artist? A grateful Ruby said yes at once. The concert, which would also include Ruby's co-stars Todd Duncan and Anne Brown, would be given over two nights. It was an important milestone for Ruby—her debut with the New York Philharmonic-Symphony. And to top it off, she would be paid a hundred dollars for her appearance.

Emma arrived in June. Ruby was overjoyed to see her mother, but it was too late for Emma to help her daughter and her son-in-law reconcile. Shortly before Emma's arrival, Gardner moved out of the Seventh Avenue apartment. After less than five years, Ruby's marriage was over, as she wrote sadly to the McCrackens:

> I sent for mother . . . (and) she came. When she got here it was too late to do anything about Gardner and me because we had already separated and he wouldn't listen to me or to mother. . . . I had to give up my nice apartment and move to a smaller one for less money, send most of my furniture to storage because my present quarters are so small. . . . I've never in all my life been so miserable. You both know how much I loved Gardner. . . . I am alone now because Gardner and I can never live together again. I like him and I want you to like him, too. There are always two sides to any question. He probably has as good an argument as I have. I realize I was very difficult when the trouble started. We have forgiven each other and are friends. But that is all. I don't love him anymore and I am sure he doesn't love me.

The all-Gershwin concerts at Lewisohn Stadium, broadcast nationally over the Mutual Broadcasting System, were presented on July 9 and 10, 1936. By now, several of the songs from *Porgy and Bess* had become hits, and the entire segment from the opera was enthusiastically applauded. Ruby's beautiful singing of her signature aria, "My Man's

Gone Now," had a special poignancy and power. Only Emma Elzy, seated in the audience, could appreciate how painfully true the words of that song must have been for her daughter to sing on this occasion.

After the second and final night at Lewisohn, Ruby and Emma went to the post-concert party. It was a huge farewell for George Gershwin, who was about to leave with his brother Ira for the West Coast, where they had signed a contract with RKO Studios to write the score for two new motion pictures starring Fred Astaire and Ginger Rogers. Before she left the party, Ruby thanked Gershwin for inviting her be part of the Lewisohn concert and wished him well in Hollywood. It would be the last time Ruby saw George Gershwin alive.

After the Lewisohn concerts, Ruby again fell into a depression. It was if she did not care whether she lived or died. For a time, she even seemed to lose all interest in singing. Close friends like Georgette Harvey and Eddie Matthews tried to help Ruby without much success.

Only one person could reach Ruby at a time like this, and that was her Mama. Thankfully, Emma Elzy was there. One night, after Ruby had spent another day secluded in her apartment, Emma finally decided it was time to act. She sat her daughter down for a stern talk.

"Ruby, when your daddy left me, I had four little children to take care of. Now how can you be any worse off than I was? All you've got to do is take care of yourself. Will laying around every day, weeping and moaning, bring your man back? Did it bring your daddy back? No. Honey, believe me, Mama knows what you're going through, and it's the worst feeling in the world. But somehow you've got to find it in yourself to carry on, just like I did. And if you think you haven't got the strength to do it alone—that's where the Lord comes in. Remember what the Bible teaches us—'I will lift mine eyes to the hills from whence cometh my help.' The Lord won't let you down, if just you ask Him. All He wants you to do is try, and He'll take care of the rest."

Emma Elzy's strong dose of common sense and prayer finally got through to her daughter. Gradually, Ruby's spirits began to rise. She started going out every day with Mama and her friends, and once again she looked forward to the future with hope. A grateful Ruby told the McCrackens, "Mother stayed here all summer with me, bless her. I should have died if she hadn't been with me."

But in September Emma Elzy had to return to Corinth and her little school. Ruby seemed to be her old self again, and Emma was especially happy that Ruby was ready to go back to work. Mama knew that singing, more than anything else, would heal the wounds, for to Ruby singing was as important and necessary as air to breathe.

Anxious to resume her singing career, Ruby began taking a lesson a week with her old teacher at Juilliard, Lucia Dunham. She also began making the rounds, looking for work. Thanks to *Porgy and Bess* and her radio and concert appearances, Ruby had become known to the top agents and producers in New York. Soon she landed a four-week contract with CBS network radio at twenty-five dollars per week.

Ruby was a guest star on four broadcasts, the highlight being her appearance on *Deep River,* a program devoted to spirituals and hosted by black conductor Willard Robinson. CBS was obviously pleased with her work: when her contract expired Ruby was offered another one, this time for three months.

Ruby's radio career was moving into high gear, but not without difficulties, as she explained to the McCrackens: "I've had two other broadcasts [since October 13] with another on Tuesday night, December 15th at 10:30. Please listen [it's on] WABC [the CBS flagship station in New York]. They are trying to-do something for me at WABC because they have me signed up for 3 months. But it seems almost impossible with me singing the type of things I sing. You know they always want Negroes to sing blues or hot songs and I can't do that. But they have been honest about everything and as nice as they can be. Maybe I'll get a break soon."

It was not the first time Ruby had felt frustrated at the narrow view people in the entertainment industry had of black talent. Nor was she alone in facing such obstacles; it was something all black performers encountered in their careers. Fortunately, CBS valued her talents and continued trying to find appropriate opportunities for her.

After her appearance on December 15 with popular bandleader Mark Warnow (later music director of radio's famed *Your Hit Parade*), CBS made her a regular on the Wednesday afternoon program *Columbia Concerts*. The star was Howard Barlow, founder and conductor of the CBS Symphony Orchestra and the network's most prestigious musical personality. It was the kind of format suited to Ruby's versatility with songs ranging from classical to popular to spirituals. Ruby would remain on Barlow's program until the end of her three-month contract.

With her December letter to Dr. McCracken, Ruby had good news to share about her first engagement of 1937:

> After I'd waited so long to write, I just waited until I was sure of what I am to tell you now. I wrote to Dr. Hughes to see if I could come to OSU for a concert, and he turned it over to the musical fraternity and they wrote me immediately. We came to terms and I am to go out there for January 25th which is a Monday night. I am so happy. I am preparing a dandy program. I take a lesson once a week. I wish it were possible for me to sing there at your little church once before I sing at OSU. I'd like to bring my accompanist and the only thing is I'd have to pay him about $20.00 and train fare. I'd pay it myself just to sing the program for your church and to an audience, but I am not making any money. If it could be done, I'd like to do it a Sunday afternoon in January.

Then, as if to reassure the McCrackens that she had indeed finally come through all her trials, she added:

> Anyway, I wish you all would let me come and see you soon. I am myself again now and well and won't be a wet blanket. (smile) Please give my love to the kiddies. I hope they are all well. I hope I can see them soon. Let me know if you forgive me.
>
> As ever your, Ruby Elzy.
>
> P.S. They are paying me $200.00 at Ohio State

On January 20, 1937, Ruby boarded the train for Columbus, joined by her good friend and accompanist Arthur Kaplan. It was Ruby's first visit to Columbus and Ohio State since her graduation nearly seven years before; but Columbus had not forgotten her in the interim, and her successes had been regularly reported in the local press. The *Columbus Citizen* ran a story in December 1935, after the opening of *Porgy and Bess:*

Local Girl Makes Good

> Perhaps she can't fairly be called a local girl, but Ruby Elzy had her musical beginnings in Columbus, and there are still enough (people) to remember her here to make news of her further progress interesting.

Ruby at last was able to take up Mrs. Rightmire's invitation and stay as her guest in the president's residence on campus. Ruby and Kaplan rehearsed at Royal Hughes's house, where she sat down with a reporter from Ohio State's student newspaper, *The Lantern*. She acknowledged the debt she owed to Dr. McCracken and Dr. Hughes and credited her education at Ohio State in preparing her for Juilliard and her professional career. She said, "My whole life has been of full of blessings. Loads of people have all contributed to making me very happy."

It was a heartfelt expression of joy that would have been impossible a few months before as she went through the agony of her separation from Gardner. Ruby finished the interview by telling the reporter of her ambition to study in Europe. It was a wish that would remain unfulfilled.

Not even a driving rain on the night of Thursday, January 21 could keep audiences away from Ruby's homecoming. University Chapel was filled to capacity. From the moment Ruby, dressed in a beautiful pearl gown, walked on stage to cheers, she had the audience in the palm of her hands. Her repertoire had vastly expanded since her graduate recital seven years before. She sang everything from operatic arias (Charpentier's "Depuis le juir" and Puccini's "Un bel di") and German *lieder* to spirituals and, of course, "My Man's Gone Now," which she offered as an encore.

The following day, Ruby received lavish praise in the *Columbus Citizen* from critic R. L. F. McCombs, who had also heard Ruby's graduating recital in 1930:

> It is a long and weary road, beset with pitfalls, that lies between singing hymn-tunes in a Mississippi kitchen and singing Gluck and Brahms and Puccini to an audience of cordial admirers. Ruby Elzy, the diminutive Negro soprano who gave a recital in the University Hall last night has been able to travel that road successfully. . . . There was a wide contrast between the shy, pink-frocked girl who gave a modest recital at the time of her graduation and the assured young singer, confident in her music and wise to the ways of her audiences, who sang last evening. But there was the same natural purity and freshness of voice and the same flair for song, the same sincerity and the same humility. . . . Miss Elzy's voice is vibrantly sweet and true . . . the arias seemed best suited to her voice, and their theatrical effectiveness lay well in her power to project . . . the spirituals were of blood and bone and she sang them with a magnificent simplicity. . . . She was the very voice of her people, exulting or sorrowful.

Two days later, Ruby and Kaplan performed together in the northern Ohio city of Norwalk, where she had given one of her first solo concerts while still a student at Ohio State. Again she sang magnificently, and the local newspaper called her concert "the musical event of the year."

Ruby returned to New York in an exuberant mood and promptly shared her recent triumphs with the McCracken family:

New York City. January 27, 1937

My dear Dr. and Mrs. McCracken,

I have just returned from Columbus. I think I can say, and be safe that I was very, very successful. I am enclosing a clipping from the

Columbus Citizen; don't you think the Critic was nice? Dr. Hughes was so pleased. He said, "a body certainly can learn a lot in seven years." Doesn't that sound just like him? The Hughes gave a reception for me after the concert, and they also had me and my accompanist to lunch on Saturday . . . we went to Norwalk . . . I gave my concert there on Sunday. Although it was a very bad snowing night we had a large very appreciative audience.

I have a very bad cold now. I caught it Monday before I left Norwalk. I think that I was very lucky to wait until after my recitals were over to get a cold if I just had to get one. You see by my address that I have moved again, I have a less expensive place and I like it much better. I shall probably keep this one for a long time. It is in a much better neighborhood and a quieter one. I hope to have a Radio contract for the spring and summer season. I will then have regular periods to broadcast.

I hope you won't get too tickled at my typing. I am taking great pains to write this letter (smile). . . . It has taken me most all day to write this much. I have to hunt so long before I find the letters, when I finally decide that the letter isn't on the keyboard at all, then it pops up right before my eyes. I can't see why they didn't put the letters on the typewriter in order anyway.

Please let me hear from you soon. Excuse my typewriter please. Sometimes it takes a notion not to write in a straight line. It's temperamental I guess (smile).

Lots of love, your Ruby

It would not be long before Ruby's efforts to find work paid off. She enjoyed singing on radio, and soon she had her biggest opportunity in the medium to date: a fifteen-minute solo broadcast recorded for Lang-Worth Feature Programs. Lang-Worth produced the large sixteen-inch disks called ET's (electrical transcriptions) for network and local radio syndication. Lang-Worth was one of the largest companies in the field, regularly producing programs with artists such as Count Basie and Fats Waller.

In the spring of 1937, Ruby went into Lang-Worth's New York studios to record five spirituals. She opened with one of her showpieces, Hall Johnson's dramatic "City Called Heaven." She followed it with the joyous "I Know the Lord," and then the mournful "Don't You Weep When I'm Gone," a song that demonstrated Ruby's exquisite *diminuendo* and *messa voce*. Fourth was "On Ma Journey Now," a short but lively number that showcased Ruby's lower register; and finally, a haunting rendition of one of the greatest of all spirituals, "Sometimes I Feel Like a Motherless Child."

It was fitting that Ruby should be accompanied on her first solo program by longtime friend and collaborator Arthur Kaplan. It was the only time they recorded together. Some of the announcements were hackneyed and to modern ears perhaps a bit offensive, as the host spoke of the "happy philosophy of the American Negro." Ruby herself was introduced as "Ruby Elzy, famous Negro soprano." White singers were identified by their type of voice ("coloratura soprano") or their nationality ("Italian tenor"). Only African American singers were identified by the hue of their skin. It was so common that sometimes even the black singers referred to themselves that way; certainly Ruby did, although she would say not long before her death, "There is no color to talent."

Lang-Worth released the program in the spring of 1937, and soon afterwards the voice of Ruby Elzy was being heard across America, in the music she loved best and sang most beautifully. She followed up with a guest appearance on one of the nation's most popular radio series.

Town Hall Tonight was NBC's highest-rated show; every Wednesday night more than half the country tuned in to enjoy the dry, laconic wit of its star Fred Allen. By turns a superb master of ceremonies, monologist, and comedian, Allen was the Jay Leno or David Letterman of his era, and *Town Hall Tonight* was the forerunner of every talk show on the air today. To be a guest on Allen's show was a feather in any performer's cap. On April 28, 1937, it was Ruby Elzy's turn.

A large part of the fun (and terror) for Allen's guests was the unpredictability of being on stage with him, live before a national radio audience. Allen frequently went off his script. He was a notorious ad-libber famous for such one-liners as "A celebrity is a person who works hard all his life to become well known, then wears dark glasses to avoid being recognized." His humor often came at the expense of his guests.

Allen introduced Ruby as one of the stars of *Porgy and Bess* and proceeded to ask her about her background. Ruby talked about coming to Juilliard from Ohio State, Dr. C. C. McCracken, and how she washed tablecloths to get through Rust College (she told Allen she washed so many that she now refused to eat on them in her own house). She found it impossible to keep from laughing as Allen interrupted her with jibes about everything from "coming back into her house as a spirit with a tablecloth," being upset with the Theatre Guild for closing *Porgy and Bess* before he had gotten to see it, and Ruby's friend, "Mr. Robeson . . . gadding about Russia." (Paul Robeson was then touring a number of European countries, including the Soviet Union.)

Finally, it was time for Ruby's song—"Summertime" from *Porgy and Bess*. Allen said, "One of the boys in the band told me you're appearing this week at the Apollo Club in Harlem." When Ruby said she had another show that night, Allen got in a final joke, "Well, then, we'd better just get to it!" Ruby did a lovely job on "Summertime," albeit in an abbreviated arrangement by the program's orchestra leader, Peter van Steeden.

Rushing out of NBC's studios in Rockefeller Center, Ruby made it to Harlem with just moments to spare before going on stage at the Apollo.

The now legendary Apollo Theater originally opened in 1914 as a burlesque house catering to white patrons coming to Harlem. In 1934, an enterprising man named Frank Schiffman (also white) took over the Apollo. It was Schiffman who began presenting leading black entertainers to mixed audiences, and in the process he made the Apollo the best known showcase in Harlem. Schiffman brought in such performers as Bessie Smith, Duke Ellington, and a then unknown young blues singer named Billie Holliday. Schiffman's "Amateur Night," held each week, was already famous for introducing new talent such as Ella Fitzgerald.

Ruby headlined the entire week of April 26, and much to Schiffman's delight her appearance on *Town Hall Tonight* that Wednesday helped bring in even larger audiences. He was a man who cared about art only insofar as it brought in customers who would pay to see the stars he booked. Ruby, being from the Broadway stage, helped bring in a wider audience, in addition to those regular fans who came out primarily to see blues singers or big bands.

Schiffman brought Ruby back that summer, her appearance announced in the black newspapers: "Star Ruby Elzy at the Apollo." Ruby headlined a revue, sharing top billing with popular radio comedian Eddie Green, the week of July 18, 1937.

The show was in rehearsal on the afternoon of July 11 when a news bulletin came over the radio: George Gershwin was dead in California. A brain tumor had taken the composer's life at the young age of thirty-eight. It was hard to believe. Gershwin had always seemed so vital and energetic; now he was gone. Like so many others who had personally known and worked with Gershwin, Ruby was stunned and saddened.

On Thursday, July 15, Ruby was one of more than 3,500 mourners who crowded into New York's Temple Emanu-El for Gershwin's funeral. Huge crowds lined the streets outside, paying silent tribute to the young immigrant Russian Jew who had changed American music forever.

Gershwin songs filled the airwaves constantly. It was inevitable that a number of memorial concerts would be planned, the first one in the composer's native New York City. On Monday, August 9, 1937, less than a month after his death, an all-Gershwin concert was presented by the New York Philharmonic at Lewisohn Stadium. Ruby, Todd Duncan, and Anne Brown joined an array of performers that included Broadway star Ethel Merman, who had gained fame in Gershwin's *Girl Crazy*, and composer Ferde Grofe, who had orchestrated Gershwin's immortal *Rhapsody in Blue*.

More than twenty thousand people packed into Lewisohn, the largest crowd in the arena's history. Among the notables in the audience were New York Governor Herman Lehman and New York City

Mayor Fiorello LaGuardia. Gershwin was represented by his mother, Rose, and his younger sister, Frances.

The *Porgy and Bess* segment was again a standout, and once more Ruby sang "My Man's Gone Now" with power and beauty. A year before, in the same place, and with the same orchestra, Ruby had sung with a special fervor as she grieved for the loss of her husband's love. Now she grieved again, this time for the loss of a friend, mentor, and collaborator, whose genius had changed the course of her life.

The New York concert was a sensational success. Now producers on the West Coast were clamoring to pay their own tribute to Gershwin, and they wanted the original stars of *Porgy and Bess* to be part of it.

The two-day journey by train from New York to Los Angeles was a wondrous experience for Ruby, who had never been farther west than Memphis and Chicago. The concert with the Los Angeles Philharmonic was set for September 8, 1937, at the Hollywood Bowl. It was a spectacular event in true Hollywood fashion with seven vocalists, seven conductors, and two pianists performing, along with actors George Jessel and Edward G. Robinson in spoken tributes. Ruby, Todd Duncan, and Anne Brown performed songs from *Porgy and Bess*. Their friend and colleague from New York, Alexander Steinert, conducted.

Joining them were the Hall Johnson Choir, famous for its appearances in films such as *The Green Pastures*. Ruby was delighted to at last meet the renowned Johnson, whose arrangements of spirituals such as "City Called Heaven" she had sung many times. She also met Merle Armitage, a close friend of George Gershwin's and the manager of the Philharmonic Auditorium. Soon both Johnson and Armitage would be playing key roles in Ruby's burgeoning career.

On the night of the concert more than twenty-two thousand people jammed into the Hollywood Bowl. Traffic on Highland Avenue was so heavy that Fred Astaire, who was singing "They Can't Take That Away from Me" on the program, had to get out of his taxi and enter the front gates on foot in order not to miss his performance. The concert was broadcast live worldwide by CBS starting at 8:30 p.m. Pacific

Time. Listeners back east had to stay up until after two in the morning to hear the entire program.

Ruby sang magnificently, the transcription recorded by CBS that night a lasting testimonial to her gifts. The entire *Porgy and Bess* segment went very well, despite a less-than-stellar opening in which "Summertime" was sung by the Metropolitan Opera's reigning diva, French coloratura Lily Pons. However brilliant she may have been at the Met, Pons had no feel for Gershwin's style, and her French accent made her pronunciation of some words unintelligible.

The Gershwin Memorial Concert was, in the words of the *Los Angeles Times,* a "colossal success." It was another personal milestone for Ruby: her debut with the Los Angeles Philharmonic. That it came at the Hollywood Bowl and was broadcast live to a national audience by CBS made it even more significant.

A few days later Ruby took the train back east. During her short stay she fell in love with Southern California's delightful climate, beautiful scenery, and warm, friendly people. She resolved to come back again. It was a wish that would be realized sooner than she imagined.

A year and a half had passed since Ruby had returned to New York from the first *Porgy and Bess* tour tired, ill, and broke. She had been deeply hurt by the breakup with Gardner. Now, with her divorce final, Ruby's emotional wounds were healing at last. The struggles to build her career after *Porgy and Bess* had also eased. She had achieved success as a radio and concert singer and had performed with two of America's premier symphony orchestras. Perhaps she was still being introduced as the "famous Negro soprano," but at least she *was* becoming famous.

Ruby decided she was ready now to take the next major step in her development. If she was going to establish herself as a serious artist, it meant one thing: a recital in New York before New York critics, the toughest in the world.

Riding back east from California, Ruby looked forward to the challenges that lay ahead. The next three months would be an exciting journey that would take her all the way to the White House.

RISING STAR

With its intimate space and perfect acoustics, Manhattan's Town Hall has been a favorite venue of both performers and audiences since its opening in 1921. Many celebrated artists have made their New York debuts at Town Hall, including almost every important black singer from Roland Hayes and Marian Anderson to William Warfield and Leontyne Price. To this stellar list Ruby Elzy added her name on Sunday, October 10, 1937.

To present a solo recital accompanied only by piano is the greatest challenge for any singer. Performing different types of music, in several different languages, is a true test of the singer's artistry. After her successful performances in the two Gershwin memorial concerts, Ruby felt the time was right for her to take on that challenge.

The time was also right for Ruby to take on a manager. Except for her years in Columbus, when Dr. McCracken and Dr. Hughes had carefully planned every step of her developing career, Ruby had for the most part been on her own. She had done a good job, as evidenced by her success both on radio and the stage. But now she was at the point where she needed someone who could devote their energies to booking her appearances, handling publicity, and attending to the other myriad business details of running a career.

In the summer of 1937, Charles L. Marshall, who himself was African American, founded the Manhattan Artists Bureau. There were many black managers and agents who served black entertainers in the popular music industry, but Marshall was one of the first to represent black artists in the field of classical music. Ruby joined Marshall's roster soon after he opened his agency, along with artists such as composer-arranger

Harry T. Burleigh and Ruby's friend and *Porgy and Bess* co-star Edward Matthews. With Marshall, Ruby at last had someone who could free her up to concentrate on her most important asset: her voice.

Returning to New York from Hollywood, Ruby went to work with Lucia Dunham to prepare her program. For this concert Ruby would not be accompanied by her friend, Arthur Kaplan, but by William Lawrence. He was among the most distinguished black musicians of the time, a well-known arranger, composer, and teacher as well as a pianist. Lawrence had accompanied Roland Hayes and Marian Anderson and had appeared several times at Town Hall. For this debut, Lawrence's reputation and experience would be invaluable to Ruby.

The Town Hall concert was as important to Charles L. Marshall and his fledgling agency as it was to Ruby; it would be the first major event Marshall had produced. It would be an expensive undertaking, and Ruby agreed to share the costs with her manager. If the concert made money, they would split the net profit after expenses. If the concert lost money, they would equally cover the shortfall.

In promoting Ruby's concert, Marshall was helped by the national exposure she had garnered as a result of the two Gershwin concerts, especially the live broadcast from the Hollywood Bowl. Marshall placed ads in the major daily newspapers and also in the black press. Tickets went on sale, priced from $2.75 for a box seat to $0.83 for the upper balcony.

October signaled the official start of the arts season in the Big Apple, from the Metropolitan Opera and the New York Philharmonic to Carnegie Hall and Broadway. Town Hall was playing host to a concert almost every evening that month. In addition to Ruby, several other artists were making their debuts. One of them, a seventeen-year-old, Russian-born violin prodigy, made his Town Hall debut on October 11, the night after Ruby's performance; his name was Isaac Stern.

Just after 8:30 p.m. on October 10, the curtains parted and Ruby, radiant in a new gown, walked onto the Town Hall stage. What the audience lacked in size (only about 500 of the hall's 1,400 seats were filled) it made up for in enthusiasm. Ruby's entrance was greeted with a rousing ovation. She bowed, then acknowledged William Lawrence, taking his place at the Steinway grand piano. Charles Marshall had arranged the use of the piano *gratis* in exchange for Ruby's endorsement in an advertisement: "I use the Steinway exclusively in my studio, because it is the only instrument which gives my voice perfect support."

The first half of Ruby's program consisted of classical airs by Rameau and Gluck, five German *lieder* by Brahms, and finally Charpentier's "Depuis le juir" from the opera *Louise*. Ruby's climatic high B in the aria came off perfectly, and she was called back for several bows before the intermission.

Except for the "Norwegian Echo Song," the second half of the program was sung entirely in English. Ruby followed her set of spirituals with "My Man's Gone Now," which brought the house down. She returned to the stage for several encores, including "Summertime," before closing with "Steal Away to Jesus."

A beaming Emma Elzy was in the audience—this time not holding her head down while Ruby sang in French. The McCrackens were there, too, along with many of Ruby's old friends and colleagues from radio and the stage. Afterwards they all went out to celebrate. Ruby was genuinely relieved it was over—never before had she felt so nervous for a performance.

Now came the reviews.

Noel Straus of the *New York Times* commented, "Miss Elzy's most pronounced asset, as she proceeded through the well-contrasted list of offerings she had selected, was her innate sense of the dramatic."

The *New York Sun*'s Oscar Thompson said, "Miss Elzy arrived at the Gershwin songs by way of a group of spirituals, one of which, 'Every Time I Feel the Spirit,' she was obliged to encore. Whether she sang Gluck's 'Ah, malgre moi,' Brahms' 'Botschaft,' or Quilter's 'Come Away Death,' Miss Elzy sang with intelligence and taste."

Robert C. Bagar wrote in the *New York World-Telegram* that "Miss Elzy's account of 'Depuis le jour' was tops for the night. Not only did she deliver the aria with warmth and devotion but her French pronunciation and diction were excellent."

The small-town soprano from Mississippi had taken on her toughest audience to date and had come out a winner. Ruby Elzy was acknowledged as one of America's most gifted young sopranos, a rising star in the worlds of both classical music and theatre.

The only downside of Ruby's Town Hall recital was financial. After all the ticket money came in and the expenses were added up, the ledger showed a deficit of nearly four hundred dollars. True to her agreement with Marshall, Ruby covered half the loss, or almost two hundred dollars. Ruby could only shrug—she had spent a month of work in preparation for her Town Hall debut. From it she now had a stack of good reviews in one hand and a pile of bills in the other.

Those good reviews would help, though, as Marshall now promoted Ruby for other concert appearances on the East Coast. In the meantime, Ruby went back to the Lang-Worth studios, this time with William Lawrence, to record two more programs for radio syndication.

The first program opened with James Bland's sentimental ballad "Carry Me Back to Old Virginny" followed by Stephen Foster's lively folk tune "Ring, Ring de Banjo." Then Ruby sang three spirituals: the dramatic "You Hear de Lambs," which she had sung at Town Hall, the humorous "Oh, Didn't It Rain?" about Noah and the flood, and finally, Rosamond Johnson's arrangement of "Nobody Knows the Trouble I've Seen," sung with all the beauty and power that had moved the McCracken family to tears when Ruby sang it in their living room. Her performance of this song alone validates what was said by nearly every critic who reviewed her—Ruby Elzy was one of the greatest of all interpreters of the American Negro spiritual.

With her third and final program for Lang-Worth, Ruby decided to go in a completely different direction, treating her audience to the more serious material she had performed at Town Hall. She opened with Flotow's aria "The Last Rose of Summer" from his opera *Martha*, one of the best-loved and most well-known pieces of the 1930s. Then Ruby sang three selections in German: Bohm's *lied* "Still wie die Nacht" and arias from two operas: Mozart's "Ah! lo so" from *The Magic Flute* and Wagner's "Elsa's Dream" from *Lohengrin*.

Lang-Worth released the programs in the fall of 1937, again bringing the voice of Ruby Elzy to countless listeners across the United States. Together, the three Lang-Worth programs provide a lasting record of her remarkable voice and of her range and versatility as an artist.

In September 1937, just after her return from Hollywood, Ruby was signed by John Krimsky (who had produced the film version of *The Emperor Jones*) for a role in his new Broadway comedy *In Clover*. The star was an up-and-coming young actor from Puerto Rico named José Ferrer. As it turned out, the timing of the show would directly conflict with Ruby's Town Hall debut, so she had to drop out of Krimsky's production.

Now, Town Hall was behind Ruby, as were several other concerts that Marshall had arranged for her to sing at black colleges in Pennsylvania. Back in New York, as Marshall worked on lining up more engagements for her, Ruby again decided to look for work on Broadway. She found it in a play called *Home Sweet Harlem*—but by the time previews began in Brooklyn, the title had been changed to *Brown Sugar*. Ruby was cast as Sarah; one of the leading roles.

The play was written by Bernice Angus, with incidental music by Haven Johnson. Ruby was especially looking forward to working with George Abbott, who was producing and directing. One of Broadway's legendary showmen, Abbott's career spanned nearly eight decades (he was 107 when he died in 1995), during which time he produced such hits as *Pal Joey, On the Town, The Pajama Game, Damn Yankees*, and *A Funny Thing Happened on the Way to the Forum*. Many of Abbott's shows would become enduring classics. Unfortunately, *Brown Sugar* was not one of them.

With a cast that also included Juano Hernandez, Canada Lee, and Georgette Harvey, *Brown Sugar* opened at the Biltmore Theatre on December 2, 1937. The reviews the next day were unanimous: *Brown Sugar* was dreadful, a tired and melodramatic reworking of by-now familiar themes: the "high yaller" girl on Lenox Avenue, loved by two rival Harlem gangsters, leading to mayhem and murder. Ruby and her fellow performers were spared the critical boos—the press put the blame strictly on Angus's script and Abbott's direction. By all accounts, the brightest spot in the show was the debut of a newcomer, an actress whose nervous energy and squeaky voice made her instantly memorable: Butterfly McQueen, who two years later would gain screen immortality as Prissy in *Gone with the Wind*.

Brown Sugar closed after only four performances. It was the least successful production Ruby ever appeared in. She never afterward listed it among her theatrical credits. It was also the biggest flop in George Abbott's otherwise brilliant career.

Ruby had taken the role in *Brown Sugar* in part because Charles Marshall had not yet lined up as many engagements as she had expected. By the time of Ruby's Town Hall recital, many concert series and producers already had their 1937–1938 seasons booked. Marshall began concentrating on the next season. Ruby, still needing to pay back Marshall for her share of the Town Hall loss, found work where she could. She had hoped for a longer run for *Brown Sugar* to regain solvency; now she was back where she started.

Had it not been for the close of her play on Broadway, Ruby probably would never have accepted the engagement offered her at New York's Kit Kat Club. Located on East 55th Street, the Kit Kat was a popular Manhattan supper club, a place where people went to have dinner, go dancing, and see a show. The owner and manager was another of New York's more colorful characters, Jules Podell, who had grown up on the poor side of town, a tough-talking, two-fisted street kid. As an adult he made it to the big time through his work in the labor unions. Podell had definite ties to the mob, and there were even some who whispered that he had once been a hitman. Jules Podell was far from being the kind of person Ruby Elzy was used to dealing with.

Podell needed a singer to fill a three-week engagement, and he needed someone in a hurry. When Ruby Elzy was recommended (how or by whom is unknown), Podell quickly agreed. He did make Ruby a generous offer: a hundred dollars a week for three shows a night, five nights a week. Ruby just as quickly agreed; after the failure of *Brown Sugar*, she was in no position to be choosy.

Ruby soon found that entertaining in a nightclub was as different from singing at Town Hall as Pontotoc was from New York City. Podell's clientele were used to hearing bluesy chanteuses, not classically-trained sopranos. Ray Durant, who led Podell's house orchestra, was empathetic to Ruby's plight. He helped her work up a forty-minute show that emphasized romantic ballads like "I'm Gettin' Sentimental Over You" and "One Never Knows, Do One?" Ruby wanted to sing something from *Porgy and Bess*, but "My Man's Gone Now" would be totally out of place. Ruby settled on "Summertime," by now a standard popular even with people who had never seen or even heard of *Porgy and Bess*.

Ruby began her engagement at the Kit Kat Club a few days after the close of *Brown Sugar*. Like Frank Schiffman at the Apollo, Podell could not care less about her voice or her artistry. The Kit Kat Club made its money on food and booze (especially the latter), and his performers were there only to keep his patrons happy and drinking. Ruby gave her best, as she always did, but this was definitely a kind of show business she was not cut out for. She was anxious for the three-week engagement to pass as quickly as possible.

Ruby was now living on West 115th Street in a sixth-floor apartment she shared with Enida Hamlett. Hamlett was a talented pianist from the West Indies and helped Ruby with her daily vocal practice each morning.

It was during this time that Ruby sang for Henry Jurge of Steinway and Sons at the request of Malvina Thompson Scheider, personal assistant to Eleanor Roosevelt. Jurge sent Scheider and Roosevelt a glowing report of Ruby's private audition in Manhattan's Steinway Hall. A few days later, as Ruby was home resting up for her show that night at the club, Charles Marshall called with the exciting news: the First Lady had chosen Ruby to sing the program to follow her luncheon in honor of the wives of the U.S. Supreme Court justices on Wednesday, December 15.

Throughout her career, Ruby's talents had taken her many places and brought her countless blessings. But to be invited to sing at the White House was truly an impossible dream.

Proud yet humbled, Ruby told a reporter for the *New York World-Telegram*, "This is the greatest recognition a colored girl could ever in her life hope for." The newspaper decided to do a feature story about Ruby's White House concert to run on the day of her appearance in Washington.

White House invitation or no, Ruby was still under contract to Jules Podell and the Kit Kat Club. Ray Durant, the Kit Kat's bandleader, helped out by covering for her last show the night of December 14, so that Ruby could catch a late train to Washington. She met Arthur Kaplan at Union Station. If Kaplan had been disappointed that Ruby had not asked him to accompany her Town Hall recital, she was certainly making up for it now. He was as excited as she was and just as nervous. They got into Washington just after midnight. Kaplan went to a hotel, while Ruby found a boarding house for blacks. She wanted to arise by 9:00 a.m. to rehearse and get her voice warmed up.

The White House concert that afternoon was a great success. Ruby looked as beautiful as she sounded. She was thrilled with the ovation she received and with Mrs. Roosevelt's request for "Everytime I Feel the Spirit" as an encore. The *World-Telegram* noted Ruby's reaction to riding in the First Lady's car: "'Goodness me, what an automobile! Official license plate and everything,' gasped Miss Elzy in delighted recollection."

Eleanor Roosevelt was equally delighted with her young musical guest. A few days later, the First Lady wrote about the lunch and concert in "My Day," her nationally syndicated newspaper column: "Washington—Wednesday . . . Miss Ruby Elzy, who has a most beautiful soprano voice, gave us a short program of songs which we greatly enjoyed."

On the train to New York, Ruby and Kaplan could not stop talking about the incredible experience they had just shared. It was a moment neither would ever forget. Malvina Scheider had given Ruby a handful of programs as souvenirs. Each was embossed in gold with the raised Seal of the United States, followed by the words:

Miss RUBY ELZY, Soprano
Mr. ARTHUR KAPLAN at the Piano
Wednesday, December 15, 1937
THE WHITE HOUSE

Ruby would need programs to send home to Mama, to her sisters Amanda and Wayne, brother Robert, and of course another one to Pennsylvania, which she inscribed: "To my beloved McCrackens, who have been responsible for programs such as this. Sincerely, Ruby Elzy".

Arriving back at Union Station, Ruby jumped into a taxi for the ride back to her apartment on West 115th Street. She still had a few hours before she had to be at the Kit Kat Club. Time to rest and relax.

Ruby went upstairs to her sixth-floor flat, where Enida Hamlett was sitting at the kitchen table. Hamlett handed Ruby a note that had been delivered earlier that day. It was a message from the Kit Kat Club.

Ruby Elzy had been fired.

Jules Podell's note said that Ruby's songs were "not the type" for his establishment. She read the message to Hamlett, and the two women broke out laughing. A few hours ago Ruby Elzy had been applauded by the First Lady and her guests at the White House. Now she was being fired because her singing was "not the type" for audiences at the Kit Kat Club.

Ruby herself had to admit that she was not meant to be a cafe singer. In that sense, she really did not mind losing her job; it was the timing that amazed her. If 1936 was the most traumatic year of Ruby's life, then 1937 was the most topsy-turvy. She had performed at the Ohio State University, the Apollo Theatre, Lewisohn Stadium, the Hollywood

Bowl, Town Hall, Broadway, the Kit Kat Club, and the White House. She had sung tributes to Gershwin, traded jokes with Fred Allen, entertained Eleanor Roosevelt—and been fired by Jules Podell. And now the rising young star was again unemployed.

Ruby and Hamlett were still laughing when the reporter from the *World-Telegram* called to do a follow-up interview about Ruby's concert in Washington. The story he ended up with was much more lively and entertaining: "Sings at the White House, Loses Her Night Club Job: Ruby Elzy, Negro, Makes a Hit at Luncheon but Now She's Dazed."

Ruby's career as a cafe entertainer was over almost as soon as it began. She came out of it wiser for the experience: she needed to stick with the kind of singing she did best. Maybe she could not sing hot jazz or the blues like Bessie Smith—but then, Bessie could not sing "Depuis le juir" or hit a high B, either.

It is not known if Jules Podell paid Ruby the balance of the three hundred dollars her engagement called for. A few years later he closed the Kit Kat Club and opened a bigger, flashier establishment on East 60th Street. Podell named his new club the Copacabana, and there he reigned as one of the kings of New York's night life for the next thirty years.

Ruby "laughed off her misfortune," as the *World-Telegram* reported. "I guess I don't live right, or something," she told the newspaper, adding, "I'll get a job somewhere, but there aren't many jobs open for colored sopranos, even if they've sung at the White House or in heaven."

But she would not be out of a job for long. Ruby Elzy's luck, and her life, were about to change.

"SERENA OUT WEST"

Mama came from Mississippi to spend the holidays with Ruby in the cramped sixth-floor apartment on West 115th Street. Together they put up a small Christmas tree, and the place was soon filled with the wonderful aroma of Mama's home-cooking.

Emma Elzy had always been proud of Ruby but never more so than now. That her daughter had sung in the White House for the First Lady was an honor Emma could not have imagined even in her fondest dreams. At the same time, Emma was not at all concerned about Ruby being fired from the Kit Kat Club. In fact, she was very pleased.

"Now Ruby," Mama said, "you know the Good Lord didn't give you that beautiful voice just so you could ruin it singing in some smoke-filled nightclub to a bunch of drunks."

"Yes, Mama, I know," Ruby replied. "I really didn't care much for singing there either. But that hundred dollars a week they paid me sure did come in handy. It's gonna be hard to find another singing job that pays me that much. And what'll I do until then?"

Ruby's agent, Charles Marshall, was trying to take advantage of the publicity about her White House concert, contacting symphony and concert managers throughout the East and Midwest. But most impresarios already had their seasons fully booked; it would be next summer or fall before they would have dates available for another artist.

Ruby could always go back to the Federal Music Project. The FMP and its sister agencies, the Federal Theatre Project and the Federal Arts Project, were part of the Works Progress Administration (WPA). Among the most innovative of Franklin D. Roosevelt's New

Deal programs, these agencies during the Great Depression brought culture to the masses while providing jobs to singers, musicians, actors, and artists. During her own lean period the year before, Ruby had been on the WPA's roster, appearing in free concerts throughout the New York area in schools, libraries, and parks. While it did give Ruby ample opportunities to perform, the pay—only twenty-four dollars a week—was a far cry from what she earned on Broadway and in her solo concerts for Marshall. Ruby did not relish the thought of going back to the WPA. Still, unless something else turned up soon she might not have a choice.

Emma tried to reassure her. "Ruby," Mama said, "you just remember what I always told you—keep on working and praying and trusting in the Lord. When He's ready, He'll let you know what you're supposed to do. So don't you go worrying too much—everything is going to turn out fine."

Mama's words proved prophetic once again. A few days later, an unexpected Christmas present arrived in the form of a phone call. It was Ruby's old friend, Bob Wachsman, who had handled publicity for *Porgy and Bess*. Wachsman was now in Los Angeles, working for concert and opera manager Merle Armitage, who was mounting the first West Coast production of *Porgy and Bess*. There would be performances in Pasadena, Los Angeles, and San Francisco, with a possible tour of other cities. Armitage wanted to cast as many of the opera's original stars as he could, and Wachsman had been put in charge of contacting them. Was Ruby interested in playing Serena again, Wachsman wanted to know, and if she was, could she be out in Los Angeles ready to begin rehearsals the second week of January? Ecstatic at the turn of good fortune, Ruby said yes at once.

Her immediate future now set, Ruby celebrated a joyful Christmas with Mama. A few days before leaving New York with Mama, Ruby met with Charles Marshall. "Ruby, I think it's just great you're getting this chance to play Serena out West. And I'll start working on next season while you're gone," Marshall told her.

"Thank you, Charles," Ruby replied. "I'll keep in touch with you and let you know as soon as I can if *Porgy and Bess* will go on tour after we close in San Francisco."

It had been three years since Ruby had been home. She decided to accompany Mama back to Mississippi before going on to California. She was delighted to be with her sisters Amanda and Wayne, both of them beginning their careers as educators. Together they celebrated the start of the new year of 1938 at Mama's house on King Avenue in Corinth. Ruby also went to see her old friends from Pontotoc. It seemed to Ruby as if everybody in Mississippi wanted to see her, eager to ask questions about her glamorous life and career. Ruby regaled her friends and neighbors with stories about Gershwin and *Porgy and Bess*, about her concerts at the Hollywood Bowl and Town Hall. She was pleased when many of them told her how exciting it was to hear her on Fred Allen's NBC radio show, singing "Summertime" and talking about Rust College. And when Ruby recounted in detail her concert at the White House and pulled out the framed photograph of Eleanor Roosevelt, personally inscribed by the First Lady, they were truly in awe. Everyone was proud of Ruby, and perhaps a few were even a little envious. Ruby Elzy was living a life most of them could only imagine.

Her brief stay in Mississippi over, Ruby said goodbye to Mama and her sisters and took the train out to California. By the time she arrived in Los Angeles, her friend and colleague Todd Duncan was already there. Soon they were joined by Anne Brown and Georgette Harvey. Wachsman had succeeded in contacting nearly everyone from the original New York company, although a number of them would not be coming out for Armitage's production. Abbie Mitchell had now retired from the stage, and a young soprano named Lois Hodnett replaced her as Clara. Eddie Matthews was on a South American concert tour, so William Gillespie was hired to take over the role of Jake. Armitage wanted very much to have John W. Bubbles repeat his celebrated performance as Sportin' Life, but the actor wanted such an outlandish salary that Armitage had no choice but to decline. Although temperamental and difficult to work with, Bubbles had left such an indelible impression in the role that Armitage was worried finding another Sportin' Life would be very difficult. Fortunately, Brown knew a talented dancer and singer named Avon Long, with whom she had grown up in Baltimore. On her recommendation Armitage auditioned Long and hired him on the spot to replace Bubbles.

There was one more cast change—one that would have far-reaching implications for Ruby personally, although she did not know it at the time. Warren Coleman, the original Crown, was concertizing back east and unavailable for the Armitage production. Bob Wachsman had a friend who had also been in the original New York cast, playing the smaller role of the fisherman Jim. Jack Carr was tall and handsome, with a rich baritone voice. When Armitage offered Carr the role of Crown on Wachsman's recommendation, the actor jumped at the chance. It would be a fateful move for both Ruby and Carr. Within a year they began to date, and in 1940 they would marry.

In addition to a great cast, Armitage also assembled a strong backstage team. Besides Bob Wachsman, the producer recruited two veterans of the original company. Rouben Mamoulian was now one of Hollywood's most distinguished film directors yet had never forgotten his experience working with Gershwin on *Porgy and Bess*. He not only came on board as stage director, but told Armitage he would do so without a salary—a magnanimous gesture. Alexander Steinert, who conducted over one hundred of the original performances and the celebrated Hollywood Bowl memorial concert, signed on as musical director and conductor. Armitage himself would design the sets and costumes.

By mid-January 1938 the entire company was in place, ready to begin an intense three weeks of rehearsal. But first they all gathered at Philharmonic Auditorium to meet with their producer. Merle Armitage was a restless, brilliant man of many interests and talents—author and book designer, theatrical designer and producer, concert manager and impresario. Among his many accomplishments he had founded the Los Angeles Grand Opera Association in the 1920s and managed the careers of a number of world-famous singers, including legendary opera divas Amelita Galli-Curci and Rosa Ponselle.

Armitage welcomed the cast and spoke about his close relationship with George Gershwin. Armitage had met the composer a number of times in New York, but their friendship had really blossomed when Gershwin and his brother Ira had come to Hollywood in the summer of 1936, hired by Sam Goldywn to write new songs for two Fred Astaire and Ginger Rogers movies being made at RKO. Armitage was then managing the Los Angeles Philharmonic Auditorium. Soon after Gershwin's arrival in Hollywood, Armitage invited him to do an all-Gershwin concert with the Philharmonic. Gershwin accepted immediately. He and Armitage planned a program that would include not only Gershwin's famous piano and orchestral works, but also an extended segment of songs from *Porgy and Bess*. As a favor to Gershwin, Todd Duncan came out to Los Angeles for the concerts, where he was joined by a local soprano named Marguerite Chapman and a chorus recruited from local black churches. The two concerts played to sellout audiences at Philharmonic Auditorium in February 1937, and the *Porgy and Bess* excerpts were especially well received.

Armitage, thrilled at the concert's success, told Gershwin he wanted to do a full-scale production of *Porgy and Bess*. Gershwin gently reminded him that the first production had lost its entire investment. "Do you dare?" Gershwin asked his friend. Yet Gershwin had faith in Armitage's abilities, and the two began making plans for a West Coast production of the opera in 1938.

There had been one ominous note to the otherwise successful Philharmonic engagement. On the second night of the concert—February 11, 1937—Gershwin stumbled twice at the piano while playing his *Concerto in F.* Conductor Alexander Smallens covered him; Gershwin quickly recovered both times and made it successfully to the end of the piece. Afterwards Gershwin told Smallens and Armitage that the sudden lapse had been caused by a stabbing pain in the head. He also felt momentarily dizzy, and had noticed a peculiar smell that he described as the odor of burning rubber. No one knew it at the time, but it was the first sign of the brain tumor that would take

Gershwin's life on July 11, 1937, four months to the day after the incident at the Philharmonic concert.

Gershwin's untimely death stunned Armitage—yet made him more determined than ever to go forward with *Porgy and Bess*. Many years later, recalling the stellar company he had brought together for the West Coast production, Armitage wrote, "Motivating our efforts was my desire to make certain that we did not let George Gershwin down. That feeling was shared by every person in the cast." It was definitely shared by Ruby, who was grateful for what Gershwin and his opera had done for her. He had given her the role of a lifetime and written some of his greatest music for her voice. Playing Serena once again gave her a chance to repay Gershwin the debt of gratitude she felt she owed him.

Ruby and the company went to work with Mamoulian and Steinert. Rehearsals went smoothly, aided in large part by the experience that the leads brought to their roles. Everyone was excited and did indeed feel that this was something special, not only a great production in itself, but a tribute to the man and the genius who had created it.

Among his other production duties, Bob Wachsman again took over publicity. The story of Ruby's discovery at Rust College by Dr. McCracken, which Wachsman had used successfully in New York, was revived. Armitage himself designed the playbill, and on the title page he gave Ruby full star billing. It was *Porgy and Bess* starring Todd Duncan as Porgy, Anne Brown as Bess, and Ruby Elzy as Serena—recognition of Ruby's rise in the music and theatre worlds and also acknowledgment of her status as one of the original stars of the opera, a fact that Armitage had Wachsman play up prominently in the press.

On February 3, 1938, after three weeks of rehearsal, *Porgy and Bess* was ready. The preview performance in Pasadena's Municipal Auditorium went well, but the true test would be the following night, when the official premiere was given in Los Angeles at Philharmonic Auditorium, the same hall where George Gershwin had performed only a year before.

The scene outside the Philharmonic on opening night had all the trappings of a big movie studio premiere. Floodlights swept across the sky, and crowds behind ropes ogled as limousines pulled up with filmdom's elite: Marlene Dietrich, Douglas Fairbanks, Jr., John Barrymore, and Eddie Cantor arrived, as did Deanna Durbin, Charles Boyer, Robert Taylor, Joan Crawford and her husband Franchot Tone, and Metropolitan Opera diva Gladys Swarthout with her husband, singer Frank Chapman. It was truly a star-filled night.

Whether or not it was the added excitement caused by so many celebrities, the performance given that evening was unforgettable. Ruby's singing of "My Man's Gone Now," always a show-stopper on Broadway, drew bravos from the audience. Todd Duncan's signature piece, "I Got Plenty o' Nuttin," elicited whistles, cheers, and the longest applause of the night. Although he was new to the role of the slippery Sportin' Life, Avon Long proved an instant hit with his rendition of "It Ain't Necessarily So." Anne Brown was haunting as ever as the tragic Bess, and her duets with Todd Duncan were beautifully sung. When the final curtain fell on the strains of "I'm on My Way," the house came down. The audience stood and applauded for twenty minutes, as the cast came out for bow after bow.

Backstage, Ruby and the cast were swamped by celebrities and well-wishers, shaking their hands and offering congratulations. One man quietly making the rounds of each star's dressing room was Ira Gershwin, accompanied by his wife Lenore. Ira had been a frequent visitor to rehearsals and had consulted with Armitage on every aspect of the production. In fact, the whole enterprise would not have been possible without Ira's blessings and encouragement. Working behind the scenes, he had made an immense contribution to the success of Armitage's production. It had been the same when Ira and George had worked together during their long partnership: Ira was content to linger in the shadows and let his brilliant younger brother bask in the limelight. Tonight had to be bittersweet for Ira—jubilation at the tumultuous reception *Porgy and Bess* had received, yet also sadness that George was not there, standing again at center stage, receiving the crowd's ovation for the opera he had worked on so devotedly and had believed in so passionately.

Merle Armitage himself believed fervently that his production would bring *Porgy and Bess* the acclaim it deserved, and ultimately he was proven right. Many theatre historians and critics consider Cheryl Crawford's 1941–1942 revival, again starring Duncan, Brown, and Elzy, as the production that firmly established the show's popularity once and for all; yet the truth is that it was Merle Armitage's 1938 production that marked the beginning of the elevation of *Porgy and Bess* to the ranks of a true American masterpiece. Much of the credit for this must go to Ruby Elzy, Todd Duncan, Anne Brown, and Avon Long for their brilliant performances.

The reviews the day after opening night were overwhelmingly positive. *Los Angeles Times* critic Virginia Wright wrote, "Merle Armitage is to be congratulated for bringing Todd Duncan, Anne Brown and Ruby Elzy here for this production." And in the *Los Angeles Examiner* Florence Lawrence wrote, "One of the outstanding performances is given by Ruby Elzy. She has an exceptional range, her upper tones are brilliant and almost haunting in evanescent beauty."

Armitage had to add extra people at the box-office to handle the volume of calls for tickets, and within a few days of the opening the three-week run at the Philharmonic Auditorium was completely sold out. Advance sales were also heavy in San Francisco, where *Porgy and Bess* would play immediately following the closing in Los Angeles. Best of all, Armitage was getting calls from promoters throughout the West and as far east as Cincinnati wanting to book the show. It was a relief for Armitage, who had sunk every cent he had personally to put the production together. The run in California would generate only enough to cover expenses. Armitage needed the show to tour in order to recoup his initial investment and make a profit for himself.

For Ruby, working once again on *Porgy and Bess* was a joy. She had grown as a singer and an actor and was able to bring even more feeling and depth to the character of Serena than she had before. She was also having a great deal more fun. The first production of *Porgy*, despite the excitement and the acclaim it brought her, had been a difficult time for Ruby. Chronic health problems, aggravated by the stress resulting from her mounting troubles with Gardner, plagued her. This time, however, things were completely different. Ruby was happy, relaxed, and enjoying herself thoroughly.

One reason was that she had never felt stronger or healthier in her life. Ever since she had left Mississippi—first to Columbus, then to New York City—Ruby had suffered every winter with a severe cold and bronchitis. She had missed a week of *Porgy and Bess*'s initial run on Broadway and had been ill several times on its first tour in 1936. But the mild climate of southern California acted like a magic elixir on her—"It reminds me of back home in Mississippi," she told her sister Wayne. Ruby even noted it when she wrote to the McCrackens after the production had moved to San Francisco: "We have one more week of 'Porgy and Bess' and we're through. It has been a wonderful run—I've enjoyed it very much. So far I've been perfectly well. Everybody else has had colds but I've sung on and on and am still feeling perfectly."

The three-week run in San Francisco's Curran Theatre began on February 21, one day after friend and fellow cast member Georgette Harvey threw a surprise party in honor of Ruby's thirtieth birthday. Again the premiere was a huge success. Everyone expected a sellout run, and Ruby and the rest of the troupe were waiting to hear where the production might go next. But a line in her letter to the McCrackens shared some news that would spell disaster for Armitage and his company: "We have been in San Francisco almost 3 weeks now, [it] will be Monday. We end our run here this Saturday, March 5. We missed the worst floods in years in Los Angeles—thank heaven!"

"The worst floods in years" turned out to be an understatement. In fact, the rains that deluged California that February and March of 1938 were the most devastating in a century: roads became impassable, bridges washed out, mudslides covered railroad tracks. It almost seemed as if the rain would never stop; travel in California came to a standstill for more than a week.

Merle Armitage was now unable to get his company on the road. Not only that, the nonstop rain was having a drastic impact in San Francisco. Despite the heavy advance sales, attendance and box-office receipts for the final week at the Curran fell sharply. Armitage had sunk every penny he had into the production and had counted on a long tour to regain solvency; now he was financially ruined. The production would be forced to close in San Francisco. Armitage was unable even to meet the final week's payroll at the Curran.

Half an hour before the closing performance, the producer called his entire company to the stage with the bad news. Armitage recalled later that, much to his surprise, there was little grumbling or anger. Several cast members even asked if they could help cover his losses. Armitage was deeply touched. He promised the actors, most of whom had come from New York, that he would help them get at least part of the money owed to them through Actors Equity. This would give them enough money for train tickets back east.

Ruby, however, had other plans. *Porgy and Bess* ended its run at the Curran, and as soon as trains could finally move again Ruby headed straight for Los Angeles. The two months she had spent in California had done wonders for her, and she decided to stay. There were as many opportunities to perform here as there were back east, where Charles Marshall was still working to get her concert bookings—so far to no avail. Los Angeles had many legitimate theatres and concert halls. It was also fast becoming the major base for network radio, with performers like Bing Crosby, Bob Hope, and Jack Benny hosting their own highly-rated shows. And Los Angeles had one thing New York lacked—movies. By now, nearly every major film studio had moved out west. Even Paramount Pictures was now leasing out its famed Astoria studios in New York, where many classic movies had been made and where only five years before Ruby had made her screen debut opposite Paul Robeson in *The Emperor Jones*.

More and more, the place to be in show business was sunny California. And Ruby Elzy felt she was ready to tackle Hollywood.

"GOING HOLLYWOOD"

Ruby returned to Los Angeles in the middle of March 1938. She settled temporarily with a family named Harris on East 42nd Street, with whom she had stayed while rehearsing and performing in Armitage's production. Thanks to the run of *Porgy and Bess* at the Philharmonic Auditorium, Ruby had met a number of key people in the entertainment industry. She began making the rounds of casting agents and producers and soon landed her first job: a small role in the MGM picture *The Toy Wife*.

In the Hollywood "dream factory" of the 1930s, there was no bigger studio than Metro-Goldwyn-Mayer. With such talents on the lot as Clark Gable, Greta Garbo, Spencer Tracy, and the singing team of Jeanette MacDonald and Nelson Eddy, MGM could truly back up its claim that it had "More Stars Than There Are in Heaven." One of the studio's top attractions at the time was a petite Austrian actress named Luise Rainer, who had just won her second consecutive Academy Award as Best Actress (the first time any actor had won more than once) for her performance in *The Good Earth*. *The Toy Wife* would star Rainer in the title role, supported by Barbara O'Neil (who a year later would play Scarlett O'Hara's mother in *Gone With the Wind*) and two of Metro's reliable "second-tier" leading men, Melvyn Douglas and Robert Young.

As a romantic drama set in antebellum New Orleans, *The Toy Wife* called for a good number of black actors. Unfortunately, nearly all the roles were the usual mammies, maids, servants, and lackeys that blacks were relegated to playing in that era, complete with all the stereotypical mannerisms and expressions. Most of the actors in these roles did not even receive on-screen credits, as was the case for Ruby in *The Toy Wife*.

She appears briefly as a mulatto at a fruit stand. It was not much of a part for someone who had just been acclaimed as one of the stars in *Porgy and Bess*, but Ruby exemplified the attitude of many black artists—work was work, an opportunity to use your talents. In addition, working brought you into contact with producers, directors, and fellow actors, which in turn could lead to bigger and better opportunities. It had happened for Ruby in *The Emperor Jones*. Doing that film had introduced her to DuBose Heyward and had ultimately led to George Gershwin and *Porgy and Bess*. In *The Toy Wife*, Ruby would strike gold again.

The movie went into production late in March 1938. Ruby's scene took only a few days to complete. While she enjoyed meeting and working with stars like Rainer and Douglas, Ruby spent most of her time getting to know the black actors assigned to the film. There was the young and beautiful Theresa Harris, joined in the cast by veterans like Clinton Rosemond and Libby Taylor. Ruby was deeply impressed by the talent and professionalism of these performers. They in turn admired her accomplishments on stage and willingly shared their insights on Hollywood and the film industry. But there was one actor in particular who would have an enormous impact on Ruby's career.

Clarence Muse, cast in the role of Robert Young's servant, enjoyed one of the longest careers of any actor, black or white, in Hollywood. He made more than two hundred movies over a period of more than fifty years. His final performance was in *The Black Stallion*, released in 1979 a few months after his death at the age of ninety. Yet Muse was more than a prolific film actor. He was also a writer, director, choreographer, and composer. One of his tunes, "When It's Sleepy Time Down South," which he co-wrote with brothers Leon and Otis Rene, became famous as the theme song of the great Louis Armstrong.

Like Ruby, Muse had come to Hollywood by way of New York. In the early 1920s he had cofounded the renowned Lafayette Players, an important milestone of the two-decades-long explosion of genius and creativity today known as the Harlem Renaissance. Now, after nearly a decade devoted to film, Muse was returning to the stage. He was to direct a musical play for the Federal Theatre Project in Los Angeles. And when Clarence Muse met Ruby Elzy during the filming of *The Toy Wife*, he knew he had found the perfect leading lady for his production. The show was Hall Johnson's *Run Little Chillun*.

The role of Ella Jones, like that of Serena, was tailor-made for Ruby Elzy: it called for a performer who was not only a fine singer but a compelling actress. The original production on Broadway in 1933 had run for more than two hundred performances. Ruby had seen it while still a student at Juilliard. She knew the powerful impact the play made on its audiences, both dramatically and musically. Here would be an opportunity to use her talents to the fullest. Best of all, Ruby would be working not only with Clarence Muse but with Hall Johnson himself, who agreed to join the production as musical director.

Born in 1888 in Athens, Georgia, Francis Hall Johnson was one of the great black musical figures of the twentieth century. As a boy Johnson was taught "slave songs" by his father, a minister. Johnson became a skilled arranger of the songs, which in the early 1900s came to called "spirituals." In 1928 Johnson—who by this time had dropped "Francis" from his name—founded his celebrated all-Negro choir. Within a few years the Hall Johnson Choir was internationally renowned, performing in live concerts, on radio and recordings, and in motion pictures, most notably 1936's *The Green Pastures*. Long before she actually met Johnson, Ruby had been singing his arrangements of spirituals; one of her signature concert pieces was Johnson's "City Called Heaven."

In a sense, one of Johnson's purposes in writing *Run Little Chillun* was to show how the Negro spiritual came to be, how it evolved naturally from the unique social, religious, and community life of blacks in America.

Run Little Chillun is the story of a young black preacher, Jim Jones, whose father, the elder Reverend Jones, is pastor of the New Hope Baptist Church. The little church is undergoing an intense monthlong revival yet is steadily losing members to a new sect, the pantheistic New Day Pilgrims. The Pilgrims are led by a charismatic and mysterious figure known as Brother Moses. Unlike the Baptists with their church and orthodox liturgy, the Pilgrims worship outdoors in the woods by moonlight. Jim Jones is married to a devout woman named Ella, but for the past year he has been carrying on a secret affair with a woman named Sula Mae, who comes from a seedy part of town called Toomer's Bottom and is a member of the New Day Pilgrims. Johnson's story unfolds almost as a morality play—the conflict between good and evil, sin and redemption, the spiritual and the carnal. The music is comprised entirely of Negro spirituals arranged by Johnson.

Audiences today would probably find such a play contrived and melodramatic; to audiences of the 1930s, *Run Little Chillun*, with its combination of music, drama, and spectacle, was spellbinding theatre. Especially powerful were the crowd-filled scenes of the two congregations as they worship. The revival scene at New Hope Baptist Church, where Ruby sings "Nobody Knows the Trouble I've Seen," was as stirring and emotional as the saucer burial scene in *Porgy and Bess* and Ruby's singing of "My Man's Gone Now."

Ruby, Clarence Muse, and Hall Johnson were the only people involved in the production who were not members of the Federal Theatre Project. All the other leads as well as the ensemble were members of the project's Negro Theatre Unit. That Ruby was the sole outsider in the cast was a testament not only to her talents as a performer but to her status as one of the leading black artists of the theatre.

After a month of rehearsals, *Run Little Chillun* opened at the Mayan Theatre on July 22, 1938. It was an immediate success with audiences, and the critical notices were sensational, particularly for Ruby:

Ruby Elzy's acting is as splendid as her beautiful singing.

Especially impressive are the lovely voice and dramatic power of Ruby Elzy.

One naturally expected a great performance from Ruby Elzy, fresh from her success in "Porgy and Bess," and she gave a great performance.

Within a week of opening *Run Little Chillun* was the hottest ticket in town, and free passes were suspended. By the end of its third month more than a hundred thousand people had seen the show—a phenomenal figure. When *Chillun* had to vacate the Mayan to make way for another show, demand was still so strong that Muse and the heads of the Federal Theatre Project in Los Angeles decided to move the production to another theatre. After closing for a week, *Run Little Chillun* reopened at the Hollywood Playhouse (renowned today as the Hollywood Palace). The new playbill at the Hollywood had a picture on the cover of Ruby Elzy as Ella Jones. It remained that way until the show closed on June 10, 1939, after nearly a year and more than three hundred performances, more than even *Porgy and Bess* had given up to that point.

With *Run Little Chillun* an unqualified hit, Ruby was ready to plant permanent roots in Los Angeles. She had lived in apartments ever since moving to New York City in 1930 but had always wanted to live in a house, preferably a large and comfortable one like the McCrackens' home in Columbus—a place of her own where she could sit out on a porch, have a yard to putter around in. Sunday was her only day off from the show, and Ruby began spending her afternoons after church driving through the black neighborhoods of Los Angeles. Finally she came upon what she'd been looking for.

The residence at 898 East 54th Street was a large, one-story house with three bedrooms in the neighborhood known as South Central. Like many houses in Southern California, the architecture was of Spanish origin, with cherry pink stucco and an earthen-red tiled roof. Six steps led from the sidewalk up to a large front porch; driveways on either side of the house led to a carport out back. Inside the house were three large bedrooms and a living room big enough for a grand piano.

It was a neighborhood of upper-middle-class blacks, including a number of prominent physicians, attorneys, and businessmen. Nearby was South Park, with lush trees and lawns and a huge playground for children. The house was only a few miles away from the theatre, and best of all, less than a half-hour drive from the ocean and the beaches. Ruby knew this was the place for her. She rented it and moved in not long after *Run Little Chillun* opened.

Wayne Elzy would later recall this as one of the happiest times in her sister's life.

"Ruby loved California," Wayne remembered. "She loved the weather, the people, living close enough to the ocean that she could swim almost every day."

Wayne came out with Mama to visit Ruby and to see *Run Little Chillun*. When it was time for Wayne to return to Mississippi, Emma stayed on, living with Ruby in the house on South Central.

Although 1938 was a very good year for Ruby, it was not completely without its dark moments. *Run Little Chillun* was in rehearsal on June 26 when the news broke that James Weldon Johnson had been killed when his car was struck by a train. It was a loss not just for Ruby but for all black Americans, as Johnson was more than just a great writer and poet. He had become one of the most eloquent and influential public figures of his time. Black Americans everywhere mourned the passing of the man who had written the words to "Lift Ev'ry Voice and Sing," the song they now proudly called the "Negro National Anthem." In church a few weeks after Johnson's death, Ruby sang the special concert version of "Lift Ev'ry Voice and Sing" that John Rosamond Johnson had arranged especially for her. (Ruby would pass away on June 26, 1943, exactly five years to the day after James Weldon Johnson.)

In November, less than six months after Johnson's death, Ruby suffered another painful loss. Her beloved teacher Dr. Royal Hughes suffered a massive heart attack while driving to his office at Ohio State. He died a few days later, only fifty-four years old. Ruby was heartbroken. She would never forget how Hughes had patiently taken a young girl from Mississippi, unable to read a note of music, and trained her to become an accomplished singer able to perform in four languages.

As the star of both *Porgy and Bess* and *Run Little Chillun*, Ruby quickly became one of the most prominent black entertainers in

Hollywood. Starting with Clarence Muse and Hall Johnson, Ruby soon became friends with many of the leading black film and radio personalities, including Eddie Anderson, already a household favorite across America as Jack Benny's gravel-voiced sidekick Rochester; Fay Jackson, Hollywood correspondent for the Associated Negro Press and one of the most powerful black journalists in America at the time; and veteran character actress Hattie McDaniel, who had just beaten out scores of other black actresses for the prize role of Mammy in David O. Selznick's forthcoming production of Margaret Mitchell's *Gone with the Wind*. That performance would win McDaniel the Academy Award as Best Supporting Actress, the first black performer to be so honored.

Ruby also became friends with black soprano Florence Cole Talbert. In Europe, where there was less prejudice and discrimination against blacks, Talbert had enjoyed a substantial career as an opera singer in the 1920s, most notably in the title role of Verdi's *Aida*. After seeing Ruby's performances as Serena and Ella Jones, Talbert encouraged her to resume serious study. Ruby's long-held dream of singing grand opera in roles such as Aida was rejuvenated by her association with Talbert.

The heavy schedule of performances in *Run Little Chillun* left Ruby little time to join the Friday and Saturday night party circuit so popular in Hollywood. But Sundays gave her a chance to enjoy herself and her new circle of friends—having cookouts in her backyard, going to Venice Beach for a swim in the ocean, or playing tennis at the house of friends like Clarence Muse or Hattie McDaniel.

Christmas 1938 was far different for Ruby from the one only a year before. *Run Little Chillun* was continuing to draw large audiences six months into its run, and Ruby was financially more secure than she had ever been. Christmas this year was spent not in a cramped sixth-floor apartment in Harlem, but in the spacious ranch house in South Central. Her brother Robert, who was now living in California and working at a chicken ranch in the San Fernando Valley, also came to spend his first Christmas with his mother and sister in many years. It was a happy time for the whole Elzy family.

The year 1939 would prove to be a momentous one, not only for Ruby but for America and the world. For the second time in Ruby's life the world was at war. Great Britain and her allies joined forces to defeat the tyranny of Hitler's Germany. Even though the United States would not become involved in combat for more than two years, America's sympathies clearly were on the side of Britain and her allies.

It was a critical time for all Americans and especially for black Americans like Ruby. Despite the indignities and discrimination they had endured, black Americans were unfailingly loyal, patriotic, and ready to serve their country. If America entered the Second World War—which most leaders, including President Roosevelt, believed it would, even if most ordinary citizens did not—the support and contribution of black Americans would be critical. Black leaders such as Claude Barnett, founder and president of the Associated Negro Press, and Thurgood Marshall, legal counsel of the NAACP, saw this as a time to advance the cause for civil rights. After all, how could any American condemn Hitler's treatment of Jews and yet be silent about the lynching of blacks in the South? How could America promote democracy to the world when most Negroes living here could not cast a vote without fear of violence?

In 1940 America would observe the seventy-fifth anniversary of the end of the Civil War and the passage of the Thirteenth Amendment, which permanently abolished slavery in the United States. Led by Barnett, Marshall, and others, and with the strong endorsement of Franklin D. Roosevelt and his entire administration, plans were laid out for a yearlong, nationwide celebration of the achievements of black Americans. Capping the observation would be the American Negro Exhibition in Chicago from July 4 to Labor Day, 1940.

Through the black newspapers affiliated with the American Negro Press, Barnett called for celebrations in every major American city and encouraged local black leaders to organize committees. In early 1939, an enterprising community leader named Claude Honeybuss began organizing efforts in Los Angeles. He formed the Negro Pageant Movement. Since Honeybuss himself was not in show business, he enlisted Spencer Williams, Jr., and Lew Payton, two of Hollywood's most celebrated black entertainers, as advisers. And to direct radio projects Honeybuss picked Ruby Elzy. That he chose Ruby is an indication of her stature and visibility in the entertainment industry. Ruby's job would be to promote the movement on radio through announcements and the presentation of special programs related to black American history and achievement. Honeybuss set up offices in Los Angeles at 939 South Van Dyke, and Ruby went to work. Now her time was divided between the movement during the day and performances of *Run Little Chillun* at night.

Despite this addition to her already busy life, Ruby still managed to find time in the spring of 1939 to appear in two more films. The first, for MGM, was *Tell No Tales*, a contemporary drama starring Melvyn Douglas as a reporter trying to solve a murder and at the same time save the struggling newspaper he works for from being sold. Once again not billed on the credits, Ruby had several lines as a woman attending the wake of a black prizefighter. Shooting required only a few days and the part was small, but Ruby was still happy to be back working in pictures.

Her second film that year was more interesting: *Way Down South,* an RKO musical set in pre-Civil War Louisiana. It was a vehicle for Bobby Breen, a child actor and singer who was second only to Fred Astaire and Ginger Rogers as RKO's biggest star. Breen played the son of a plantation owner who is kind and generous to his slaves. When Breen's father is killed in an accident, the lawyer who takes over as the boy's guardian and head of the plantation begins beating the slaves and plans to sell them all so he can become rich. The boy foils the plot with the help of his father's black houseservant and a kindly innkeeper from New Orleans. While it may sound contrived and hokey, the story was in fact the creation of Clarence Muse in collaboration with Langston Hughes, one of the United States' most celebrated black writers. Hughes, one of the great figures to come out of the Harlem Renaissance, was almost always strapped financially, at which times he wrote not for art's sake but for money. Such was the case with *Way Down South*, a project which, with its characterizations of shuffling and grinning slaves happy to labor tirelessly for their benevolent white masters, would be a source of great criticism aimed at both Hughes and Muse. But it marked an important milestone in the annals of film history: Clarence Muse and Langston Hughes were the first black men to write the screenplay for a mainstream Hollywood film. They also collaborated on two original songs—one of which, "Good Ground," includes a solo by Ruby with the Hall Johnson Choir. Unbilled for the third time, Ruby also had lines as a pipe-smoking mammy. Muse himself co-starred as the houseservant, Uncle Caleb, while other black actors in the cast included child actor Charles "Stymie" Beard from the popular "Our Gang" comedies. Jack Carr had a large supporting role as Luke, although he and Ruby had no scenes together. *Way Down South* debuted in August 1939 but was completely overshadowed by another film that premiered the same day—*The Wizard of Oz*, the MGM musical fantasy that made a star out of seventeen-year-old Judy Garland.

Ruby was in preparation for *Way Down South* when one of the singular moments in civil rights history occurred. On April 9, 1939—Easter Sunday—contralto Marian Anderson gave her triumphant concert on the steps of the Lincoln Memorial. A crowd of seventy-five thousand was on hand for the event, and millions more—including Ruby at home in Los Angeles—listened on radio.

Anderson's manager, Sol Hurok, had wanted to book the singer for a concert in Washington's renowned auditorium, Constitution Hall. But the hall was owned by the Daughters of the American Revolution (D.A.R.), which was dominated by conservative women from the South. Blacks at Constitution Hall might be employed to clean the floors— but to be presented there as an artist, to stand upon their hallowed stage and sing a concert as a white artist might do? No way. The D.A.R. refused Hurok's request. Of course, Anderson's color was not the reason given for the refusal; it was a "scheduling conflict." But when Hurok produced a series of alternative dates and every one turned out to be "unavailable," the real reason became clear. Hurok, furious, had his considerable press resources go to work, and the ensuing story made national headlines. The leaders of the D.A.R. were swamped with calls and telegrams of protest. Despite this enormous pressure, or perhaps because of it, they obstinately refused. No matter how great an artist, no matter how acclaimed—Marian Anderson would not sing at Constitution Hall.

It was Eleanor Roosevelt who brought things to a head and, in the process, became the most recognized white champion of civil rights at that time in America. Herself a member of the D.A.R., the First Lady resigned in a letter to the organization's members published in newspapers across the nation. Not content with that, Mrs. Roosevelt called in Secretary of the Interior Harold Ickes. Was there a public place in Washington appropriate for an Anderson concert? It was Ickes who suggested the Lincoln Memorial, and Roosevelt, recognizing the symbolism in having a black artist sing there, immediately agreed.

Among those in the crowd of seventy-five thousand who jammed the Washington Mall on that Easter Sunday was Todd Duncan, Ruby's co-star from *Porgy and Bess*. Years later, Duncan would recall the thrill of hearing Anderson in this setting and of the stirring impact made by the words of her opening song:

> *My country, 'tis of thee*
> *Sweet land of liberty,*
> *Of thee I sing!*
> *Land where my fathers died,*
> *Land of the pilgrim's pride,*
> *From ev'ry mountain side,*
> *Let freedom ring!*

It was a watershed moment for all black Americans. Ruby, listening in Los Angeles, was proud and deeply moved. She felt a close affinity to the famed "Lady from Philadelphia." Like Anderson, Ruby was not comfortable as a militant. Both women could be best described as "quiet rebels." Perhaps because of their deep religious backgrounds, both believed in the ultimate goodness of man; both believed they could do more good and wield more influence through the use of their talents than by any other means. Anderson's Easter Sunday concert made a deep impression on Ruby and would stimulate her own thinking and actions in the next few years.

On June 10, 1939, the curtain finally came down on *Run Little Chillun*. By then, Ruby and the company had given more than three hundred performances to a total of more than 250,000 people. The production was one of the greatest successes of the Federal Theatre Project. Sadly, the Project itself was coming to an end; the fall elections of 1938 had produced a more conservative Congress eager to dismantle some of Franklin D. Roosevelt's New Deal agencies. The Federal Theatre Project, long criticized by conservatives as a hotbed for left-wing thinkers and intellectuals, was one of the first programs they went after. On June 30, less than three weeks after *Run Little Chillun* closed, the most ambitious government program ever undertaken in the U.S. in support of the theatre and the arts came to an end.

Now at loose ends for the first time in a year, Ruby signed on to play the lead in a revival of Noble Sissle and Eubie Blake's classic musical revue, *Shuffle Along*. When first produced in 1921, it was hailed as a theatrical landmark and became recognized as one of the highlights of the early years of the Harlem Renaissance. The tuneful score included "I'm Just Wild about Harry" and "Love Will Find a Way," which was Ruby's big number in the revival.

But the times had changed considerably, and the tastes of audiences in 1939 were vastly different from those of 1921. *Shuffle Along* played a limited number of dates in California before closing in Los Angeles in early November 1939.

But Ruby was not disappointed by the show's demise. She had gotten a call from New York from the producers of a new musical set to open on Broadway. It would be about the legendary black folk hero John Henry, and the star would be a man who was quickly becoming a legend himself—Paul Robeson. The producers wanted an accomplished singer and actress who could hold her own as leading lady opposite the formidable Robeson.

They wanted Ruby Elzy.

"WHERE IS DIS ROAD A-LEADIN' ME TO?"

When Ruby stepped off the train at Grand Central Station shortly before Thanksgiving of 1939, it had been nearly two years since she had left New York. She had not particularly missed having to contend with its cold winters and living in high-rise flats. California was now home, with its perpetually sunny weather and her own little house in South Central. Charles Marshall had tried enticing Ruby back for some concerts to no avail. But when the opportunity came to star on Broadway with Paul Robeson, it was too good for Ruby to pass up.

Robeson was at the peak of his popularity in the fall of 1939. For more than a decade, he had lived in London, returning to the United States periodically to give concerts or to make films like *The Emperor Jones* and *Showboat*. But the start of World War II prompted him to move with his wife Eslanda and their son, Paul Jr., back to the U.S. Soon after his return, Robeson thrilled the nation when he sang Earl Robinson and John LaTouche's stirring anthem "Ballad for Americans" on the CBS radio program *The Pursuit of Happiness*. The studio audience was so moved at Robeson's performance that they were still applauding more than fifteen minutes after the show had gone off the air, and calls came in from across the country asking for the program to be repeated. Robeson's recording of the song became a best-seller, second only to his unforgettable "Ol' Man River."

Ironically, despite the patriotic fervor of the "Ballad for Americans," there were many who were beginning to question the patriotism of the man who sang it so magnificently. In the years since Ruby had worked with Robeson on *The Emperor Jones*, the actor had become increasingly outspoken on a wide range of issues—from civil rights for American Negroes to the Spanish Civil War to European colonialism in Africa and Asia. Robeson had made three highly publicized trips to the Soviet Union (a fact Fred Allen remarked about when Ruby was his guest on NBC's *Town Hall Tonight* program in April 1937), and his effusive praise of the Russian system of socialism had made international headlines. He had even enrolled Paul Jr. in a Soviet Model School. Robeson's words and actions made him a hero to many the world over, especially in Europe; but to many others, particularly the right-wing movement in the United States, he was a dangerous radical. A decade later, as America entered the dark years of the Cold War and McCarthyism, Paul Robeson's enemies would seek to destroy him.

The saga of John Henry, often called the "Black Paul Bunyan," had delighted several generations of youngsters before New Orleans author Roark Bradford wrote a novel based on the legendary hero in 1931. The book was an instant best-seller and spawned a popular CBS radio adaptation in the mid-1930s with black Puerto Rican actor Juano Hernandez as the "steel-drivin' man." It was only a matter of time before Broadway would seek to turn Bradford's book into a play, as had been done with his *Ol' Man Adam and His Chillun*, adapted by Marc Connelly into the Pulitzer Prize–winning drama (and later film) *The Green Pastures*.

The role of John Henry was tailor-made for Paul Robeson. Six feet, three inches in height, weighing 230 pounds, with a muscular frame honed in his years as an All-American football star and athlete at Rutgers, Robeson was an imposing figure on stage. Adding to this the rich, resonant voice that was recognizable the world over, he was the embodiment of Bradford's hero.

If Robeson was the perfect John Henry, then Ruby Elzy was the ideal Julie Anne, the sweet country girl who remains faithful to her man and kills herself in grief after he dies trying to beat the steam engine in a contest. Ruby loved the role, which was unlike that of the bereft Serena or the anguished Ella James. Julie Anne was a strong woman, as the other characters had been, but she was also something more—a young woman in love. Ruby Elzy was finally getting to play the romantic heroine.

Bradford himself adapted *John Henry* into the play, which was being produced by Sam Byrd. Don Voorhees would direct the music, written by Jacques Wolfe, a Romanian-born composer best known for "Shortnin' Bread," which popular film baritone Nelson Eddy had chosen as the theme song for his weekly radio series. Anthony Brown, whose previous credits included the long-running *Tobacco Road*, was assigned to direct. The production was officially launched with a photo that ran in New York newspapers in late November of a smiling Robeson and Ruby, looking over the script with Brown.

The cast of *John Henry* featured a number of other fine black performers in supporting roles, among them Musa Williams (as Julie Anne's rival), Minto Cato, and Joe Attles. Next to Robeson and Ruby, the most prominent musical character was Josh White as the strolling minstrel, Blind Lemon. White, then in his mid-twenties, was already on his way to becoming one of America's greatest bluesmen. In the chorus was a young folk singer named Bayard Rustin; like his hero Paul Robeson, Rustin would become a major civil rights activist. In 1963, he would organize the March on Washington, which culminated with Dr. Martin Luther King, Jr.'s immortal "I Have a Dream" speech at the Lincoln Memorial.

Behind the scenes were several other gifted black artists, working as assistants to musical director Don Voorhees. The show's chorusmaster, Leonard dePaur, soon went on to become one of America's most renowned choral conductors. Dean Dixon, a twenty-year-old musician from Harlem who conducted the orchestra for *John Henry*'s out-of-town tryouts, moved to Europe after World War II and become the first black conductor of a major symphony orchestra.

Wolfe's score for *John Henry* boasted more than two dozen musical numbers, including two beautiful solos for Ruby—"Careless Love" and

"Lullaby." She also had a duet with Robeson, "I've Trampled All Over." Robeson's solos included "Got a Head like a Rock" and "I'm Born into This Country," which showed off his booming voice to the fullest.

Despite a fine score and a first-rate cast, problems seemed to plague *John Henry* from the outset, mostly resulting from the poor libretto. Although Roark Bradford was a good novelist, he lacked the dramatic gifts of a DuBose Heyward when it came to adapting his book for the stage (nor was he fortunate to have a talented partner, as Heyward had in his wife, Dorothy). *John Henry*, as many critics would point out, seemed less a musical play than a series of musical vignettes without much plot connecting them.

Rehearsals were held at the West 44th Street Theatre, where the show would have its Broadway opening in January 1940, following previews in Philadelphia and Boston. Sam Byrd also wanted the show to have a pre-Broadway run at Washington's National Theatre, where Ruby and the original *Porgy and Bess* company had finished their tour in March 1936. Robeson adamantly refused to perform at the National because of its segregation policy.

When *John Henry* opened in Philadelphia on December 10, 1939, the house was filled to capacity for Robeson's return. Ruby had her own cheering section in the audience, led by the McCrackens. The *New York Times* noted the occasion, saying: "After an absence of seven years from the American stage, Paul Robeson was welcomed back tonight in Roark Bradford's new play 'John Henry,' which opened at the Erlanger Theatre for a limited engagement. Sharing applause with him was Ruby Elzy as Julie Anne."

Returning to New York, producer Sam Byrd made several major changes, including bringing in a new director, Charles Friedman. After more rehearsals, the show went on to Boston where it opened on Christmas Day for a final week of previews before the Broadway premiere.

John Henry opened at the 44th Street Theatre on January 10, 1940, playing to a full house. When the reviews came out the following day, Bradford's script was universally panned. But there was lavish praise for the performances, especially by Robeson and Ruby. Except for one reviewer who said she "tended to wax shrill and hard on her top notes," Ruby was applauded by critics as enthusiastically as her illustrious leading man:

Mr. Robeson sings beautifully and acts with directness and force. Ruby Elzy, as his true love, also sings extremely well and acts with simplicity and gentleness.

Ruby Elzy is all that Mr. Bradford envisioned as the loyal and loving Julie Anne. Mr. Wolfe has [provided] melodies that will take their place with the best of our Negro folk songs and Mr. Robeson and Miss Elzy sing them superbly.

Mr. Robeson plays what there is in the role of John Henry with deep feeling and great sincerity. . . . Ruby Elzy is excellent as the faithful Julie Anne.

Pressing him [Robeson] closely for first honors is Ruby Elzy, who can act and sing in superb fashion. She has several solo numbers and several with Mr. Robeson and she merited the applause bestowed upon her at the end of each song.

The performance also provided a triumph, from a musical standpoint, for another member of the cast, Ruby Elzy, playing opposite Mr. Robeson. Miss Elzy's voice—clear, powerful, but with a touch of plaintiveness no white singer can achieve—was at its best in a delightful melody called "Careless Love."

With acclaim for both its stars and music, and the box-office draw of Robeson in the lead, *John Henry* could and should have run a long time. The weaknesses of the script could probably have been fixed, but unfortunately there was never a chance to do so. In a repeat of what Ruby had seen happen in Merle Armitage's West Coast production of

Porgy and Bess, Sam Byrd had overextended himself financially with numerous personnel and other changes made after Philadelphia and Boston. Receipts from the show's opening week on Broadway were not enough to pay both the cast (Robeson's salary alone was $1,500 a week) and Byrd's backers. No other "angels" (people who put up money for Broadway productions) stepped forward. After only seven performances, *John Henry* was forced to close.

Ruby was deeply disappointed. Not only did she relish performing with Robeson, but she felt Julie Anne was one of her best roles, an opinion validated by the praise she received from critics. Now, with the show's demise, Ruby was again at loose ends, and she debated what to do next. There were several opportunities in New York. Charles Marshall, trying to keep his struggling agency alive, was eager to book her for concerts on the East Coast. A new all-black musical was being planned for Broadway that would ideally suit Ruby's talents—*Cabin in the Sky*, by composer Vernon Duke and lyricist John LaTouche (who had written the words for Robeson's "Ballad for Americans"). The show was to open in October 1940 with an all-star cast that included Ethel Waters, Dooley Wilson, Todd Duncan, Katherine Dunham, and J. Rosamond Johnson.

But Ruby decided against staying in New York. She was anxious to get back to California—and to Jack Carr.

Eight years her senior, Jack Carr, like Ruby, was a child of the Jim Crow South. Born in North Carolina, Carr had left the state when he went to serve overseas in the first World War. Upon his return he began his career as an actor and singer. Tall and lean with a rich, mellow baritone voice, Carr attracted the attention of Hall Johnson when he formed his first choir in the 1920s. Carr created the role of Brother Moses in Johnson's *Run Little Chillun* on Broadway in 1933, and two years later was cast by George Gershwin as the fisherman Jim in *Porgy and Bess*. Carr also understudied the larger role of Crown. When Warren Coleman, the original Crown, was unable to join Armitage's West Coast production in 1938, Bob Wachsman recommended Carr as his replacement.

It was during that 1938 tour that Ruby and Jack Carr had begun to date. Although they had known each other in the first production of *Porgy and Bess*, Ruby was still married at the time. In California, her marriage to Gardner Jones now over, Ruby began to date the handsome and personable Carr. When she chose to stay in Hollywood after the Armitage production closed, Carr decided to remain, too. Carr wanted to marry Ruby, but she resisted.

While Ruby starred in the Federal Theatre Project's *Run Little Chillun* (ironically without Carr in the cast, despite his role in the original Broadway production), Carr began working steadily in films. He often played the stereotypical roles to which blacks were usually consigned, like the downtrodden slave Luke in *Way Down South* (in which Ruby had also appeared); but sometimes he would get a good part, such as the boxer Tiger in *One Hour to Live*, that showed him to be a fine actor.

When Ruby went to New York to play in *John Henry*, it was the first time she and Carr had been apart since they began dating. Perhaps the two-month separation made Ruby realize how much she loved Jack Carr and that she was ready at last to put the painful experience of her failed first marriage behind her. Ruby returned to Los Angeles in February 1940, and within a few months she and Jack Carr were married.

They settled happily into Ruby's house on East 54th Avenue, which she fortunately had held on to while in New York working on *John Henry*. Soon they would be joined by a new addition—a six-year-old boy named Buster.

A few years earlier, before he moved west, Ruby's brother Robert had dated a young woman in Mississippi named Mary (May) Lawhorn. When Robert went back home for a visit from the California ranch where he was working, May now had a son—and she told Robert that he was the boy's father. Robert decided at once to marry May. He named the boy Edward after his uncle (Charlie Elzy's brother), who played professional baseball in the Negro Leagues. Robert took his family back to California, where he and May went to work together as the chauffeur and maid in the Beverly Hills home of a wealthy couple.

Robert and May lived during the week at their employer's home, and the little boy, whom everybody called "Buster," could not stay with them. Ruby was overjoyed when Robert asked if she and Jack could take Buster in to live with them.

"Staying with Aunt Ruby and Uncle Jack was like a dream come true," Buster recalled. "Here I was, living in this big house, with my own big room, in this beautiful neighborhood. I would walk to my school, and every day, on my way home, I could hear Aunt Ruby's voice coming up the street as she practiced."

On their weekends off, Robert and May came over to stay at Ruby's house and see their son. Buster remembered the constant flow of people, including the many celebrities who were his aunt's friends.

"I'd be listening one night to Rochester on the *Jack Benny Show*, and then the next day he'd be over at our house. One of Ruby's best friends was Clarence Muse, who had this big ranch out in the valley where he threw a party almost every weekend. Aunt Ruby and Uncle Jack took me with them all the time, and I got to ride horses and play with the children of all the other famous black movie stars. I felt I was the luckiest kid alive."

Ruby, who never had a child of her own, doted on Buster, as did Emma, who by now was living most of the time with Ruby and Jack. Buster recalled there was only one time he had to be quiet in the house—when his aunt was practicing.

"Aunt Ruby had an accompanist whom I remember had a strange accent. He didn't seem to particularly like children, so I would hide under the piano and try to stay very quiet while he played for Aunt Ruby. Her voice was so beautiful it made chills run up my spine."

Soon that voice would be heard again in a new venture: Ruby was about to make her first, and sadly her only, commercial recording.

Composer Harold Arlen had just won the Academy Award for Best Original Song with lyricist E. Y. "Yip" Harburg for their "Over the Rainbow," immortalized by Judy Garland in MGM's *The Wizard of Oz*. Like his close friend George Gershwin, Arlen was a composer deeply influenced by the music of black Americans.

In the fall of 1939, Arlen and another of his frequent collaborators, lyricist Ted Koehler, began work on an original "American Negro" suite of songs that they entitled *Reverend Johnson's Dream*. Completed in 1940, the suite consisted of a dream (the title song), a lullaby, and four spirituals.

Decca Records decided to record the work, with Arlen in charge of the production. The suite called for three voices—bass-baritone, mezzo-soprano, and soprano. Assisted by Bob Wachsman, Arlen chose three singers who had appeared in Merle Armitage's West Coast production of *Porgy and Bess*: William Gillespie, Lois Hodnett, and Ruby Elzy.

"Where Is Dis Road A-leadin' Me To?" was a sinner's prayer for salvation, a difficult piece with an ascending scale that called for a dramatic soprano voice. Ruby, who with "My Man's Gone Now" had proven herself the specialist in such songs, was the perfect choice to record Arlen's spiritual.

On June 29, 1940, Ruby and her fellow artists went to Decca's Hollywood studios, where the recordings for *Reverend Johnson's Dream* were completed in one session. Leon Leonardi was the accompanist, and a group called the Jubilee Singers (not the famous choir with the same name from Fisk University) provided choral backing. Decca released the album on three 78 r.p.m. records later that year.

When the 33⅓ long-playing record was introduced in the late 1940s, many albums that were recorded earlier were re-released in the new format. *Reverend Johnson's Dream* was not. In large part this was due to the lyrics of several of the songs, such as the unfortunately titled "Little Ace o' Spades," sung by Lois Hodnett, with such rhymes as "inky head" and "kinky head." In the 1980s, Broadway star Judy Kaye recorded the work, re-titling it *Americanegro Suite*. Arlen, still alive, gave his approval to have any offensive words changed. "Little Ace o' Spades" became "Little Angel Mine."

Ruby was rehearsing for the session when sad news came from back east. On June 16, 1940, DuBose Heyward suffered a massive heart attack while driving home from his doctor's office, where he had just had a physical exam. He was rushed back to the doctor, but it was too late. The man who had written *Porgy*, put Ruby in his first movie, and recommended her to George Gershwin for her greatest role was dead at the age of fifty-five.

In November 1940, Ruby gave a huge benefit concert in Los Angeles for Wesley Methodist Church. It was a splendid success with many of her friends, including the Eddie Andersons, the Clarence Muses, Hattie McDaniel, and opera star Florence Cole Talbert, in attendance. Harold Arlen and his wife Rita were also there, and Ruby sang Arlen's "Where Is Dis Road A-leadin' Me To?" in his honor. She also sang "My Man's Gone Now" in tribute to DuBose Heyward.

Following the Wesley program, Ruby went home to Mississippi for a two-month visit—the longest since she left for Juilliard in 1930. Whenever she came home, Ruby would sing at the services for Mama's church, Mount Moriah, but she had not given a complete concert in Mississippi in more than six years. Ruby decided it was time to perform again for the people and the state whence she had come. Concerts were arranged in Corinth, at Rust College, and in Pontotoc.

Her first performance was in Corinth, where her concert was advertised in the newspaper:

Ruby Elzy
Noted Soprano
Radio, Stage and Screen Star
(formerly of Corinth)
In Recital in the
Corinth Negro High School Auditorium
Thursday December 12, 1940—8:15 p.m.
Gideon May at the Piano
Adm: 50 c – 35 c and 25 c
Reservations for Whites

Ruby's Corinth program was a hit, as was the next program in Holly Springs. The last concert would be after the new year in her native Pontotoc. But first came Christmas. Ruby had not celebrated Christmas at home in more than a decade. On Christmas Eve, she went to Pontotoc for a holiday party hosted by the Furrs, the white family who had helped Mama so much. When Ruby arrived at their house, she instinctively headed for the back door, where she had always entered with the laundry her Mama had done for the family.

Eva Furr stopped Ruby and took her hand. "No Ruby," she said, "from now on, you enter through the *front* door." Ruby smiled with satisfaction. It was an affirmation of what her mother had taught her and what Ruby had always felt in her heart: if white people can get to know you first as a *person*, they will soon realize how foolish it is to be prejudiced.

One of the Furrs, twelve-year-old Martha Jo, sat close by Ruby at the party. Martha Jo was already a talented pianist, and when the Furrs asked Ruby if she would sing, Martha Jo spoke up immediately, "I'll accompany her!" As Martha Jo played, Ruby sang "Silent Night."

Martha Jo (now Fisk) still lives in Pontotoc and is still active as a pianist, church organist, and music teacher. She says, "I've lived more than seventy years, and I tell everyone that one of the things I am most proud of in my life is to say that I knew Ruby Elzy. She was a great singer and a great lady, and was absolutely loved by everyone in this town, black *and* white."

Another child on whom Ruby made a lasting impression was nine-year-old Walter Bates, whose mother Mildred had been a close friend of both Ruby and Amanda in their childhood. Walter was with his mother when they bumped into Ruby outside the Pontotoc post office. "I saw my Mother talking to this beautiful woman who was wearing this enormous fur coat. I'd never seen a fur coat before, not even on a white woman. When we said goodbye to the woman, I was very excited and said, 'Mama, who is that?' And Mama told me it was the famous singer, Ruby Elzy, who was from right here in Pontotoc and had come back to give a concert. You can bet I was *mighty* impressed!"

On January 7, 1941, Ruby's concert in the new auditorium at Pontotoc High School was filled to capacity by an audience of both blacks and whites—seated in separate sections, of course. The town's newspaper headlined its story "Triumphant Ruby Elzy Comes Home," noting: "Ruby Elzy has sung in the White House and she has been acclaimed by critics, but she has never had a group who were more appreciative in their hearts. . . . She knows many celebrities, but back home she is as simple and unaffected as the day she went away."

Ruby's concert was sponsored by the Pontotoc Music Club. Before she left town, Ruby gave the club a copy of one of her programs from *Porgy and Bess*, on which she inscribed: "No matter how far we go or how much recognition we may get, one never forgets her hometown and the dear folks who were kind to her when she needed kindness most. May God bless and keep you all forever healthy and happy. Sincerely with love, Ruby Elzy."

Soon after returning to Hollywood Ruby was at work on an exciting new film, Paramount's *Birth of the Blues*. It would turn out to be Ruby's final screen appearance and her most memorable.

Based in part on the story of the Original Dixieland Jazz Band, the film starred Bing Crosby as a white clarinetist in New Orleans who had grown up listening to the music of blacks in the French Quarter. Crosby forms a band with his friends, determined to bring jazz music to the respectable white folks and in the process gives "birth to the blues." It was pure hokum, not to mention another example of white people taking credit for the contributions of blacks; but as entertainment, *Birth of the Blues* was pure gold.

Besides Crosby, the cast included singer Mary Martin in one of her rare screen appearances, actor Brian Donlevy (in a break from his usual tough-guy roles) as Crosby's best friend, and one of the truly great jazz musicians of all time, trombonist Jack Teagarden.

For Ruby (playing a character also named Ruby), performing with Crosby and Martin was a wonderful experience. And she had the added joy of working for the first time with her good friend, Eddie "Rochester" Anderson, who in the film played her husband Louie. Anderson was at the height of his popularity as Jack Benny's sidekick, and the producers of the movie capitalized on it by simply billing him as "Rochester."

As with any Crosby film, there was plenty of music—both new songs and jazz and blues standards. Ruby's shining moment comes with her singing of W. C. Handy's "St. Louis Blues," in a scene where "Louie," injured and nearly killed in a fight, is brought home to his loving wife by Crosby's band. An emotional Ruby asks the band to play, to help bring Louie out of his unconscious state. Crosby starts the song; when he is overcome and unable to continue, Ruby takes over. Even though Ruby always protested that she could not do blues songs, her rendition of the Handy classic—done in her own style—is powerful. Despite a brief but annoying interlude where Crosby and Martin engage in some inane and unnecessary dialogue as she sings, Ruby Elzy's performance of "St. Louis Blues" remains the musical highlight of *Birth of the Blues*.

Paramount's publicity department went to work, touting Ruby as a "new screen find" and reporting that she and Mary Martin had a "mutual admiration" society for each other. Martin supposedly said, "Ruby, I'd give anything if I could hit those high notes in that soft, clear tone of yours," to which Ruby replied, "Honey, I'd give anything if I could swing 'My Heart Belongs to Daddy' like you." It was hype as only Hollywood could do.

By comparison to *Birth of the Blues*, Ruby's next engagement might have seemed unimpressive. Yet it was something very dear to her heart and in many ways more important to her than any plum stage or screen role: a week with the Methodist Youth Organization at its summer camp in California's San Bernardino Mountains.

Ruby had always loved working with young people and tried to spend time each July with the teenaged campers. They admired and respected her immensely, knowing how she had overcome the obstacles of her race to achieve the success she now enjoyed. And she had a unique ability to communicate with them, through her enthusiasm, sense of humor, optimism, and most of all, her voice.

On a late afternoon this particular year, Ruby was coming down from Sunset Rock with some of the camp girls. She looked resplendent in an all-white hiking outfit. As Ruby and the girls walked the path downhill, a group of boys passed on the other side. One of the boys, in a loud voice, said to the others, "Well, if that ain't a nigger!"

The girls with Ruby halted at once and looked at her. To their surprise, Ruby drew herself up proud and erect; and as she resumed walking, began to sing an old, rousing spiritual, "The Old Ark's a-Moverin'." The boys on the other side stopped to listen, and the one who insulted Ruby said, "But, gee whiz, she can sing!"

Sitting around the campfire that night, Ruby spoke to one of the girls, who was white. "You're still unhappy about this afternoon," Ruby said to her.

"Yes, I am," the girl replied. "It was so unkind and unnecessary. It hurts to think that such a thing should happen here."

Ruby consoled her. "Yes, I know, but really it didn't hurt me so much."

The girl said, "I noticed that. You didn't show you were hurt, but how could you help it?"

Ruby smiled. "There was a time when I'd stiffen up with resentment just as you felt I did. But not any more. Now I just relax and say to myself, 'Poor soul, he doesn't know as I do that we are all children of one Father.' Then I lift a quick prayer that God will help me to show that I have no grudge myself."

"Is that why you went singing down the path?" the girl asked Ruby.

"Yes," came the reply. "I wanted him to know I understood and didn't blame him."

The girl said, "Also, you gave the impression that you were proud and happy to be a Negro."

Ruby again smiled and said, "I'm glad, for that is the way I feel. Now please don't feel badly any longer. Probably it hurt you more than it did me."

Years after Ruby's death, the incident at the camp would be used in a story about her in a Sunday school lesson for the Methodist Church. The subject was tolerance.

On November 1, 1941, Ruby appeared on a nationwide broadcast from Hollywood to promote *Birth of the Blues*. Billed as a tribute to the

"Silver Anniversary of the Blues," the thirty-minute show starred Bing Crosby, who hosted and was joined by Ruby, Rochester, songwriter Johnny Mercer, and singer Betty Jane Rhodes (substituting for Mary Martin). Crosby introduced Ruby as a "truly great artist." With John Scott Trotter's orchestra and the Paramount Studio Chorus accompanying her, Ruby's broadcast performance of "St. Louis Blues" surpassed even her screen version; and her high B-flat at the end, with its diminishing *messa di voce*, was stunning.

Birth of the Blues opened a month later as Paramount's big holiday release. It was acclaimed as one of Crosby's best films (Bing himself would later say it was one of his favorites). Many critics singled out Ruby's performance:

> This department would like to hear more of one Ruby Elzy, who sings "St. Louis Blues" like an angel from heaven.

> Ruby Elzy, dusky vis à vis to Rochester, croons "St. Louis Blues" like an indigo aria.

> The one sign of honest feeling for the Negro's music is Ruby Elzy's splendid singing of "St. Louis Blues." It comes through with a piercing sad-sweet quality that lifts the sequence far above the rest of a routine musical comedy.

> In this cast is Ruby Elzy, Negro singer, whose rendition of "St. Louis Blues" will be remembered as long as the song will live.

One person who shared the critics' enthusiasm for Ruby was Bing Crosby. His introduction of Ruby as a "truly great artist" on the radio show was no mere flattery. The crooner had always had high regard for black performers and had credited many of them with influencing his own style. Following *Birth of the Blues*, Crosby signed Ruby to the agency headed by his brother Everett to represent Ruby for future work in motion pictures.

Ruby's mood was definitely upbeat in the last few months of 1941. She wrote to the McCrackens on November 3, a few days after the broadcast with Crosby:

> Dear Dr. and Mrs. McCracken and Mary,
>
> We left New York Sunday and got here Friday night because we went by to see mother. We also stopped at New Concord for a moment, as you perhaps know by Mrs. Florence's letter. So disappointed we couldn't see the boys, but it was our fault because we didn't know we would pass through. I do hope you heard the broadcast. It was very successful according to the Studio and to others who heard it.
>
> I suppose you have seen ads about the picture, "Birth of the Blues." It is to be premiered here this Thursday evening. I have been invited to a private preview of it, however on the Paramount movie lot; some "pumpkin" eh? Wish you were here to enjoy with me my first big movie premiere. Anyway you have your wonderful selves to thank for whatever success might come my way. I hope I have definite news to tell you about my several plans in the next letter. There will be a next and soon. (smile).
>
> Your Sister Florence has invited us to stop a while with her even over night if we pass through New Concord again. Nice wasn't it? I will be sure to let you know if I am to come to New York or whatever I am to do. I did so enjoy my visit with you. It was a real pleasure. Jack is better and sends best regards.

Ruby did indeed have "several plans," prompted by offers that were now coming her way. The *Hollywood Reporter* ran an item that she was to appear in MGM's upcoming film *Mokey*, starring Donna Reed and Robert Young. Her friend Clarence Muse had been approached about directing a revival of *Run Little Chillun* on Broadway, and of course he wanted Ruby to again play Ella James.

But these tempting offers would be set aside for another. On November 26, 1941, Ruby signed a contract to return to Broadway, to once again play the role that had made her a star—Serena in *Porgy and Bess*.

PORGY AND BESS TRIUMPHANT

When Merle Armitage's production of *Porgy and Bess* came to its abrupt end in San Francisco in March 1938, many people in the theatre world—perhaps even Ruby—thought that was the end of Gershwin's opera. Although a number of its songs, especially "Summertime," had become popular on the radio, the show itself seemed too huge and costly an undertaking for any sensible producer to take on. The general consensus that *Porgy and Bess* was an interesting but ultimately unprofitable work was validated even by Gershwin's own estate. After his death in 1937, attorneys cataloging the worth of his compositions put the value of *Rhapsody in Blue* at twenty thousand dollars; *Porgy and Bess* was valued at less than five thousand dollars.

One woman who did not share this dim view was Cheryl Crawford. In 1941, she was already one of Broadway's most distinguished producers even though only in her thirties. A native of Akron, Ohio, Crawford was stagestruck at an early age. She went to work as a secretary for the Theatre Guild immediately after graduating from college in 1925. Less than a decade later, she was part of the Guild's management and one of the first important women producers with such hits as Clifford Odets's *Golden Boy* to her credit.

In 1940, Crawford and her associate John Wildberg opened a regional theatre in the town of Maplewood, New Jersey. It could hardly be called a summer stock company—the theatre boasted a twenty-week season from May to mid-October, and featured stars such as Ethel Barrymore in *The School for Scandal*, Paul Robeson in *The Emperor Jones*, Helen Hayes and Maurice Evans in *Twelfth Night*, and Ingrid Bergman in *Anna Christie*. Only twenty miles from the heart of Manhattan, the

Maplewood Theatre was a spectacular success from the start, drawing huge audiences from New York who enjoyed the scenic drive and the small-town setting as much as they did the first rate productions.

With the onset of gas rationing (mandated by the federal government as America prepared for World War II), Crawford knew that 1941 would be the last year for her company. She wanted to close the final season on a high note with a work by her favorite composer, George Gershwin. She chose *Porgy and Bess.*

Crawford had fallen in love with Heyward's story when she was an assistant stage manager on the Theatre Guild's first *Porgy* in 1927, later accompanying the production to London. Crawford was part of the Guild's management by the time it produced Gershwin's operatic version in 1935.

Although Crawford greatly admired Gershwin and was impressed by *Porgy and Bess*, she was not surprised by its lack of success. To her manager's eye, it was too big and expensive to turn a profit, even with sold-out houses. Crawford felt Gershwin's use of sung recitatives, versus spoken dialogue, seemed creatively awkward and slowed the production down.

For her Maplewood production, Crawford reduced the number of characters. She also trimmed the orchestra from forty-four musicians to twenty-seven. And she found an ally in her quest to change the troublesome recitatives when she hired Alexander Smallens, the opera's original conductor, to be her musical director. Like Crawford, Smallens disliked the recitatives and had told Gershwin so in 1935. Gershwin was undeterred—*Porgy and Bess* was an opera, and operas had recitatives. But now Gershwin was gone, and Smallens and Crawford, working together, made a number of judicious cuts. The result was a shorter (by forty-five minutes) show that moved along much more swiftly and coherently.

Like Merle Armitage, Crawford wanted to assemble as many of Gershwin's original company as she could. Ruby, Todd Duncan, Anne Brown, Georgette Harvey, and Edward Matthews were all signed to recreate their roles. Avon Long was hired to reprise his Sportin' Life from the Armitage production, and a newcomer, Harriet Jackson, was cast as Clara. To Ruby's delight, Crawford engaged Jack Carr to play the menacing Crown.

The Maplewood Theatre closed for a full week of rehearsals with Smallens and stage director Robert Ross. Unlike many of the managers Ruby had worked for, Crawford was as sharp a businesswoman as she was a talented producer: her Maplewood *Porgy and Bess* was budgeted to break even at thirteen thousand dollars, versus the seventy thousand dollars of the 1935 production.

Advance publicity for *Porgy and Bess* generated such excitement that all eight performances were sold out even before the show's opening on October 13, 1941, with a demand for more tickets than Crawford was simply unable to fulfill. The opening night was a thrilling success, with endless bravos and curtain calls.

More importantly, many of the critics who had previously dismissed the opera now hailed *Porgy and Bess* as a masterpiece. Among the most critical before had been Virgil Thomson; reviewing the Maplewood production for the *New York Herald-Tribune*, he now admitted that Gershwin had created "a beautiful piece of music and a deeply moving play for the lyric theatre." Gershwin's prophecy that his opera would endure was finally realized, although sadly after both he and DuBose Heyward were gone.

Thomson's review also noted, "Miss Ruby Elzy, as Serena, gives the single loveliest performance in the cast."

For Ruby, Crawford's production would be significant for another reason. One night after the show a man came backstage to tell Ruby how much he had enjoyed her performance. Ruby and the man chatted for several minutes, and before leaving he gave Ruby his business card:

MARK BYRON, JR.
30 ROCKEFELLER PLAZA
NEW YORK, NEW YORK

The address was certainly familiar to Ruby—it was the headquarters of NBC. Byron was a former advertising executive turned agent who now represented a number of important concert artists, including famed Irish tenor John McCormack. When Byron learned that Ruby had no manager (Charles Marshall had closed his agency the year before), he offered his help. Ruby liked the amiable Byron and felt he was someone to whom she could entrust her career. Before she left Maplewood, Ruby signed with Byron.

The success of Crawford's production brought out the major impresarios from Broadway, each clamoring for her to bring *Porgy and Bess* to their theatre that season. Ruby knew, even before she and Jack returned to California for the *Birth of the Blues* broadcast and premiere, that a Broadway revival was possible. It was part of the "plans" she hinted at in her letter to the McCrackens. A few weeks later, the plans became a reality when Crawford agreed to present *Porgy and Bess* at Lee Shubert's Majestic Theatre.

Ruby signed a run-of-the-play contract at a guaranteed salary of two hundred dollars per week. Jack was also signed, but not to play Crown; Crawford had hired Warren Coleman to reprise the role he created in 1935. Jack would play the smaller role of Jim, as he had in the original production, and would understudy Crown for Coleman. For his services, Jack would be paid fifty dollars a week.

Ruby and Jack returned to Mississippi from Hollywood for a short visit with her mother and sisters. Amanda was now supervisor of Negro schools in Leflore County, the heart of the Delta. Wayne was teaching home economics in the town of Amory and was engaged to be married.

As she always did when she came to Corinth, Ruby sang at her mother's church, Mount Moriah, a few blocks from Emma's home at 505 King Street. Ruby, Jack, and Mama had just come back from Sunday services on December 7, 1941, and, like millions of other Americans, they were relaxing after lunch and listening to the radio when the announcer broke in with news of the Japanese attack on Pearl Harbor. The United States had entered World War II.

A week later, Ruby and Jack caught the train to New York. When Ruby arrived to begin rehearsals for *Porgy and Bess*, many of her fellow cast members came up to offer congratulations: *Birth of the Blues* had just opened as the Christmas attraction at New York's Radio City Music Hall. Ruby's performance in the film was winning her rave reviews and new admirers.

Rehearsals went smoothly, as nearly everyone in the company, with the exception of Warren Coleman, had recently performed together at Maplewood. *Porgy and Bess* was to have a three-week run in Boston before opening in New York. Once again, Crawford's managerial touch was magic: she spent sixteen thousand dollars on the Broadway-bound production of *Porgy and Bess*; advance ticket sales were so strong that the entire cost was recovered in Boston even before the show opened there on December 30, 1941.

On January 22, 1942, the curtain went up at the Majestic Theatre for the triumphant return of *Porgy and Bess*. Nothing before had prepared Ruby or the company for the tumultuous reception they and the production received. Critical praise was lavish, Ruby's performance once again receiving acclaim:

> Ruby Elzy, who sang the melancholy "My Man's Gone Now" with such sweet humility in 1935, has recaptured her original delicacy of feeling.

> Ruby Elzy, as a particularly appealing Serena, could scarcely be improved upon.

> Ruby Elzy is there to sing the mournful songs of the unhappy Serena, with all their weird cadences, and if Serena has put on a pound or two and looks less miserable than she used to, she still is doing full justice to her songs.

The last review had to sting a bit, despite the critic's enthusiastic praise for Ruby's vocal performance. Ruby *had* put on weight in recent years, and it was noticeable on screen in *Birth of the Blues*. Still, Ruby could not help but be pleased, as *Porgy and Bess* seemed destined for a long run.

There was more to do now than just appearing in one's own show, however—there was a war going on. On January 16, 1942, while Ruby was still in Boston for *Porgy and Bess*, film actress Carole Lombard and her mother were killed when their plane crashed while returning to Hollywood from a campaign to sell war bonds in the Midwest. Entertainers from every part of show business were being called upon to do their part, and the stars of *Porgy and Bess* and other Broadway plays were no exception.

On Monday, April 6, 1942—the twenty-fifth anniversary of America's entry into the First World War—Ruby, J. Rosamond Johnson, Harriet Jackson, and Eddie Matthews went to Washington, D.C., to sing a benefit performance at the Annual Army Day Dinner, given "in honor of the American citizen soldier." There were other benefit performances such as these throughout the run of *Porgy and Bess* on Broadway and the tour that followed. Ruby and her colleagues also helped with war bond drives and entertained troops at camps and hospitals—especially where the troops were black.

A month after the Army Day appearance in Washington, the *Porgy and Bess* company gave what was one of its most unusual and memorable performances. The U.S. Treasury Department, to promote the sale of war bonds, was sponsoring an eight-week summer series on the Mutual Broadcasting Network entitled *The American Opera Festival.* To inaugurate the series, there could be only one choice—*Porgy and Bess.* On May 7, 1942, the curtain at the Majestic Theatre was held for an hour and a quarter so the opera could be presented live from WOR studios. Jean Dalrymple, Crawford's publicity director, adapted the opera to fit the broadcast's one-hour format. There would be dialogue and music with narration by Dalrymple to bridge the gaps in the storyline. The WOR Symphony Orchestra, conducted by Alfred Wallenstein, accompanied the cast.

The shorter version meant some songs were abbreviated, among them "My Man's Gone Now" and "I Got Plenty o' Nuthin.'" Some music was cut altogether, including "Oh, Doctor Jesus." But the performance, preserved on record, is magnificent. From this broadcast, one can get a glimpse of the superb acting and singing of Ruby Elzy, Todd Duncan, Anne Brown, and Edward Matthews in the roles they created, as well as the fine performances of later cast members like Avon Long and Harriet Jackson. Warren Coleman was unable to appear, and Jack Carr took over the role of Crown. The *American Opera Festival* marked the last time Ruby performed on radio.

A few weeks later, Decca assembled nearly the entire cast to record six selections from *Porgy and Bess*. Two years before, Decca had recorded eight songs from the opera, with Todd Duncan doing not only Porgy's solos but also "It Ain't Necessarily So," sung in the show by Sportin' Life, and Anne Brown singing all the solos for Bess, Clara, and Serena—including "My Man's Gone Now." The 1942 session would have been the perfect opportunity for Decca to record Ruby in the song she'd made famous and Harriet Jackson and Avon Long in their numbers. But Decca chose instead to keep the earlier recordings with Duncan and Brown. The six new recordings, along with those from 1940, were released by Decca as a single "Original Cast Album," but it was not. The album became a best-seller and in later years was released on LP and CD. Although Anne Brown does a fine version of "My Man's Gone Now," the woman who introduced the song was never given the chance to record it in the studio.

However disappointing it must have been for Ruby to be left out of the Decca session, she had no time to be downcast. In addition to playing eight performances a week at the Majestic Theatre, Ruby was working closely with Mark Byron, planning her career beyond *Porgy and Bess*. In fact, they decided not to wait for the opera to end—Byron booked Ruby, accompanied by Arthur Kaplan, for her Boston recital debut on June 21, 1942. The *Boston Globe* announced her appearance: "Ruby Elzy, who sings the role of the widow Serena in George Gershwin's 'Porgy and Bess,' will appear in concert at the Isabella Stewart Gardner Museum (Sunday) at 2 o'clock. . . . Miss Elzy, who was also in the original production . . . has never missed a performance, and will fly to Boston Sunday morning, flying back that afternoon in time for the Sunday night show at Broadway's Majestic Theatre."

The day after Ruby's performance, critic Rudolph Elie, Jr., wrote a glowing review in the *Boston Herald*:

> Ruby Elzy, whose singing of the role of Serena in "Porgy and Bess" is by no means the least important part in making the American folk opera a success, is also a concert singer of considerable achievement. She appeared yesterday (the first time) as a solo artist in Boston; attracted a capacity audience and rewarded it with a distinctly superior song recital.
>
> Possessed of a naturally fine voice, an accurate ear for the vocal line and an emotionally mature and intelligent grasp of the essential moods of the songs she sings, Miss Elzy has a running start on the majority of the younger singers appearing today. Moreover, her training in the theatre has given her a sense of drama (which she fortunately does not overdo) and an important sense of timing.

It was the kind of critical praise that every artist—and artist's manager—hopes to achieve. The reaction to Ruby's concert in Boston convinced Mark Byron to go ahead with his plans for a major solo tour for Ruby.

Ruby signed another run-of-the-play contract with Cheryl Crawford on June 1, 1942, that would carry her through the end of the run of *Porgy and Bess* on Broadway and the national tour that Crawford was arranging to follow. One performer who chose not to remain was Anne Brown. Anxious to begin a concert career, Brown bowed out of the show. Replacing her as Bess would be Etta Moten, who had appeared with Ruby more than a decade earlier in the short-lived revue *Fast and Furious*.

Not long after *Porgy and Bess* returned to Broadway—and perhaps spurred on by the barbed comments of the critic who wrote that Serena had "put on a pound or two"—Ruby went on a diet and began to exercise. It was not simply to lose weight; she also needed greater strength and stamina for the grueling schedule of performances in *Porgy and Bess*.

Within a few months, Ruby was physically in excellent condition. Byron was creating a promotional brochure for Ruby and arranged a portrait sitting for her with renowned theatre photographer James Abresch. Ruby bought a new evening gown that complimented her more slender, shapely figure. She completed the makeover with a stylish new hairdo. Captured in the lens of James Abresch's camera, Ruby Elzy never looked more beautiful than she did that summer of 1942.

Byron also had Abresch photograph Ruby in costume as Aida. The photo appeared in the brochure, which announced, "The grand opera debut of Miss Elzy will be in the title role of Verdi's *Aida*."

Ruby as Aida would be mentioned not only in Byron's brochure, but in several articles in the coming months and also in obituaries at the time of Ruby's death. The only information missing is where and for whom she was to sing *Aida*. The Metropolitan Opera excluded blacks from their roster until 1955, and the New York City Opera (the first New York company to break the color barrier) had not yet been founded.

Black soprano Caterina Jarboro had sung Aida for Italian-born conductor Alfred Salmaggi's Chicago Civic Opera in the late 1930s. Salmaggi was more than receptive to black artists, and it is possible that he would have engaged Ruby. But more likely is that she would have performed for Mary Cardwell Dawson's National Negro Opera Company, which presented *Aida* in Chicago and Washington, D.C., in 1944.

Dawson was a unique figure in black classical music, not only a gifted choral director and teacher but a tireless organizer and entrepreneur. In 1941, at the convention of the National Association of Negro Musicians, Dawson had presented *Aida* starring another gifted black soprano, La Julia Rhea. The tremendous reception to the production convinced Dawson to create a company that she envisioned as a vehicle for black artists who were otherwise being denied the chance to use their talents on the operatic stage. Thus was born Dawson's National

Negro Opera Company, which performed in Pittsburgh, Philadelphia, Chicago, and Washington.

Ruby met Dawson in 1936; she and Anne Brown were the guests at a reception Dawson gave in their honor when *Porgy and Bess* played Pittsburgh on its first national tour. A few years later, Dawson and Ruby met again when Ruby was in New York working on *John Henry*. Certainly, if Dawson hoped to build a major black opera company, then the stars of *Porgy and Bess*—like Ruby Elzy—would be great assets, not only on stage but at the box office.

Dawson's records, now part of the Library of Congress, are unfortunately incomplete. In her business files, there is no contract for Ruby Elzy to appear in any opera. But in Dawson's photo collection, there is one of James Abresch's full-length portraits of Ruby, with the handwritten inscription: "To Mary Cardwell Dawson with sincere admiration—Ruby Elzy, 1942."

In March 1943, Ruby and her fellow *Porgy and Bess* stars gave a benefit concert for the National Negro Opera Company in Pittsburgh. A newspaper article about their performance noted, "Many of those artists will appear in the all-Negro cast of an opera to be presented in the near future." Whether or not that opera was *Aida*—with Ruby in the title role—is unknown. When Dawson presented *Aida* in 1944, a year after Ruby's death, the star was Minto Cato, who had appeared with Ruby in *John Henry*.

Porgy and Bess closed at the Majestic on September 26, 1942, after 286 performances (more than double the number given by the first production), the longest-running revival of any play that year. Although some members of the Gershwin family derided it as "the bargain basement production," Cheryl Crawford had done what no one else had: she had made *Porgy and Bess* a success at last.

The national tour opened two days later in Rochester, New York. In the long months on the road, Ruby would become good friends with the new Bess, Etta Moten. After she and Ruby had appeared together in 1931 in *Fast and Furious*, Moten had left New York for Hollywood. She appeared in several films, including *Gold Diggers of 1933* and the Astaire-Rogers hit, *Flying Down to Rio*, in which she introduced "The Carioca." Moten's husband, Claude Barnett, was the founder and owner of the Associated Negro Press and one of America's most influential black leaders of the time.

Moten, who celebrated her hundredth birthday in 2001 at a huge party hosted by Harry Belafonte and Halle Berry, fondly remembered her friend, Ruby Elzy. "She was a beautiful woman," Moten recalled, "and a great singer. I loved her voice."

The *Porgy and Bess* company had already been to five cities in as many weeks when it arrived in Chicago in November 1942 for a two-month run at the Studebaker Theatre. Cast members who had been separated from their families for more than a month were now joined by their husbands and wives. Of course, Ruby and Jack were fortunate—as the only married couple in the show, they never had to be apart. Etta Moten and Claude Barnett lived in Chicago and frequently hosted Ruby and Jack, Todd and Gladys Duncan, Eddie Matthews and his wife, mezzo-soprano Altonell Hines, the Avon Longs, and the Warren Colemans. Mama Elzy, her teaching in Corinth now over for the winter, joined Ruby and Jack.

Back in New York, Mark Byron was busy booking Ruby's concert and opera appearances for the following season. Up to that time, there was only one man in whom Ruby had placed her confidence, as far as her life and career were concerned, and that was Dr. C. C. McCracken. When the new promotional brochure was at last ready, Ruby asked Byron to get in touch with Dr. McCracken:

> November 19, 1942
>
> Dear Dr. McCracken,
>
> Judging by a letter Ruby Elzy wrote me immediately after she had received the first copy of this four-page letterhead, only God and her mother stand higher in her esteem than you. Previously, she had told me how very grateful she felt towards you because of your great aid in guiding

and helping her to build a solid foundation for her future. This unusual characteristic in her artistic make-up highly impressed me for, as you may know, most artists do not know the meaning of the word "appreciation."

In another letter, I received today, Miss Elzy requested me to mail you a number of these letterheads. I am glad to send you 25 under another cover and will be pleased to send you as many as you like.

Doubtless, you will be interested to learn that I am working with the heads of the Methodist Church in New York and Chicago in promoting Miss Ruby. Their principal official organ, the Christian Advocate, has a circulation of 250,000 weekly. The editor has accepted an article about her with her picture, for a November issue.

Another story is being prepared for the Etude magazine which has 150,000 monthly circulation.

I find it a genuine pleasure to work with Miss Elzy and keenly appreciate the cooperative attitude of her unselfish husband.

Yours sincerely, Mark Byron, Jr.

Byron's skills as a promoter, learned from his many years in the advertising business, were invaluable to Ruby. His wife, Florence Smith Vincent, also played an important role. A skilled journalist, Vincent wrote the profile on Ruby that appeared in the *Christian Advocate*. Vincent's narrative was interspersed with comments from Ruby that were by turns sad, touching, humorous, and inspirational. Yet there was also a serious tone, unlike any other article that had ever appeared about Ruby.

Now in her mid-thirties, Ruby Elzy had risen far beyond the "little colored girl" who came from the backwoods of Mississippi. Although she was still, as the *Pontotoc Progress* wrote a year before, "as simple and unaffected as the day she went away," her experiences as a woman, as an artist, and as a black American had given her a poise and maturity, even a sense of purpose, that she had never had before.

Perhaps it was an effect of the sobering times in which Ruby was living, with the nation at war and its effect on her people. The Depression was over, and good-paying jobs in wartime factories were open to everyone—except blacks, who were only hired to do the most menial labor. It took civil rights leader A. Phillip Randolph's threat of a march on Washington by a hundred thousand black Americans to force President Roosevelt to sign an executive order outlawing discrimination in the defense industry. Young black men—among them Ruby's brother Robert and sister Wayne's new husband—were going off to defend freedom around the globe when all too often it was denied to them at home. Whatever reasons compelled her, in the *Christian Advocate* Ruby Elzy spoke out publicly for the first time as a member of her race, on behalf of her race: "I believe prejudice is based altogether on misunderstanding and fear, and I pray that the day will come when my race will find the way to let it be known that what they want is not the sort of thing the white people fear. In the new world for which we are fighting, Negroes ask only to be considered as men and women with the right to work out their own salvation with, as Mr. Lincoln put, 'malice toward none,' with liberty and justice for all."

The *Christian Advocate* issue featuring Vincent's profile of Ruby was released on December 31, 1942. That night Ruby, Jack, and Mama went to a New Year's Eve party hosted by the Barnetts. For Ruby, 1942 had been incredible, yet the coming year promised to be even more exciting and memorable. Tonight was a time to relax and enjoy herself, and she did; raising her voice with everyone else as they jubilantly counted down the final seconds to midnight.

No one at that happy celebration knew, nor would even have guessed, that time was also running out for Ruby. The ambitious plans, the hopes and aspirations she had that New Year's Eve would never be realized.

It was now 1943. Ruby Elzy had exactly 177 days to live.

"I'M ON MY WAY"

Ruby had not seen Dr. McCracken's eldest son in several years. Bill McCracken was now twenty-six years old and following in his father's footsteps as an educator. While Ruby was still in Chicago appearing in *Porgy and Bess*, Bill came to town for a conference. He called Ruby, and they agreed to meet for lunch.

"We must've walked sixteen blocks from the heart of downtown," Bill recalled, "trying to find a restaurant where a white man and a black woman could be served together." Finally, they did find a place and over lunch enjoyed a happy reunion.

The long stay at the Studebaker Theatre finally came to a close on January 16, 1943. It was time for Mama to go back to Corinth and her school. Ruby, Jack, and the company went on to St. Louis, where *Porgy and Bess* would play for two weeks. The city had long been home to Charlie Elzy. Ruby wondered if her father might come to see her in performance. Thirty years had passed since Charlie walked out on his wife and children. In the ensuing years, they had heard virtually nothing from him. She sent tickets for her aunts Ada and Amanda—and one for Charlie.

"At Christmas or on our birthdays, we'd get a little card and present sent by our aunts in St. Louis," Wayne recalled. "And they'd always say, 'this is from your Daddy for your birthday' or whatever special occasion it might be."

"He didn't even *know* when our birthdays were," Amanda added. "We knew it was our aunts who'd remembered. But they'd tell us it was from Daddy, because they didn't want us to feel bad that he'd left us."

Before Ruby came to St. Louis for *Porgy and Bess*, Amanda had visited the town for her work as a school administrator. She told her aunts that she wanted to visit their house and see her father—but they were not to tell him she was coming.

"I came into the house, and he was sitting in the kitchen. We started talking, and I asked him, 'Are you married?' and he said, 'Yes, I was married once.' I asked him if he had a family, and he said, 'We had four children, and I just couldn't stand being there, all those little kids with their crying and runny noses and all. So I left. But my wife, she was a real Christian woman, and she did a fine job raising them all by herself.' And I asked him, 'What were the children's names?' He had to stop and think a moment. He said, 'Well, I have one son, named Robert. Then there's Ruby, the oldest, and next to her is Amanda. And there's one more girl, too—if I remember correctly, her name is Wayne.'"

Throughout their conversation, Charlie looked Amanda up and down, as if he she looked familiar but he could not quite place her. When he finished talking, Amanda asked him, "Do you know who I am?" Charlie shook his head no. "Daddy, I'm your second daughter, Amanda Belle." With that, Charlie Elzy broke down crying.

"He just threw his arms around me and held me like he'd never let go," Amanda remembers, stunned at his outburst of emotion. She began to cry, too.

"I told him it was all right, Mama had taught us never to hate him or judge him harshly for having left," she said. Charlie finally calmed down, and he and Amanda visited a little longer before it was time for her to leave.

"He knew what he'd done was wrong, but I think it was just too hard for him to admit it and go back," Amanda said. "He was just glad that we didn't hold his leaving against him, even though it made things so difficult for Mama."

Charlie knew Ruby had become a renowned singer. He had even heard her on the radio, but had never seen her perform live. Amanda and Ada persuaded him to come with them to the American Theatre to see the celebrated daughter who had carried his name to stardom. Charlie, who had never before been in an opera house, took his seat next to his sisters. When the first scene was over, he turned to Ada. "Which one is Ruby?" he asked.

Backstage after the final curtain, Ruby warmly greeted her aunts. Charlie stood back several paces, seemingly nervous and uncomfortable. There were a few awkward moments of silence. Finally, Ruby spoke to him.

"What did you think of the show?" she asked her father.

"Good, real good. I told Ada and Amanda you must've gotten that voice from your mother," Charlie said.

Jack Carr stepped out of his dressing room. "Daddy, this is my husband," Ruby said, introducing Charlie to his son-in-law.

Gradually, everyone relaxed a little. After a few more minutes, it was time to say goodbye. As Ruby's sisters had said, their mother had taught them not to hate Charlie. Whatever he had done, he was still their father. Ruby embraced her father at her dressing room door. As Charlie walked toward the exit, Ruby took her aunts aside.

"Thank you for coming," she said, adding, "and thank you for bringing Daddy, too."

From St. Louis, the tour passed like a whirlwind through the Midwest—four days in Kansas City, four days in Minneapolis, two days in St. Paul. Then there was a full week in Milwaukee, where the closing night, February 20, fell on Ruby's thirty-fifth birthday.

In Detroit on the following Saturday, the occasion was even more auspicious, as Ruby gave her seven hundredth performance as Serena. Among the leading players, only Georgette Harvey as Maria had given more performances. A special release was sent out to the press, and a party was held in Ruby's honor after the show.

Strangely, Ruby did not feel like celebrating. She was suddenly irritable and moody, which was not like her at all. Only the summer before, after working hard to lose weight and build up her stamina, she had never felt better. Now every performance left her feeling drained and depleted. Clearly, something was wrong.

Concerned, Ruby went to see a Detroit physician, Dr. Samuel H. C. Owen. He ran tests and took X-rays, which revealed the source of Ruby's problem: a benign tumor had developed in her uterus. It was causing a greater loss of blood during her menstrual period. This in turn caused anemia and fatigue and the resulting irritability and mood swings.

The news surprised Ruby; thankfully, the tumor was benign. But when Dr. Owen told her she would need an operation, she hesitated— not that she was afraid of surgery, but because it would mean leaving *Porgy and Bess*. Ruby talked it over carefully with Mama and Jack. The *Porgy and Bess* tour would close in Denver on June 19. Could the operation wait until after then? she asked Owen. Knowing the tumor was benign, the doctor agreed. He gave Ruby medications to help alleviate her symptoms and instructions to call a physician at once if she developed complications. Ruby would be allowed to finish the tour, returning to Detroit for the operation in late June.

Now feeling better, Ruby went on with the tour to Indianapolis. Then it was Canada, and the Royal Alexander Theatre in Toronto. It was the first and only time Ruby Elzy ever sang outside of the United States.

The two-week run in Pittsburgh was highlighted by the benefit concert on March 25 for Mary Cardwell Dawson's National Negro Opera Company. Ruby, Todd Duncan, Etta Moten, Harriet Jackson, and Edward Matthews all appeared at midnight—after they finished the evening performance of *Porgy and Bess*. The benefit was to help launch Dawson's ambitious drive to attract 125,000 supporters nationwide for her fledgling company, established, according to the *Pittsburgh Courier*, "to afford the general public a chance to enjoy the talents of those artists who, because of their race, are denied the opportunity of appearing in many of the familiar operas in New York, Chicago, and other cities."

On the road and between shows, Ruby worked on the article Mark Byron had arranged for her to write for *The Etude* magazine, one of the largest and most prestigious magazines covering classical music. The article would appear in August 1943, timed to coincide with the start of Ruby's solo concert tour. Her subject was one dear to her heart—the Negro spiritual. But, like the article in the *Christian Advocate*, she also wanted to make a statement about race in America: "Music and religion, I profoundly feel, are two very great assets in the national life of our country. By this, I mean the Negro's natural love of music and his instinctive reverence for God are so deep seated that, if fostered, they will always be a power for good. It must be obvious that this is the common ground upon which an understanding, resulting in harmony in life between the two races which must exist side by side, will unquestionably be resolved. It is to this end that I hope to dedicate my life and talents."

Ruby was ready to put her words into action. Byron had been working with Methodist Church leaders in Chicago and New York to arrange Ruby's concert tour. Ruby decided that a portion of the proceeds from each appearance would go to support local churches in the cities where she sang and to help Rust College. The college's five-story building— where Ruby attended class and was discovered by Dr. McCracken—had been destroyed in a fire in 1940; Ruby wanted to help the school build a new, better facility where young blacks could be given a chance, just as she had been given a chance so many years before.

In Philadelphia, Ruby had a happy reunion with her sister, Wayne, who had moved to nearby Trenton, New Jersey, to be close to her husband Harry Reynolds, now stationed with the U.S. Army at Fort Dix. Trenton was just across the river from Philadelphia. Far from her home in Mississippi, with her husband only allowed a few days leave a month, Wayne was lonely. When Ruby came to Philadelphia for the three-week run of *Porgy and Bess*, the sisters spent nearly every day together, and Wayne came several times to the Forrest Theatre to see *Porgy and Bess*. Before leaving Philadelphia, Ruby gave Wayne one of the Abresch portraits, inscribed: "To my precious baby sister, Wayne Elzy Reynolds, with loads of love and affection—Your Ruby."

The photograph would remain on Wayne's bedroom dresser to the end of her life, a treasured keepsake of the last time she and her sister shared together.

After Philadelphia, the tour went on a brief hiatus before moving west. The school year had finished in Corinth, so Emma once again joined Ruby and Jack on the road. The West Coast tour opened in San Francisco's Curran Theatre—where Merle Armitage's production had prematurely folded five years before.

From San Francisco it was on to Los Angeles. Ruby had missed Southern California and was happy to be back. *Porgy and Bess* was presented in Philharmonic Auditorium by the Los Angeles Civic Light Opera; its director asked Cheryl Crawford's road manager for permission to include Ruby's name in the advertising, noting that "Ruby Elzy is very well known here." But Todd Duncan's contract guaranteed him sole billing with the title in all advertising, and it was impossible to deviate from the agreement. Nonetheless, Ruby proved a huge draw, as the many friends she had made in Hollywood came out in force.

Ruby also sang at her old church in Hollywood, Wesley Methodist, where she had given the huge benefit concert two years before. Even though Sunday was Ruby's only day off from the show, if a local church asked her to appear, she would be there. It was that way in almost every town on the tour. Ruby never seemed to mind, telling a friend, "I want to sing. It's my way of saying 'Thank You' for the chance God gave me through the church. It has done everything for my Mother and her family. I can't say 'No.' I want to sing for them."

The end of the tour was now in sight. From Los Angeles it moved on to Portland, where, in addition to the regular performance of *Porgy and Bess*, Ruby and the company gave a show for the troops at Fort Stevens. The tour went back to Oakland before the final stop—Denver, playing from June 16 to 19.

Writing in the *Denver Post* on June 20, 1943, Frances Wayne praised the production and especially the "saucer burial scene": "There are crap games, there is murder, there is a wake in Serena's room, with unforgettable color and shadow effects, where Ruby Elzy as Serena lifts her voice in the spiritual ('My Man's Gone Now') . . . giving a stinging reality to the finality of death."

Porgy and Bess gave its final performance on Saturday, June 19, 1943. It was a bittersweet night, as Ruby said goodbye to friends and colleagues, some of whom, like Todd Duncan, Georgette Harvey, and Eddie Matthews, she had performed with since the opera's beginning nearly eight years before.

The finale has the anguished Porgy hitching up his goat to the dilapidated little wagon for the journey to "Noo Yawk," where he is determined to find his Bess, who has run off with Sportin' Life. As she had more than eight hundred times before, Ruby as Serena joined with Duncan and the company to sing the words written by DuBose Heyward and set to music by George Gershwin: "Oh, Lord, I'm on my way, . . ."

The tour was now over, and Ruby was relieved. The grind of being on the road for nine months, living out of a suitcase, and constantly traveling by train from one town to the next had taken its toll. Amanda remembers Mother Elzy's concern at Ruby's condition as they prepared for the trip back east.

"Mama told me Ruby was just plain worn out," Amanda said. Not only was she worn out, she was still suffering the effects of the tumor, despite the medications Dr. Owen had prescribed. She was actually looking forward to going into the hospital.

As Ruby, Jack, and Mama made the trip to Detroit, the city exploded in one of the worse race riots of the 1940s. A small skirmish between white and black youths at an amusement park along the lakefront erupted into a wild melee that spread throughout black neighborhoods. For two days there were shootings and brawls, fires and looting. When order was finally restored, nearly fifty people had been killed and more than seven hundred injured, mostly black. Ruby arrived in Detroit just as the riots were ending.

There were only two hospitals that exclusively served the black community in Detroit. Most of the city's hospitals catered to whites only or at best had small wards that cared for black patients. The three days of rioting had strained the resources of every black doctor and hospital in Detroit to the limit. Dr. Owen admitted Ruby to Parkside Hospital, located at the corner of Brush and Illinois Streets. Parkside was known to local blacks as "the place you go to die," but Ruby was unaware of that.

Ruby entered Parkside on Thursday, June 25. The next morning, she was taken to the holding room to await the operation. Dr. Owen had reassured her the procedure was routine, and the chances of anything going wrong were small. Ruby seemed relaxed and unconcerned. Emma vividly described that morning in a letter to Dr. McCracken sent the following month:

> You and the family were the last folks she talked about the morning she was operated on. She told me you all were in Florida and she hoped you, the girls, and Mrs. McCracken were happy as could be without the boys. She said, "Mama, you didn't know our precious little baby, Edward, was in camp, did you?" Then she said, "Mama do you know I have never seen or found any man that was as perfect a father, husband, or a Christian gentleman as Dr. C. C. McCracken and I don't believe his equal is in the world." She ended by saying, "the best people in the world."
>
> Then we heard footsteps that proved to be Jackie, her husband. She began laughing and talking with him and was so jolly and happy. The time was near for the operation. I didn't think so much about it then, but in her conversation all the morning, she talked and touched on everything that concerned her in life. She even mentioned her personal things she wanted each sister, myself, and her husband to have. Even the amount of money Jack would need to take care of the extra expenses, and then she looked at me very strange, but I just wouldn't accept anything that pointed to her not going through all right.
>
> She even said, "Mama, you and Jackie love me so much, don't you?" Finally she said, "If anything should happen to me, I'm a pretty good Christian. I love the Lord, and everything will be all right." And when they had her all ready to go to the operating room, she vocalized just a

little, gave the sweetest *smile*, and said, "my voice is all right," and just
jumped on the carriage, seemingly so happy.

The operation would take a couple of hours at most, after which
Ruby would be moved into the recovery room. Emma and Jack decided
to go out for a bite to eat and to wait. When they returned to the hospital, they were hardly prepared for the shock that awaited, as Emma
recalled to McCracken: "They had finished the operation and were
sewing her up and she just quit breathing. They said she asked for a
drink of water and they told her she couldn't have the water and she quit
breathing. They did everything in man's power, but nothing helped."

Something went terribly wrong that summer morning in Parkside
Hospital; exactly what will probably never be known. All that is certain is that on Saturday, June 26, 1943, at 12:18 p.m., Ruby Pearl Elzy
Carr was pronounced dead by Dr. Owen. It was just one week after her
final performance in *Porgy and Bess*. She was only thirty-five years old.

Emma and Jack were stunned. For Ruby to be dead seemed impossible, incomprehensible. In the waiting room outside where Ruby's
body lay, Emma Elzy and Jack Carr held each other and wept.

If any woman could carry on in the face of such tragedy, it was
Emma Elzy. Her trust in God would see her through this loss, as it had
so many other times in her life. If Emma's beloved child was gone,
then she knew with the inner calm of a woman whose faith is unshak-
able that it was the will of the Almighty. There was much to do, and
first of all she had to take her baby home. Ruby Elzy had been born in
the red clay hills of Mississippi; now it was time for her to return.

While Emma took charge of Ruby's funeral, it was left to Jack to
deal with official matters. Her death certificate stated that Ruby had
been a resident of Detroit for "14 years" and that her occupation was
"housewife." The official cause of death was listed as "cardiac dilata-
tion" (enlargement of the heart) and "shock following operation."

Jack signed the certificate despite the errors. Perhaps he was still too
upset to read the document as carefully as he should have, but it was

more likely that he did not want to cause any further delays in taking Ruby back to Mississippi for burial, as Emma was anxious to do.

Emma knew that there was one person, besides her children, that she had to contact as soon as possible. When she and Jack arrived in Corinth with Ruby's body, Emma sent a telegram:

> Cornish, Mississippi via Columbus, Ohio. June 28, 1943.
> Dr. C.C. McCracken, Tavares, Florida.
> Our darling Ruby passed during operation. Answer Western Union.
> Mrs. Emma Elzy

Unfortunately, C.C. and Cleo McCracken were away at the time and would not receive the news until after Ruby's funeral had already taken place. The man who had discovered Ruby Elzy, and his entire family, grieved at the loss.

"Ruby's death hit all of us hard," Ed McCracken recalls, "but especially my Dad. He never got over it." Bill McCracken had been the last member of the family to see Ruby, just five months earlier in Chicago. "It was a waste," he said, "a tragic waste. She had done so much, yet there was so much more she could have done had she only lived."

Lusk Funeral Home in Corinth took over all the arrangements at Emma's request. On Tuesday, June 29, a wake for Ruby was held at the house on King Street.

"You could hardly move in that place—it was filled wall to wall with people," Oneida Vanderford remembers. "The crowds spilled onto the street and down the block. And it was like that all night long."

One of the youngest mourners was Robert's son, ten-year-old Edward "Buster" Elzy. "I'll never forget it," he said. "I was too short and had to get up on a little stool, so I could look into the casket. Aunt Ruby looked so beautiful, just like she was asleep. It was hard for me to believe she was really dead."

Outside Mississippi, the wire services carried news of Ruby's passing across the country, generating headlines and coverage that probably would have surprised her (although the accounts inaccurately reported her age). The announcement of her death led the obituaries in *Variety*, the entertainment industry's "bible," and in every major newspaper from the *New York Times* on down. The *New York Amsterdam News* ran a three-column story with Ruby's photograph that ran in black newspapers across America: "Ruby Elzy's Death at 33 Shocks Concert, Theatre World."

In August, Ruby's article "The Spirit of the Spirituals" was published posthumously in *The Etude*. The magazine's editors paid tribute to her in an editorial: "The passing of Ruby Elzy on June 26, at the age of 33, after an operation in Detroit, removes a very unusual figure of great potential value to her race and to her country. She was just starting upon a concert tour under the management of Mark Byron, Jr., and had a list of important appearances scheduled. Her aspect of the race question was one of the sanest and most sincere we have ever known."

But probably the most fitting announcement came in the newspaper of the town where Ruby was born. The *Pontotoc Progress* headline read simply: "Ruby Elzy Has Come Home Again."

Ruby was buried in Pontotoc City Cemetery, the largest in the county. Here was the final resting place of the area's most renowned citizens, from the earliest settlers to Confederate heroes of the Civil War. Like nearly all cemeteries in the South of the time, Pontotoc City Cemetery segregated the races in death as they did in life. Blacks were relegated to a separate section, smaller and more remotely located than the section where whites were buried. But an exception was made for Ruby Elzy. In a gesture of respect and recognition by the cemetery's trustees, Ruby's grave would be located in a central place previously reserved for whites only, less than fifty yards from the front gates.

On Wednesday, June 30, 1943, the Lusk hearse arrived in front of Emma's house to take Ruby on her final journey. A long caravan of cars would follow all the way to Pontotoc. McDonald Methodist

Church, where four-year-old Ruby Elzy had once startled the congregation with her remarkable voice, would be the setting for her funeral.

Dr. L. M. McCoy, the president at Rust College who had once told Ruby he would pray for God to grant her wish to become a singer, gave the eulogy. Natalie Doxey and the Rust A Cappella Choir led the congregation in song. There were telegrams and messages of condolence from Ruby's friends and colleagues, from Bing Crosby to the cast of *Porgy and Bess*, from the Ohio State University to the young campers from the Methodist Youth Organization in California.

Emma Elzy sat in the front pew, her other children and Jack Carr by her side. As the final notes of the opening hymn were sung, the rear door of the church opened and a slight man entered, taking the end seat in the last row. It was Charlie Elzy. Thirty years after he had left his family and Pontotoc, he had returned home to bid his firstborn child farewell.

Young Walter Bates was in awe of the crowd at the church. "They had roped off an entire section just for the white people," he remembers, "and every seat was taken. The sections for the black folks was all filled up, too, and people were standing outside the doors. It seemed like everybody in town—black and white—was there."

People of both races coming together in harmony. No other tribute could have pleased Ruby Elzy more.

EPILOGUE

A few weeks after Ruby's funeral, Emma Elzy finally sat down to write a heartfelt letter to Dr. McCracken, an outpouring of affection and gratitude for all that he had done to help Ruby to achieve her dream.

> July 19, 1943. Corinth, Mississippi.
>
> Dr. CC McCracken and Family,
>
> I have wanted to write you for several days, but just couldn't write. Hope this finds you and family well. Ruby attempted to write you the day before the operation. It was so hot and they wanted her to relax. So she didn't write anyone. She told me where you were but I didn't remember the place and thought probably someone in Columbus would know and they did and I was so thankful.
>
> Yes, I must say she was a precious child. And it's so hard to give her up. It is the hardest blow I ever had, but I am trying to be brave and submissive to God's will. Dr., I've never been able to express myself in words just how much it meant—your finding Ruby way down in the hills of Mississippi, where opportunity unborn had died for Negro children, and giving her a chance. In your wonderful Christ-like way, it didn't just help Ruby, but it has helped thousands of Negro boys and girls throughout America. And as long as time shall be, that wonderful kind deed you did for her will forever serve as a sign pointing to others helping them to do likewise and she did appreciate it in every way she could (bless her heart). . . . I'll miss her presence, but her work will go on forever.

The work did indeed go on. In the coming years, many young black singers would follow in the paths that Ruby Elzy, her co-stars in *Porgy and Bess*, and other artists like Marian Anderson and Paul Robeson had laid out for them.

In 1945, her friend and colleague Todd Duncan became the first black artist to appear with the New York City Opera. Ten years later, Marian Anderson made her historic debut at the Metropolitan Opera as Ulrica in Verdi's *Un Ballo in Maschera*.

Six years after Anderson came Leontyne Price. Like Ruby Elzy, Price was a soprano, a small-town Mississippi girl (from Laurel) who'd gone to college first in Ohio and then on to Juilliard. Price's sensational debut at the Met firmly established once and for all the legitimate right of gifted black singers to take their places on the great opera stages. No longer would a singer's race be a barrier. It was an affirmation of the words Ruby Elzy had written in *The Etude* in 1943: *There is no color to talent.* The roster of great black artists since Price has grown steadily and includes such venerated names as Grace Bumbry, Shirley Verritt, Jessye Norman, Kathleen Battle, and Denyce Graves.

Porgy and Bess is more popular today than ever before. In 1976, the Houston Grand Opera had tremendous success when it presented the first complete production of the work since Boston in 1935. The opera's long road to glory culminated with its production on the stage of the Metropolitan Opera in 1985, fifty years after its initial premiere. *Porgy and Bess* is now included in the repertoire of nearly every major opera house in the world.

The towering legacy of George Gershwin has long overshadowed the contributions of others with whom he collaborated on the opera. But there is no question that DuBose Heyward, with his memorable libretto and lyrics (along with those of Ira Gershwin), and the phenomenal cast of unknown talents Gershwin handpicked—especially Todd Duncan, Anne Brown, Ruby Elzy, and John Bubbles—were all equal partners in bringing *Porgy and Bess* to glorious life.

If, over the years, *Porgy and Bess* has been elevated to the status of a legitimate opera, it also elevates the status of those who perform in it. The roles of Porgy, Bess, and Serena are no less operatic roles than are Figaro, Tosca, or Carmen.

One singer who has done both Carmen *and* Serena is American Cynthia Clarey. Clarey is probably the best known Serena of recent years, having played the role in Trevor Nunn's acclaimed production at the Glyndebourne Festival in the late 1980s. That production, also starring Willard White and Cynthia Haymon in the title roles, was filmed for the BBC and America's PBS, and has been a best-seller on video.

Said Clarey of her role as Serena, "We gave eighteen performances of *Porgy and Bess* over a fifty-four-day period. I had three days of rest between each performance, and believe me, I needed it! Serena's music is so difficult to sing, and when you have to act the role too, it's overwhelming."

Clarey admires the incredible feat pulled off by Ruby Elzy and the original cast. "I can't imagine having to do a role and an opera this difficult, and then have to perform in them *eight times a week*."

Asked if she feels Serena is an operatic role, like the many others she has done, including her acclaimed Carmen, Clarey responds with one word: "Absolutely."

Ruby Elzy dreamed of a career as an opera singer. In eight hundred performances as Serena in *Porgy and Bess*, she became—she *was*—a true opera singer, a pioneer black diva whose talents and artistry helped pave the way for those who would follow her.

In 1998, the centenary of George Gershwin's birth, the 1937 Hollywood Bowl Memorial Concert was released on CD for the first time. Pulitzer Prize–winning critic Lloyd Schwartz, in his review for the *Boston Phoenix*, said that one of the highlights of the CD was "Ruby Elzy, the first and best Serena, in a hair-raising 'My Man's Gone Now,' which she never recorded commercially."

The ultimate tribute came on April 1, 2000, at a gala ceremony in Jackson, Mississippi. Ruby Elzy was named by her native state as one of the first twenty-seven inductees into the new Mississippi Music Hall of Fame, part of an illustrious roster that also included Leontyne Price, William Grant Still, Elvis Presley, B.B. King, and Tammy Wynette.

Sadly, many of those closest to Ruby did not live to see the honors and recognition she is finally receiving. Jack Carr continued to perform, most notably creating the role of Sergeant Brown in Oscar Hammerstein's *Carmen Jones*. Carr eventually remarried, yet remained close to Emma Elzy. He was appearing in a Broadway revival of *The Green Pastures* in April 1951 when he collapsed and died at his home while dressing for the evening's performance. Jack Carr was fifty.

Dr. C. C. McCracken retired from his long career as an educator in the late 1940s. In 1952, he began working with Emma Elzy on a biography of Ruby, but ill health forced him to stop work on the project before it was completed. He died in 1957 at age seventy-five. Cleo McCracken died in 1965. Two of the McCracken children—Mary Ruth and Bill—passed away in 2000. The McCrackens' eldest daughter Janet died in 2003. Ed McCracken, Ruby's favorite, is still going strong in his eighties. A former college president, Ed and his energetic and devoted wife Ruth live happily in retirement in the Florida Panhandle.

Charlie Elzy outlived his daughter by many years. When he died, Emma and Amanda went to his funeral in St. Louis. Ruby's only brother Robert was eighty-one when he died in 1993. Wayne's marriage to Harry Reynolds ended in divorce after only a few years. More than two decades would pass before Wayne married again: Silas Bankhead was a widower with eight children when he and Wayne were wed in 1969. Their union lasted until Silas's death in 1993, after which Wayne and Amanda moved in together. They shared a house in Columbus, Mississippi, until Wayne died in 2000 at the age of eighty-eight.

Amanda Elzy's prolific career in education spanned more than fifty years and brought her distinction not only in Mississippi but throughout the United States. From supervisor of Negro schools in LeFlore County, she rose to become the county's first black assistant superintendent. In the late 1940s she was one of the founders of Mississippi Valley State University, the first college for blacks in the Delta. In 1959

Leflore County dedicated Amanda Elzy High School in her honor, located on Elzy Avenue in Greenwood. In 1970 she was named Outstanding Educator of America and her alma mater, Rust College, bestowed an honorary doctorate degree upon her. Amanda passed away in February 2004 at the age of ninety-four.

Emma Elzy outlived her beloved Ruby by more than four decades. She died in 1985, one month shy of her ninety-ninth birthday, and was buried in Pontotoc beside Ruby. To the end of her long life "Mother Elzy," as she was known to countless Mississippians, remained a dynamic and caring woman who was devoted to her community, to the Methodist Church, and to Rust College. Even in her nineties Emma never tired of talking about the accomplishments of her firstborn daughter and her remarkable career on stage.

Ruby Elzy's final resting place lies at the top of a gentle knoll not far from where the little house on Church Hill, now long gone, once stood, where Ruby, as a child, neatly folded the warm clothes Mama had just ironed for the white families in town and listened intently as Grandma Belle and Aunt Fannie told her the stories of her people and taught her the songs she would love so much and sing all her life:

Steal away, steal away
Steal away to Jesus.
Steal away, steal away home!
I ain't got long to stay here.

The stone monument over Ruby's grave bears an inscription, the epitaph written by her Mother:

Ruby Elzy
February 20, 1908
June 26, 1943
"Now Singing in the Celestial Choir"

RESEARCH AND REFERENCES

Author Interviews and Correspondence

Raoul Abdul, New York, New York (author of *Blacks in Classical Music: A Personal History*; music critic for the *New York Amsterdam-News*)

Wayne Elzy Bankhead, Columbus, Mississippi (Ruby Elzy's youngest sister; deceased April 2000)

Etta Moten Barnett, Chicago, IL (Bess in *Porgy and Bess*, 1942–1943; deceased January 2004)

Walter Bates, Pontotoc, Mississippi (son of Mildred Bates, Elzy family friend)

Clarence Bolton, Milwaukee, Wisconsin (originally from Pontotoc; father Pinson presented Ruby Elzy's 1934 concerts)

Anne Wiggins Brown, Oslo, Norway (original Bess in *Porgy and Bess* 1935–1942; friend and classmate at Juilliard)

Dr. Karen M. Bryan, Tempe, Arizona (assistant professor of music history and literature, Arizona State University; authority on Mary Cardwell Dawson and the National Negro Opera Company)

Joe Carroll, Jr., Corinth, Mississippi (stepson of Robert Elzy; Ruby's nephew; lived with her in California 1940–1941)

Cynthia Clarey, Binghamton, New York (opera singer; performed Serena in Glyndebourne Festival production of *Porgy and Bess*, 1989, filmed for BBC-TV and PBS)

Mildred (Johnson) Edwards, New York, New York (daughter of J. Rosamond Johnson)

Amanda Elzy, Columbus, Mississippi (Ruby Elzy's younger sister; deceased February 2004)

Martha Jo (Furr) Fisk, Pontotoc, Mississippi (granddaughter of family for whom Emma Elzy worked; Martha Jo at age twelve accompanied Ruby singing)

Rosalie Furr, Pontotoc, Mississippi (daughter-in-law of family for whom Emma Elzy worked)

Madge Cooper Guthery, Marion, Ohio (classmate at Ohio State University, 1928–1930)

Norman Harris, Columbus, Ohio (son of family with whom Ruby Elzy lived while at Ohio State, 1929–1930)

Ellistine Perkins Holly, Jackson, Mississippi (professor of voice, Jackson State University; author; singer; wrote and performed in *Mississippi's African American*

Divas, about Elizabeth Taylor Wakefield, Ruby Elzy, and Leontyne Price; chair of the selection committee, Mississippi Music Hall of Fame)

Edward Jablonski, New York, New York (noted biographer of George Gershwin and Harold Arlen; met Ruby Elzy during run of *Porgy and Bess*, 1942)

Michael Kaplan, New York, New York (father Arthur Kaplan was Ruby's accompanist, 1934–1942, including 1937 White House concert)

Oneida (Vanderford) Lasley, Corinth, Mississippi (classmate at Rust College; family were longtime friends of Emma Elzy)

Janet Leeder, Columbus, Ohio (member of Delta Omicron sorority that brought Elzy back to Ohio State for 1937 concert; visited Ruby Elzy and her husband in New York, 1935)

Josephine (Herrald) Love, Detroit, Michigan (classmate and accompanist at Juilliard, 1933–1934; accompanied Elzy's *Porgy and Bess* audition for George Gershwin; deceased September 2003)

J. Edward (Ed) McCracken, Valparaiso, Florida (son of Dr. C. C. McCracken; knew Ruby Elzy from 1927)

Charles W. (Bill) McCracken, Fort Walton Beach, Florida (son of Dr. C. C. McCracken; knew Ruby Elzy from 1927; deceased October 2000)

Janet M. McCracken, Fort Walton Beach, Florida (daughter of Dr. C. C. McCracken; knew Ruby Elzy from 1927; deceased July 2003)

Dale (Dalili) Pierson, Los Angeles, California (grandmother Fay M. Jackson was journalist for Associated Negro Press and Elzy's publicity agent in Hollywood, 1938–1939)

Mary Katherine Rose, Columbus, Ohio (mother Katherine Weatherington was Elzy's best friend at Ohio State, 1927–1930)

Mary Tolbert, Circleville, Ohio (assistant to Dr. Royal Hughes, 1936–1937, Ohio State University)

Oral History: Recorded Interviews

Emma Kemp Elzy, Pontotoc, Mississippi (Ruby Elzy's mother; interview recorded with Elliott Thompson at Pontotoc County Library in 1975)

Works by Ruby Elzy

"The Spirit of the Spirituals." *The Etude* magazine, August 1943 (condensed in *The Negro Digest*, October 1943).

Stumbling Upward, a play in two acts (performed and copyrighted but not published), Columbus, OH: 1927.

Books

Abdul, Raoul. *Blacks in Classical Music: A Personal History*. New York: Dodd, Mead, 1978.

Alpert, Hollis. *The Life and Times of Porgy and Bess: The Story of an American Classic*. New York: A. A. Knopf, distributed by Random House, 1990.

American Film Institute. *The American Film Institute Catalog of Motion Pictures Produced in the United States: Feature Films, 1931–1940*. Berkeley: University of California Press, 1993.

———. *The American Film Institute Catalog of Motion Pictures Produced in the United States: Feature Films, 1941–1950*. Berkeley: University of California Press, 1999.

Armitage, Merle. *George Gershwin*. New York, London: Longmans, Green & Co., 1938.

———. *George Gershwin: Man and Legend*. New York: Duell, Sloan and Pearce, 1958.

Bergan, Ronald. *The United Artists Story*. New York: Crown Publishers, 1986.

Bogle, Donald. *Blacks in American Films and Television: An Encyclopedia*. New York: Fireside/Simon & Schuster, 1989.

Boyd, Valerie. *Wrapped in Rainbows: The Life of Zora Neale Hurston*. New York: Scribner, 2003.

Buckland, Michael, and John Henken, eds. *The Hollywood Bowl: Tales of Summer Nights*. Foreword by Ernest Fleischmann. Los Angeles: Balcony Press, 1996.

Bundles, A'lelia Perry. *On Her Own Ground: The Life and Times of Madam C. J. Walker*. New York: Scribner, 2001.

Carlton, Jackson. *Hattie: The Life of Hattie McDaniel*. Lanham, MD: Madison Books, 1990.

Craig, Evelyn Quita. *Black Drama of the Federal Theatre Era: Beyond the Formal Horizons*. Amherst, MA: University of Massachusetts Press, 1980.

Crawford, Cheryl. *One Naked Individual: My Fifty Years in the Theatre*. Indianapolis, IN: Bobbs-Merrill, 1977.

Crosby, Bing (as told to Pete Martin). *Call Me Lucky*. New York: Da Capo, 1993.

Duberman, Martin Bauml. *Paul Robeson*. New York: Alfred A. Knopf, 1988.

Durham, Frank. *DuBose Heyward, the Man Who Wrote Porgy*. Columbia: University of South Carolina Press, 1954.

Eames, John Douglas. *The MGM Story: The Complete History of Fifty-Seven Roaring Years*. 2nd revised edition. New York: Crown Publishers, 1982.

———. *The Paramount Story*. 1st edition New York: Crown, 1985.

Ewen, David. *The Complete Book of the American Musical Theater*. New York: Holt, 1958.

Flaherty, Lanny. *Ruby Elzy: Pontotoc's Singing Daughter*. Published by the author, 1994, revised 1999.

Green, Stanley. *Broadway Musicals Show by Show*. 5th edition, revised and updated by Kay Green. Milwaukee, WI: H. Leonard Publishing Corp., 1996.

Hamalian, Leo, and James V. Hatch, eds. *Lost Plays of the Harlem Renaissance, 1920–1940*. Detroit, MI: Wayne State University Press, 1996.

Hirschorn, Clive. *The Hollywood Musical*. New York: Crown, 1981.

Hutchisson, James M. *DuBose Heyward: A Charleston Gentleman and the World of Porgy and Bess*. Jackson: University Press of Mississippi, 2000.

Jablonski, Edward. *Harold Arlen: Happy with the Blues*. New York: Da Capo, 1985.

———. *Gershwin*. Northeastern University Press edition. Boston: Northeastern University Press, 1990.

Jablonski, Edward, and Lawrence D. Stewart. *The Gershwin Years*. Garden City, NY: Doubleday, 1973.

Jewell, Richard B. *The RKO Story*. New York: Arlington House, a Division of Crown, 1982.

Keiler, Allan. *Marian Anderson: A Singer's Journey*. New York: Scribner, 2000.

Kellner, Bruce, ed. *The Harlem Renaissance: A Historical Dictionary for the Era*. Westport, CT: Greenwood Press, 1984.

Lewis, David Levering. *When Harlem Was in Vogue*. 1981. New York: Oxford University Press, 1989.

McMillen, Neil R. *Dark Journey: Black Mississippians in the Age of Jim Crow*. Urbana, IL: University of Illinois Press, 1989.

Peyser, Joan. *The Memory of All That: The Life of George Gershwin*. New York: Billboard Books, 1998.

Rampersad, Arnold. *The Life of Langston Hughes*. New York, NY: Oxford University Press, 2002.

Robeson, Jr., Paul. *The Undiscovered Paul Robeson: An Artist's Journey, 1898–1939*. New York: Wiley, 2001.

Smith, Eric Ledell. *Blacks in Opera: An Encyclopedia of People and Companies, 1873–1993*. Jefferson, N.C.: McFarland, 1994.

Story, Rosalyn M. *And So I Sing: African-American Divas of Opera and Concert*. New York: Warner Books, 1990.

Suriano, Gregory R., ed. *Gershwin in His Time: A Biographical Scrapbook, 1919–1937*. Foreword by Marvin Hamlisch. New York: Gramercy Books, 1998.

Woll, Allen L. *Black Musical Theatre: From* Coontown *to* Dreamgirls. Baton Rouge: Louisiana State University Press, 1989.

Articles (arranged chronologically)

"Teachers to Work on Labor Day—Institute for All Teachers in County Will Open Monday," *Bellefontaine Daily Examiner* (OH), September 3, 1927.

"Only Eight Teachers Absent from Institute—Miss Ruby Elzy Delights Large Audience of Educators by Her Singing of Many Numbers," *Bellefontaine Daily Examiner* (OH), September 6, 1927.

"Recommendations Approved," Board of Trustees October Meeting, *Ohio State University Monthly*, December 1928.

"Cotton Field Singer, Find of Professor, Groomed at University for Concert Career," by Anne E. Schatenstein, *Columbus Dispatch*, April 21, 1927.

"Ohio State Senior Dramatizes Her Life," *Columbus Dispatch*, May 8, 1930.

"Ohio State Offers Graduate Soprano," *Columbus Dispatch*, May 25, 1930.

"Ruby Elzy to Give Soprano Recital in Chapel Tuesday," Ohio State University *Lantern*, May 26, 1930.

"Co-Ed Making Musical Debut, Says Mother Sings Better," Ohio State University *Lantern*, May 28, 1930.

"Ruby Elzy Sings at University," by R. L. F. McCombs, *Columbus Citizen*, May 28, 1930.

"Singer Heard in Campus Recital," by H. E. Cherrington, *Columbus Dispatch*, May 28, 1930.

"Campus News," *Ohio State University Monthly*, July 1930.

"Institute News: Student Activities," by Albert Kirkpatrick, *The Baton*, Juilliard School of Music, March 31, 1932.

"The Class of 1932: Graduates on Parade," *The Baton* (graduation issue), Juilliard School of Music, May–June 1932.

"To Give Recital," *New York Amsterdam-News*, February 8, 1933.

"Music Notes," *New York Times*, February 9, 1933.

"Leading Lady in Less Than a Day," publicity release from *The Emperor Jones* pressbook, United Artists, 1933.

"Fifth Meeting," *Dynamics*, Juilliard Student Club, May 21, 1934.

"Negro Opera Company Opens at Mecca Temple," unidentified New York newspaper, July 7, 1934.

Review of *Porgy and Bess*, by Olin Downes, *New York Times*, October 11, 1935.

Review of *Porgy and Bess*, by A. Walter Kramer, *Musical America*, October 1935.

Review of *Porgy and Bess*, by Marcia Davenport, *Stage*, December 1935.

Review of *Porgy and Bess*, by Ruth Woodbury Sedgwick, *Stage*, December 1935.

"Story of 25-year-old Woman's Rise Dramatic," by Floyd J. Calvin, *California Eagle* and *Philadelphia Tribune*, November 21, 1935.

"*Porgy and Bess* Cast on RCA 'Magic Key' Hour," NBC press release, November 27, 1935.

"One Benefactor after Another Paved the Road for Ruby Elzy," *New York Herald-Tribune*, December 1, 1935.

"Ruby Elzy, Negro Soprano, Joins 'Melody Master' Cast," NBC press release, December 5, 1935.

"Carrie Jacobs Bond Is Guest Star of 'Melody Master' Program," NBC press release, December 9, 1935.

"Local Girl Makes Good," *Columbus Citizen*, December 28, 1935.

"Stage Stars Honored Here," *Pittsburgh Courier*, February 1936.

"Ruby Elzy Will Give Recital at O.S.U. on January 21," *Columbus Dispatch*, January 14, 1937.

"Ruby Elzy to Give Recital Thursday," by Robert A. Watson, Ohio State University *Lantern*, January 15, 1937.

"Two Faculty Members Aided, Says Ruby Elzy," by Nathan B. Zahm, Ohio State University *Lantern*, January 21, 1937.

"Ruby Elzy Returns for Home Concert," Ohio State University *Lantern*, January 22, 1937.

"Ruby Elzy Gives Excellent Song Recital at O.S.U.," by Samuel T. Wilson, *Columbus Dispatch*, January 22, 1937.

"Ruby Elzy, Soprano, Returns for Recital at Alma Mater," by R. L. F. McCombs, *Columbus Citizen*, January 22, 1937.

"Elzy Concert Was Musical Treat of the Year," *Norwalk Reflector-Herald* (OH), January 25, 1937.

"Star Comes Home," *Ohio State University Monthly*, February 1937.

"Variety Parade on Fred Allen's 'Town Hall Tonight,'" NBC press release, April 20, 1937.

"Star Ruby Elzy at the Apollo," *New York Amsterdam-News*, July 19, 1937.

Steinway piano advertisement, *Town Hall Concert Program*, October 10, 1937.

Review of Town Hall Concert, by Oscar Thompson, *New York Sun*, October 11, 1937.

Review of Town Hall Concert, by W.C.C. *New York Amsterdam-News*, October 16, 1937.

Review of Town Hall Concert, by Noel Straus, *New York Times*, October 11, 1937.

"Negro Soprano in White House Sings for Mrs. Roosevelt," *New York World-Telegram*, December 15, 1937.

"Sings at the White House, Loses Her Night Club Job," *New York World-Telegram*, December 16, 1937.

"Mrs. Roosevelt Entertains Wives of Supreme Court Justices at Luncheon," *Washington Evening Star*, December 16, 1937.

Review of *Porgy and Bess*, by Virginia Wright, *Los Angeles Times*, February 5, 1938.

Review of *Porgy and Bess*, by Florence Lawrence, *Los Angeles Herald-Examiner*, February 5, 1938.

"*Porgy and Bess* Star Discovered Singing at Work," *San Jose Mercury Herald*, March 3, 1938.

"Gets Another Important Role," *Los Angeles Journal & Guide*, June 18, 1938.

Review of *Run Little Chillun*, *News-Guardian*, July 28, 1938.

Review of *Run Little Chillun*, *Evening News*, July 23, 1938.

Review of *Run Little Chillun*, *Hollywood Variety*, July 23, 1938.

"Ruby Elzy Guest Soloist at Second Baptist Sunday," *California Eagle*, May 6, 1939.

"Paul Robeson in on *John Henry* Rehearsal," unidentified New York newspaper, November 1939.

Review of *John Henry*, by Richard Lockridge, *New York Sun*, January 11, 1940.

Review of *John Henry*, by Robert Coleman, *New York Daily Mirror*, January 11, 1940.

Review of *John Henry*, by Richard Watts, Jr., *New York Herald-Tribune*, January 11, 1940.

Review of *John Henry*, by Kelcey Allen, *Women's Wear Daily*, January 11, 1940.

Review of *John Henry*, by Sidney B. Whipple, *New York World-Telegram*, January 11, 1940.

"Triumphant Ruby Elzy Comes Home," *Pontotoc Progress* (MS), January 8, 1941.

"Mutual Admiration," publicity release from *Birth of the Blues* pressbook, Paramount Pictures, 1941.

Review of *Birth of the Blues*, by Kenneth McCaleb, *New York Daily Mirror*, December 11, 1941.

Review of *Birth of the Blues*, *Variety*, September 3, 1941.

Review of *Birth of the Blues*, by Milton Meltzner, *Daily Worker,* New York, December 11, 1941.

Review of *Birth of the Blues*, by Virginia Oakley, *Richmond News-Leader* (VA), November 21, 1941.

"*Porgy* in Maplewood," review by Virgil Thomson, *New York Herald-Tribune*, October 18, 1941.

Review of *Porgy and Bess*, by Brooks Atkinson, *New York Times*, January 23, 1942.

Review of *Porgy and Bess, Musical America*, February 10, 1942.

Review of *Porgy and Bess*, by Burns Mantle, *New York Daily News*, January 23, 1942.

"Ruby Elzy of *Porgy and Bess* to Give Recital Here," *Boston Globe*, June 20, 1942.

"Ruby Elzy," by Florence Smith Vincent, *Christian Advocate*, December 31, 1942 (reprinted in *Methodist Woman*, March 1943).

"700th Performance," unidentified newspaper, February–March 1943.

"National Negro Opera Company to Open Membership Campaign," *Pittsburgh Courier*, April 3, 1943.

Review of *Porgy and Bess*, Francis Wayne, *Denver Post*, June 20, 1943.

"Ruby Elzy, Soprano, of *Porgy and Bess*," obituary, *New York Times*, June 28, 1943.

"Noted Soprano Dies in Detroit," *Columbus Dispatch*, June 29, 1943.

"Ruby Elzy Dies at 33 after Detroit Operation," *Variety*, June 30, 1943.

"Ruby Elzy Has Come Home Again—A Tribute," by Mildred B. Caldwell, *Pontotoc Progress* (MS), July 1, 1943.

"Ruby Elzy's Death at 33 Shocks Stage, Music World," *New York Amsterdam-News*, July 3, 1943.

"Ruby Elzy Is Dead," *Ohio State University Monthly*, July 1943.

"Ruby Elzy—An Editorial," *The Etude*, August 1943.

"Her Song Lingers On," *Lessons for Intermediates*, Methodist Publishing House, April 18, 1948.

"An Evening to Remember," by Douglas Watt, *New York Daily News*, June 14, 1959.

"Mother of Former Stage Singer Returns for Visit," *Pontotoc Progress* (MS), by Elliott Thompson, February 27, 1975.

"*Porgy and Bess*'s Original Serena," by Lanny Flaherty, *Mississippi*, July–August 1995.

"Gershwin Golds: 100th Anniversary Finds," by Lloyd Schwartz, *Boston Phoenix*, September 17–24, 1998.

"State Inducts 27 into Musicians Hall of Fame," by Donnie Snow, *Jackson Clarion-Ledger* (MS), April 2, 2000.

Documentary Films

Aida's Brothers and Sisters: Black Voices in Opera. Korbinian Meyer and David Horn, Executive Producers. A production of PARS Media and Thirteen/ WNET New York. © Pars Media, 2000.

Marian Anderson. Produced by Dante J. James; written by Juan Williams. A production of WETA-TV. © WETA, 1991.

Porgy and Bess: An American Voice. Charles Hobson, Executive Producer; James A. Standifer, Producer and Project Director. A presentation of the University of Michigan in collaboration with Vanguard Films and Mojo Working Productions, Inc. © University of Michigan, 1997.

Websites

"Afrocentric Voices in Classical Music," www.afrovoices.com.

"Art of the Negro Spiritual," www.artofthenegrospiritual.com.

ACKNOWLEDGMENTS

Research Sources

Black History Museum of Corinth, The Webb House, Corinth, MS, Betty L. Fry, Chairperson.

Columbia College, Center for Black Music Research, Suzanne Flandreau, Librarian and Archivist.

Columbus Metropolitan Library.

University of Connecticut, Charles C. McCracken Presidential Papers, 1930–35, Archives and Special Collections, Betsy Pittman, Archivist.

Detroit Public Library, E. Azalia Hackley Collection, Barbara Martin, Collection Specialist.

Howard University, Moorland-Spingarn Research Center, Jean Currie Church, Chief Librarian.

Fay M. Jackson House, Los Angeles, CA, Dale Lya Pierson.

Juilliard School Archives, Jeni Dahmus, Archivist.

Library of Congress: Federal Theatre Project Collection, Music Division, Walter Zvonchenko, Curator; George and Ira Gershwin Collection, Music Division, Raymond A. White, Curator; National Negro Opera Company Collection, Music Division, Walter Zvonchenko, Curator; NBC Collection, Recorded Sound Division, Jan McKee and Wynn Matthias, Librarians.

New York Public Library for the Performing Arts, Billy Rose Theatre Collection, Billy Taylor, Curator; Annette Marotta, Assistant Curator.

Northeast Mississippi Museum, Corinth, MS, Kristy White, Executive Director.

Ohio State University Archives, Raimund Goerler, Director; Bertha Inhat, University Manuscripts; Julie Peterson, University Photo Archives.

Ohio State University Libraries, Robert A. Wachsman Collection, Jerome Lawrence & Robert E. Lee Theatre Research Institute, Alan Woods, Director; Nena Couch, Curator.

Pontotoc County Historical Society, Pontotoc, MS. James Mogridge, President.

Pontotoc County Library, Pontotoc, MS. Regina Graham, Librarian.

Pontotoc Music Club, Pontotoc, MS. Judy Maxey, President.

Franklin D. Roosevelt Presidential Library and Museum, Hyde Park, NY, Eleanor Roosevelt Papers, Raymond J. Teichman, Supervisory Archivist and Virginia H. Lewick, Archives Technician.

Rust College, Holly Springs, MS, David Beckley, President; Paula Clark, Public Relations Associate.

Schomberg Center for Research in Black Culture, New York, NY. Charles Marshall Collection, Diane Lachatanere, Curator, Manuscripts, Archives, and Rare Books Division.

Western Connecticut State University, Howard Barlow Papers, Meg Moughan, Archivist and Special Collections Librarian.

Worthington Public Library, Worthington, OH. Meribah Mansfield, Director.

Yale University, John Rosamond Johnson Papers, Irving S. Gilmore Music Library, Suzanne Eggleston Lovejoy, Assistant Music Librarian for Public Services.

Personal Acknowledgments

In addition to the people and organizations listed in the preceding pages, there are many others who have provided encouragement and support during the years it has taken to research and write this book.

Special thanks to the Elzy and McCracken families, not only for all they did to help me but for their kind hospitality and friendship; and to Madge Cooper Guthery, who started me on the project and was an unfailing champion throughout.

I thank Madge, the S. O'Donnell family, and Ed Orlett for generously sponsoring several important activities and events connected to the project; Nena Couch for her personal support and for the help she provided through the Jerome Lawrence and Robert E. Lee Theatre Research Institute at Ohio State University; Chiquita Mullins-Lee, who not only edited my original manuscript but became an enthusiastic partner in the project; Randye Jones, a gifted singer herself, who helped me through her two marvelous websites, "Afrocentric Voices in Classical Music" and "The Art of the Negro Spiritual"; Ray Norman, Jerry Haendiges, and Lance Bowling, who provided from their archives of rare broadcasts copies of Elzy's performances on radio; Jordana Y. Shakoor, who introduced me to University Press of Mississippi not long after it published *Civil Rights Childhood*, a memoir of her remarkable father, Andrew Jordan; and all the people at University Press—Seetha Srinivasan, Craig Gill, Anne Stascavage, Steve Yates, Kathy Kerr Burgess, and Will Rigby.

Many others in Mississippi helped me, including Walter Bates, Virginia Dillard, Mary Jo Fisk, Rosalie Furr, Regina Graham, and Gertrude Kimp in Pontotoc; Mrs. Oneida Lasley, Sonny Boatman, Jebb Johnston of the *Daily Corinthian*, Ann Walker, and Rosemary Williams in Corinth; Sam Givhan in Columbus; Clara Jones Davis in Greenvill, and Claudine Brown and Cedell Pulley in Greenwood.

Ellistine Perkins Holly and Lanny Flaherty preceeded me in writing about Ruby Elzy; in addition Ellistine has presented lectures and performances about Ruby and

Mississippi's other black divas-Elizabeth Taylor Greenfield and Leontyne Price-throughout the South. I thank both Ellistine and Lanny for sharing their insight and offering their enthusiastic encouragement to my own research and writing.

Several other writers also gave their advice and encouragement, including Rosalyn Story, author of *And So I Sing*, the first important book about the contributions of black women to the operatic and concert stages; Edward Jablonski, who as a young Army Air Corps recruit met Ruby Elzy in a memorable backstage encounter during the 1942 revival of *Porgy and Bess* and who later became the definitive biographer of George Gershwin, Harold Arlen, and Irving Berlin; and my friend, Derek Mannering, who has written several splendid biographies on my boyhood musical hero, the great American tenor, Mario Lanza.

I thank my brothers: Richard, the family's computer expert, for helping scan photographs, and Robert, who on his rare days off drove me on numerous excursions related to the project.

Special thanks go to the staff of the WOSU stations of Ohio State University, especially Beverly Ervine, Brent Greene, Susan Johnson, Christina Morgan, Christopher Purdy, and Jody Williams.

In her book *Wrapped in Rainbows*, Valerie Boyd thanked her subject, Zora Neale Hurston, "for choosing me." I feel the same way about Ruby Elzy, for I have sensed from the beginning that she has been close by my side, helping and guiding me. I thank Ruby Elzy for choosing me.

Finally, I thank my wife Aina and my daughter Julia for their unwavering love and support. I dedicate this book to them and also to the loving memory of my parents, Edgar and Loretta Weaver; my sisters Darlene and Carol; and my mother-in-law, YuYing Sun. I know they would all be very proud.

Index

Abbott, George, 118, 119
Abresch, James, 171, 172, 180
Addams, Jane, 74
Allen, Fred, 109, 110, 123, 126, 148
American Opera Festival, 168, 169
Anderson, Eddie "Rochester," 140, 154, 156, 158, 161
Anderson, Marian, viii, 5, 58, 97, 114, 115, 143–45, 188
Angus, Mrs. Bernice, 118
Arent, H. W., 63–67
Arlen, Harold, 154–56
Arlen, Rita, 156
Armitage, Merle, 112, 125–34, 151, 152, 163, 164
Armstrong, Louis, 135
Astaire, Fred, 103, 112, 128, 142, 172
Atkinson, Brooks (*New York Times*), 90
Attles, Joe, 149

Bagar, Robert C. (*New York World-Telegram*), 117
Bankhead, Silas, 191
Barbour, Rebecca, 20–22
Barlow, Howard, 105
Barnett, Claude, 141, 173, 175
Barrymore, Ethel, 163
Barrymore, John, 130
Bates, Mildred, 157
Bates, Walter, 157, 187
Battle, Kathleen, vii, 188
Beard, Charles "Stymie," 143

Becker, Ella M., 20–22, 24, 25, 29–35, 41, 43, 44, 52, 56, 58
Belafonte, Harry, 173
Benny, Jack, 133, 140, 158
Bergman, Ingrid, 163
Berlin, Irving, 89
Berry, Halle, 173
Birth of the Blues (film), 158, 159, 161, 162, 167
Black, Frank, 93
Blake, Eubie, 69, 145
Bledsoe, Jules, 78
Bond, Carrie Jacobs, 94
Boyer, Charles, 130
Bradford, Roark, 148–51
Brandeis, Alice, 7, 8
Brandeis, Louis, 8
Breen, Bobby, 142
Brown, Anne (Wiggins), viii, 62, 63, 72, 77, 78, 85–87, 89, 91, 93, 97, 98, 102, 111, 112, 126, 127, 129–31, 164, 169, 170, 172, 189
Brown, Anthony, 149
Brown, Dr. Harry, 62
Brown Buddies (musical play), 60
Brown Sugar (play), 118, 119
Bubbles, John W., 86, 96, 99, 126, 127, 189
Buck, Ford (Buck & Bubbles), 86
Bumbry, Grace, 188
Burleigh, Harry T., 74, 77, 115
Byrd, Sam, 149, 150, 152

Byron, Mark, Jr., 165, 166, 169, 170, 173, 174, 179, 180, 186

Cantor, Eddie, 130
Carr, Jack (second husband), 127, 143, 152, 153, 162, 165, 166, 169, 173, 175, 176, 178, 179, 181–84, 187, 188, 191
Cato, Minto, 149, 172
Chapman, Frank, 130
Chapman, Marguerite, 128
Clarey, Cynthia, 189
Cole, Bob, 60
Coleman, Warren, 86, 127, 152, 166, 167, 173
Cole-Talbert, Florence, 140, 156
Connelly, Marc, 148
Cooper (Guthery), Madge, vii, viii, 49, 53
Crawford, Cheryl, 131, 163–68, 170, 172, 181
Crawford, Joan, 130
Creatore, Giuseppe, 78
Creatore, Peter, 78, 79
Crosby, Bing, 133, 158, 159, 161, 187
Crosby, Everett, 161

Dalrymple, Jean, 168
Damage, Matthews S., 22
Damrosch, Dr. Frank, 58, 59, 73, 77
Damrosch, Walter, 58
Davenport, Marcia (*Stage*), 91
Davis, Henrietta, 50, 63–67
Dawson, Mary Cardwell (National Negro Opera Company), 171, 172, 179
DePaur, Leonard, 149
Dietrich, Marlene, 130
Digges, Dudley, 76
Dixon, Dean, 149
Donlevy, Brian, 158
Douglas, Melvyn, 134, 135, 142
Dowdy, Helen, 95

Downes, Olin (*New York Times*), 91
Doxey, Natalie, 23, 24, 187
Duke, Vernon, 152
Duncan, Gladys, 173
Duncan, Todd, 78, 85–89, 91, 93, 96–98, 102, 111, 112, 126, 128–31, 144, 152, 164, 169, 179, 181, 182, 188
Dunham, Katherine, 152
Dunham, Lucia, 6, 62, 63, 67–69, 71, 72, 85, 90, 104
Durant, Ray, 120, 121
Durbin, Deanna, 130

Eddy, Nelson, 134
Elie, Rudolph, Jr. (*Boston Herald*), 170
Ellington, Duke, 110
Elzy, Ada (aunt), 10, 15, 176–78
Elzy, Amanda (aunt), 10, 15, 176–78
Elzy, Amanda Belle (sister), 10, 11, 23, 50, 122, 126, 166, 176, 177, 182, 191, 192
Elzy, Beatrice Wayne (sister), 10, 11, 23, 50, 122, 126, 132, 139, 166, 176, 177, 180, 181, 191
Elzy, Charlie (father), 10–15, 20, 153, 176–78, 191
Elzy, Ed (uncle), 10, 153
Elzy, Edward "Buster" (nephew), 153, 154, 185
Elzy, Emma Kimp (mother), 9–23, 29–31, 37, 39, 40, 45, 50, 51, 53, 54, 56, 66, 77, 90, 101–4, 116, 122, 124–26, 139, 166, 175, 176, 179, 181–87, 191, 192
Elzy, Robert Isaac (brother), 11, 23, 50, 122, 140, 153, 154, 175, 177, 185, 191
Elzy, Ruby Pearl: ability to handle prejudice, 42–44; in Merle Armitage production of *Porgy and Bess*, 126–33; auditions for George Gershwin, cast as Serena, 84, 85; birth in Pontotoc, 9,

10; in *Birth of the Blues*, 158, 159, 161, 162, 167; burial in Pontotoc City Cemetery, 186; CBS radio appearances, 104, 105; closeness to her mother, 16; in Columbus and at Ohio State, 33–56; concerts at Ohio State and in Norwalk, 105–8; in Cheryl Crawford production of *Porgy and Bess*, 163–70; dies following surgery, 184; discovered by Dr. C. C. McCracken, 26–28; engagement at Kit Kat Club, 119–23; engages Mark Byron, Jr., as her manager, 165, 166; enters Parkside Hospital in Detroit, 183; epitaph by mother, 192; expresses her views on civil rights, 175, 180; faces lawsuit over *Stumbling Upward*, 63–67; family background, 10–12; farewell to Pontotoc, 31, 32; father abandons family, 15; films *Tell No Tales* and *Way Down South*, 142, 143; films *The Toy Wife*, meets Clarence Muse, 134, 135; final concerts in Mississippi, 156–58; final performance as Serena, 181, 182; final tour in *Porgy and Bess*, 172, 173, 176–82; fired by club owner Jules Podell, 122, 123; in first production of *Porgy and Bess*, 85–93, 95–98; first sings in public, 9; first solo on Broadway in *Fast and Furious*, 69, 70; funerals in Corinth and Pontotoc, 185, 187; gives 700th performance as Serena, 178; guests on *Town Hall Tonight*, 109, 110, 126; headlines at Apollo Theatre, 110, 111; home life in Los Angeles, 138–40, 153, 154; illness diagnosed, 179; inducted as inaugural member of the Mississippi Music Hall of Fame, 190, 191; in *John Henry*, 147–52; joins Rosamond Johnson Choir, debuts on Broadway in *Brown Buddies*, 61; at Juilliard, 58, 59, 61–63; Lang-Worth radio programs, 108, 109, 117, 118; learns spirituals from great-grandmother, 17; legacy, 188–90; life in Pontotoc, 12–19; makes debut on radio, 48; makes film debut in *The Emperor Jones*, 74–77; marries Jack Carr, 153; marries Gardner Jones, Jr., 70; Charles Marshall becomes manager, 114, 115; meets DuBose Heyward, 76; moves to Los Angeles, 134; on NBC radio program *The Melody Master*, 94, 95; and Negro Pageant Movement, 141, 142; plans concert tour and operatic debut in *Aida*, 170–72; press coverage of her death, 186; receives Julius Rosenwald Fellowship, 57, 58, 63; records "Where Is Dis Road A'leadin' Me To?" for Decca, 155; relationship with the McCracken family, 41–43, 55; reunion with her father, 178; in *Run Little Chillun*, 136–38, 145; at Rust College, 20–32; separation and divorce from Gardner Jones, Jr., 99–103; sings for Roland Hayes, 47, 48; and song, "My Man's Gone Now," viii, 86, 87, 89, 91, 102, 103, 107, 112, 120, 130, 137, 155, 156, 167, 169, 182, 190; Town Hall debut, 114–17; White House concert, 3–8, 120–23, 126; writes *Stumbling Upward*, 50, 51

Embree, Dr. Edwin, 57, 58, 63, 71, 72
Emperor Jones, The (film), 4, 75–77, 118, 133, 136, 147, 148
Evans, Maurice, 163

Fairbanks, Douglas, Jr., 130
Fast and Furious (revue), 69, 70, 172
Ferber, Edna, 82, 89
Ferrer, Jose, 118

Flagstad, Kirsten, 89
Friedman, Charles, 150
Furr, Eva, 157
Furr family (Pontotoc, Miss.), 12, 13, 157
Furr (Fisk), Martha Jo, 157

Gable, Clark, 134
Galli-Curci, Amelia, 36, 45, 78, 127
Garbo, Greta, 134
Garland, Judy, 143, 154
Gershwin, Frances, 112
Gershwin, George, vii, 5, 13, 75, 79, 80,
    82–89, 93, 102, 103, 111, 122, 127–29,
    135, 152, 154, 156, 164, 182, 188
Gershwin, Ira, 80, 103, 130, 188
Gershwin, Lenore, 130
Gillespie, William, 126, 155
Goldwyn, Sam, 128
Gordon, Mack, 70
Graves, Deniece, 188
Green, Eddie, 111
Grofe, Ferde, 111
Grombach, Jean V., 87

Hamlett, Enida, 120, 122, 123
Hammerstein, Oscar, II, 70, 82, 83, 191
Handy, W. C., 159
Harburg, E. Y. "Yip," 154
Harris, Greene, family (Columbus,
    Ohio), 51, 52
Harris, Norman, 51
Harris, Theresa, 135
Harvey, Georgette, 86, 103, 119, 126,
    132, 164, 178, 182
Hayes, Helen, 163
Hayes, Roland, 5, 47, 48, 114, 115
Hayes, Rutherford B., 11
Haymon, Cynthia, 190
Heifetz, Jascha, 89, 119
Hernandez, Juano, 69, 148

Heyward, Dorothy, 75, 82, 150
Heyward, DuBose, 4, 5, 13, 75–77,
    79–86, 88, 135, 150, 155, 156,
    182, 188
Hines, Altonell, 173
Hodnett, Lois, 126, 155
Holiday, Billie, 110
Honeybuss, Claude, 140
Hope, Bob, 133
Hughes, Mrs. Charles Evans, 6
Hughes, Langston, 59, 142, 143
Hughes, Dr. Royal D., 35, 36, 38, 44,
    45, 47–50, 52–54, 62, 105, 106, 108,
    114, 139
Hurok, Sol, 143, 144
Hurst, Fannie, 74, 89
Hurston, Zora Neale, 59, 69, 95

Ickes, Harold, 144

Jackson, Fay M., 140
Jackson, Harriet, 164, 168, 169, 179
Jarboro, Caterina, 171
Jessel, George, 112
Jessye, Eva, 93
John, Dr. Walter C., 26, 27, 37, 92
John Henry (play), 146, 149–53
Johnson, (Francis) Hall, 112, 136, 137,
    140, 152
Johnson, Haven, 118
Johnson, James Weldon, 59, 60, 95, 139
Johnson, John Rosamond, 60, 61, 63, 69,
    70, 73–77, 84, 139, 152, 168
Jolson, Al, 83
Jones, Gardner, Jr. (first husband),
    68–71, 73, 77, 90, 92, 93, 98, 100–2,
    106, 113, 132, 153
Jones, Olive, 53
Jubilee Singers, 155
Jurge, Henry, 5, 120

Kaplan, Arthur, 5, 6, 8, 62, 106, 107, 109, 115, 121, 122, 169
Kaye, Judy, 155
Kern, Jerome, 70, 75, 82, 83
Kimp, Belle (grandmother), 4, 9, 10, 16, 50, 192
Kimp, Fannie (great-grandmother), 10, 16–18, 50, 192
Kimp, Henderson (great-grandfather), 10
King, B.B., 191
King, Dr. Martin Luther, 149
Koehler, Ted, 155
Kramer, A. Walter (*Musical America*), 91
Kreisler, Fritz, 89
Krimsky, John, 118

LaGuardia, Mayor Fiorello, 111
Lathan, June, 19
Lathan, Mrs. (Clyde), 19, 78
LaTouche, John, 147, 152
Lawhorn, Mary (May), 153, 154
Lawrence, Florence (*Los Angeles Herald-Examiner*), 131
Lawrence, Jacob, 59
Lawrence, William, 115–17
Lee, Canada, 119
Lehman, Governor Herbert, 111
Leonardi, Leon, 155
Lincoln, Abraham, 4
Lombard, Carole 168
Long, Avon, 127, 130, 131, 164, 169, 173

Mabley, Jackie, 69, 76
MacDonald, Jeanette, 134
Magic Key, The, 94
Mamoulian, Rouben, 87–89, 92, 127, 129
Marshall, Charles L., 114–19, 121, 124–26, 133, 147, 152, 166
Marshall, Thurgood, 141
Martin, Mary, 158–60

Matthews, Edward, 86, 87, 103, 115, 126, 164, 168, 173, 179, 182
May, Gideon, 156
McClendon, Rose, 85, 91, 95
McCombs, R. L. F. (*Columbus Citizen*), 101
McCormack, John, 166
McCoy, Dr. L. M., 22–31, 33, 38, 50, 53, 58, 187
McCracken, Dr. Charles Chester (C. C.), ix, x, 12, 25–31, 33–55, 57–60, 63–69, 71–73, 92, 93, 96, 99, 100, 105–7, 110, 114, 129, 162, 173, 180, 183–85, 188, 191
McCracken, Charles William (Bill), ix, 41, 42, 55, 176, 185, 191
McCracken, Cleo Fulton (Mrs. C. C. McCracken), 33–36, 41, 42, 45, 48, 51–53, 55, 93, 107, 185, 191
McCracken, James Edward (Ed), ix, x, 41, 42, 55, 93, 96, 100, 183, 185, 191
McCracken, Janet May, ix, 41, 42, 55, 93, 191
McCracken, Mary Ruth, ix, x, 41, 42, 55, 162, 191
McCracken, Ruth (Mrs. James Edward McCracken), ix, x, 191
McDaniel, Hattie, 140, 156
McQueen, Butterfly, 119
Melody Master, The, 95–99
Mercer, Johnny, 161
Merman, Ethel, 111
Micheaux, Oscar, 75
Mitchell, Abbie, 78, 86, 87, 93, 126
Moore, Tim, 69
Moten (Barnett), Etta, viii, 69, 170, 172, 179
Murphy, Dudley, 76, 77
Muse, Clarence, 135–38, 140, 142, 143, 154, 156, 162

Nast, Conde, 90
Norman, Jessye, 188
Norworth, Jack, 94
Nunn, Trevor, 190

O'Neill, Barbara, 134
O'Neill, Eugene, 75
Owen, Dr. Samuel H. C., 179, 182–84

Paley, William, 87
Parade of the States, 70
Payton, Lew, 142
Podell, Jules, 119–23
Pons, Lily, 89, 113
Ponselle, Rosa, 127
Porgy (novel and play), 75, 81, 82, 164
Porgy and Bess (Cheryl Crawford pro-
    duction, 1941–43), 131, 163–70, 172,
    173, 176–82
Porgy and Bess (Merle Armitage produc-
    tion, 1938), 125–34, 139, 152
Porgy and Bess (Theatre Guild produc-
    tion, 1935–36), vii, viii, x, 80, 83 98,
    128
Presley, Elvis, 191
Price, Leontyne, 24, 114, 188, 191

Rainer, Luise, 134, 135
Randolph, A. Philip, 175
Randolph, Forbes, 69
Reed, Donna, 162
Rene, Leon & Otis, 135
Revel, Harry, 70
Reverend Johnson's Dream
    ("Americanegro Suite"), 155, 156
Reynolds, Harry, 180, 191
Rhea, La Julia, 171
Rhodes, Betty Jane, 161
Rightmire, Dr. George, 53, 93, 100, 106
Robeson, Eslanda, 147

Robeson, Paul, viii, 4, 5, 75, 76, 78, 95,
    110, 133, 146–52, 163, 188
Robeson, Paul, Jr., 147, 148
Robinson, Bill "Bojangles," 61
Robinson, Earl, 147
Robinson, Edward G., 112
Robinson, Willard, 104
Rodgers, Richard, 89
Rogers, Ginger, 102, 128, 142, 172
Roosevelt, Eleanor, 3–7, 120, 121, 123,
    126, 144
Roosevelt, Franklin D., 124, 140, 145,
    175
Roosevelt, Theodore, 11
Rosemond, Clinton, 135
Ronselle, Rosa, 127
Rosenwald, Julius, 57
Run Little Chillun (play), 136–39, 142,
    152, 162
Rustin, Bayard, 149

Salmaggi, Alfred, 171
Schatenstein, Anne, 49
Scheider, Malvina Thompson, 5, 8,
    120, 122
Schiffman, Frank, 110, 111, 120
Schwartz, Lloyd (*Boston Phoenix*), 190
Sedgwick, Ruth Woodbury (*Stage*), 91
Selznick, David O., 140
Shepperd, Carmen, 77
Shuffle Along (revue), 69, 145
Sissle, Noble, 69, 145
Smallens, Alexander, 87, 128, 164, 165
Smith, Bessie, 110, 123
Sokoloff, Nikolai, 74
Sousa, John Philip, 78
"Spirit of the Spirituals, The" (article by
    Ruby Elzy), 179, 180, 186
Steinert, Alexander, 87, 89, 112, 127, 129
Stern, Isaac, 115
Still, William Grant, 5, 191

Stone, Julius F., 49
Stovall, Reverend, 10
Straus, Noel (*New York Times*), 116
Stumbling Upward (play by
   Ruby Elzy), 50, 51, 63–67
Swarthout, Gladys, 130

Taft, Helen Herron, 6, 7
Taft, William Howard, 6
Taylor, Libby, 135
Taylor, Robert, 130
Taylor family (Columbus, Ohio), 45,
   46, 51
Teagarden, Jack, 158
Tell No Tales (film), 142
Thompson, Oscar (*New York Sun*), 116
Thomson, Virgil (*New York Herald-
   Tribune*), 90, 165
Tone, Franchot, 130
Town Hall Tonight, 109–11, 148
Toy Wife, The (film), 134, 135
Tracy, Spencer, 134
Trotter, John Scott, 161

Van Steeden, Peter, 110
Van Vechten, Carl, 94, 95
Vanderford family (Corinth, Miss.),
   21, 22
Vanderford (Lasley), Oneida, 21, 185
Vardaman, James K., 12
Verritt, Shirley, 188

Vincent, Florence Smith, 174
Voorhees, Don, 149

Wachsman, Robert, 125–27, 129, 152,
   155
Walk, Lillian D., 73
Walker, A'Lelia, 59
Walker, Madame C. J., 59
Wallenstein, Alfred, 168
Waller, Fats, 108
Warfield, William, 114
Warnow, Mark, 105
Washington, Booker T., 22
Washington, Fredi, 76
Waters, Ethel, 152
Way Down South (film), 142, 143
Wayne, Francis (*Denver Post*), 181
White, Josh, 149
White, Willard, 190
Wildberg, John, 163
Williams, Musa, 149
Williams, Spencer, Jr., 142
Wilson, Dooley, 152
Wilson, Frank, 76
Wilson, Woodrow, 7
Wolfe, Jacques, 149, 151
Wright, Virginia (*Los Angeles
   Times*), 131
Wynette, Tammy, 191

Young, Robert, 134, 135, 162